A new world order is in the making. Vietnam, Afghanistan, *glasnost, perestroika,* the yen, the mark, the Four Tigers of the Pacific: all these signal the eclipse of a world dominated by two superpowers. But none of the emerging powers appears ready or inclined to succeed the United States and the Soviet Union as world leaders.

The unformed lines of power and interest in the world today present the United States with great opportunities. If America's power has experienced a relative decline, it is still considerable and can be effective if exercised wisely. The new administration in Washington can take a decisive role in shaping a new world order in which democracy is more firmly rooted and military tensions relaxed. But first it must realistically assess America's global interests and the means the nation has to achieve them.

In this new volume from the American Assembly the experts address the choices facing America's policymakers as the world moves into a new era.

America's
Global Interests

THE AMERICAN ASSEMBLY was established by Dwight D. Eisenhower at Columbia University in 1950. Each year it holds at least two nonpartisan meetings which give rise to authoritative books that illuminate issues of United States policy.

An affiliate of Columbia, with offices at Barnard College, the Assembly is a national, educational institution incorporated in the state of New York.

The Assembly seeks to provide information, stimulate discussion, and evoke independent conclusions on matters of vital public interest.

CONTRIBUTORS

GRAHAM ALLISON, Harvard University

C. FRED BERGSTEN, Institute for International
Economics

HAROLD BROWN, Johns Hopkins University

SEYOM BROWN, Brandeis University

WILLIAM P. BUNDY

LAWRENCE S. EAGLEBURGER, Assistant Secretary
of State, Designate

EDWARD K. HAMILTON, Hamilton, Rabinovitz &
Alschuler, Inc.

ARTHUR B. LAFFER, A.B. Laffer & Associates

JOHN MARTTILA, Marttila & Kiley

PAUL CRAIG ROBERTS, Center for Strategic and
International Studies

THE AMERICAN ASSEMBLY
Columbia University

America's Global Interests

A New Agenda

EDWARD K. HAMILTON
Editor

92-296

W · W · NORTON & COMPANY
New York   London

The text of this book is composed in Baskerville.
Composition and manufacturing by The Haddon Craftsmen, Inc.

First Edition

Library of Congress Cataloging-in-Publication Data

America's global interests: a new agenda / edited by Edward K. Hamilton.
    p.   cm.
  Includes index.
    1. United States—Foreign relations—1945-   2. World politics—1945
I. Hamilton, Edward K.
E840.A637   1989
327.73—dc19
                                                        88–35227

ISBN 0-393-02702-3

ISBN 0-393-95820-5 pbk.

W. W. Norton & Company, Inc., 500 Fifth Avenue, New York, N.Y. 10110
W. W. Norton & Company Ltd., 37 Great Russell Street, London WC1B 3NU

1 2 3 4 5 6 7 8 9 0

Contents

STEERING COMMITTEE AND ADVISERS   *ix*

Preface
    DANIEL A. SHARP   *3*

Introduction and Overview
    EDWARD K. HAMILTON   *5*

1. The 1950s Versus the 1990s
    WILLIAM P. BUNDY   *33*

2. America in the World Economy: A Strategy for the 1990s
    C. FRED BERGSTEN   *82*
    Commentary: Paul Craig Roberts   *113*
    Commentary: Arthur B. Laffer   *122*

3. Choices for the 1990s: Preserving American Security Interests through the Century's End
    HAROLD BROWN   *126*

4. Inherited Geopolitics and Emergent Global Realities
    SEYOM BROWN   *166*

5. National Security Strategy for the 1990s
   GRAHAM ALLISON   *198*

6. The 21st Century: American Foreign Policy
   Challenges
   LAWRENCE S. EAGLEBURGER   *242*

7. American Public Opinion: Evolving Definitions
   of National Security
   JOHN MARTTILA   *261*

   Final Report of the Seventy-fifth American
   Assembly   *316*

   Index   *337*

America's
Global Interests

Preface

The world has been changing around us faster in the last few years than perhaps at any time since the end of World War II. The most salient examples of these changes are Mikhail Gorbachev's *glasnost* and *perestroika* in the Soviet Union; China's pragmatic efforts toward "communism with Chinese characteristics"; the emergence of major regional trading blocs; Europe's moves to become a unified economic force; the emerging strength of many Asian countries; and the escalating world debt problem. U.S. hegemony is being replaced by the need for shared management of the global economy and the global environment, and shared responsibility for peace and security.

Against this background is a prevailing debate concerning whether the United States is in a state of relative decline or simply experiencing a long-overdue adjustment to the success of its efforts to help the recovery of allies and adversaries devastated by World War II. The American Assembly saw a clear need for the United States to help create a new international order and to share its management—and prosperity—with other global powers.

In an effort to identify a long-term vision for U.S. policy through the end of the 1990s, The American Assembly formed a steering committee, whose names are listed in an appendix, to help design a series of programs. The first of these meetings was convened at Arden House, Harriman, New York, from November 17–20, 1988. Participants attended from government, business, academia, the law, and the media. In preparation for that meeting, The American Assembly retained Edward K. Hamilton, president of Hamilton, Rabinovitz & Alschuler, Inc. in Los Angeles, as editor and director of the undertaking. Under his editorial guidance, a team of authors prepared the papers in this volume to serve as background reading for the participants in the Arden House discussions.

The participants addressed many difficult policy choices for the United States in the coming decade and achieved substantial consensus on recommendations concerning economic, political, security, and environmental issues. Their proposals are contained in a report entitled *U.S. Global Interests in the 1990s: A New Approach,* which appears as an appendix to this volume. Additional copies of the report can be obtained by writing to The American Assembly, Columbia University, New York, NY 10027.

Funding for this project was provided by:

- The Benton Foundation
- The Ford Foundation
- Ford Motor Company
- Olin Corporation
- Rockefeller Family and Associates
- The Xerox Foundation

The opinions expressed in this volume are those of the individual authors and not necessarily those of the sponsors nor of The American Assembly, which takes no position on subjects it presents for public discussion.

Daniel A. Sharp
President
The American Assembly

Introduction and Overview

EDWARD K. HAMILTON

D espite the swirl and tumult of events, a strong case can be made that the past four decades have witnessed remarkably little change in either the fundamental factors that define the most basic American international interests or the broad policy directions adopted by the United States to protect and enhance those interests. The essays in this volume examine whether these fundamentals are likely to remain essentially unchanged as we move into the 1990s and onward to the beginning of the third millennium A.D. From varying per-

EDWARD K. HAMILTON has been president of the policy and management consulting firm Hamilton, Rabinovitz & Alschuler since 1976, and, for two years prior to that, was president of Griffenhagen-Kroeger public management consultants. From 1970 to 1973 Mr. Hamilton served as director of the budget and then first deputy mayor of the city of New York. He was vice president and senior fellow in foreign policy studies at the Brookings Institution from 1969 to 1970. Mr. Hamilton has held several positions with various departments in the federal government, including the National Security Council and the Bureau of the Budget. He has written numerous articles on a broad range of topics, from public finance and management to foreign economic policy.

spectives and through differing disciplinary lenses, the authors explore the agenda of coming challenges to American foreign policy makers, and the decisions that these challenges will require them to make.

The unifying thread that runs through all of these explorations is whether the great tectonic plates of geopolitics and economics upon which post–World War II American foreign policy has been based are shifting—and, if so, how this change will affect U.S. interests and policy choices. Looking back two decades hence, will it be generally agreed that the altered context addressed by American policy during this period led to a transition from the postwar era of American foreign policy to a new era fitted to fundamentally new conditions? Or, will this interval be seen as a period of American adjustment to near-term stresses and opportunities that, though requiring some important new initiatives and retrenchments, served primarily to renew the nation's capacity to realize the basic policy objectives and principles that were largely established during the decade following the end of the war? Or, will hindsight reveal no visible seam, however temporary, between the last decade and the next?

If there were a single, high-probability answer to this question, as was true at the turn of each of the last four decades, this focus would not be necessary. Rather than dwelling on basics, the discussion could simply repeat the familiar postwar verities as briefly as possible and then turn to the issues of priority, degree, means of implementation, and cost/benefit efficiency that have generally dominated the American marketplace for foreign policy ideas in the latter half of the twentieth century. Secure in the knowledge that the fundamental structure of international realities and American goals and concerns remained firmly in place, Americans would be free once again to focus their attention on the "how" questions—how best to achieve a given long-term policy objective within a global framework dominated by such fixtures as the cold war—rather than on the "what" and "why" questions that inevitably arise when the very ground begins to move underfoot.

Moreover, it is too much to expect a clear, consensual determination whether the ground is in fact shifting in a time of peace between the dominant powers in the world. The Second World War set the boundary between the last two eras of American policy in unmistakable terms. By transforming power relations, distributions of wealth and economic capacity, rates of technological advancement, public attitudes, and a myriad of other factors that define the interests and capabilities of the nations of the world, that war forced Americans not only to recognize a point of fundamental discontinuity in global affairs, but to adjust to it with what, as seen from a peacetime perspective, was truly blinding speed. Today, without the self-defining quality of a world order torn asunder by war, discerning whether things really are changing in basic ways, and if so to what extent, is a much subtler enterprise. Not only is any assertion along these lines much less subject to definitive proof, but the capacity to change current trends and thereby disprove current forecasts is much more diffused among a larger number of national players, none of whom has been recently debilitated by world war.

It follows that reasonable people can and do differ about what is changing, how much the change matters, how fast change is proceeding, and what it means for U.S. interests and policies. Many such differences are evidenced in the essays that follow. Nevertheless, although the volume does not intend nor attempt to resolve these wide differences in view, the reader will note certain common and recurring themes that demarcate the areas where the issue of fundamental change is most clearly joined.

There is certainly no difficulty in identifying the two clusters of long-term American assumptions and policy responses where fundamental change is most widely suspected. One is the long-prevailing American view of Soviet international intentions, internal dynamics, and receptivity to agreements to reduce nuclear weaponry and otherwise normalize relations, and the corollary assumption of a basically bipolar world in which the core reality that most affects American security interests, and thereby American foreign policy, is the state of cold war between East and West. The other is the presumption that the depth, vitality, and capacity for innovation that characterize the American economy ensure that the United States can improve its domestic well-being and maintain its international competitiveness without wrenching changes in the nature of its economy, in the international economic system, or in the scope and priority of other U.S. foreign policy objectives. All of the authors implicitly agree that, whatever conclusions one draws after reviewing recent history, there is sufficient evidence of change in each of these two areas to warrant serious consideration of how basic it is and what effect it is likely to have on American interests and options in the 1990s.

These broad common themes of shared concern aside, each essay in this collection takes its own angle on the central issue of the volume. The first chapter maps and contrasts the international picture of the 1950s with the scene as we enter the 1990s. The next three chapters review the current situation through the eyes, respectively, of a former shaper of international economic policy (and some equally experientially qualified critics of his views), an experienced maker of security policy, and a long-time academic observer of the broad evolution of the global sociopolitical system. In each case, the central question at issue is what major decisions American policy makers will face in the years immediately ahead. The fifth chapter presents a full-blown portrait of the past record and the proper future aspirations of U.S. foreign policy through the year 2000, as the author sees them. The sixth chapter concentrates on a number of the central focal points of impending change in the character of U.S. relations—with both sectors of Europe, the Soviet Union, and Japan. The concluding chapter explores the now critically important topography of American public opinion on security and other foreign policy issues, as it was revealed in an unprecedentedly rich lode of survey data gathered during the course of 1988.

Taken together, these thoughtful voyages toward a shore yet very dimly seen equip the reader to undertake his or her own intellectual passage. The works are not artificially trimmed to avoid any overlap among them. Neither are they conformed to any particular interpretation of past or future.

Several of the authors draw very different policy lessons from the same historical fact or sequence. Like the real world of policy making, the essays are long on diversity of reasoned opinion and very short on certainty and on single repositories of whole truth. What emerges from these pages is not revealed or unitary wisdom, therefore, but shafts of light generated by powerful and highly informed minds focused on some of the issues most pivotal to the future of the American polity. Though each shaft illuminates the foreign policy universe from a different angle, the factual base that they together provide enables serious readers to address the issues in their own terms, weighing the author's interpretations on their own scales and reaching their own conclusions.

Despite their differences, the essays trace a discernible path when read in sequence. William Bundy, former *Foreign Affairs* editor and assistant secretary of state, provides the indispensable—but all too rare—starting point for any sensible discussion of the presence or absence of fundamental change. He takes a hard look at the essentials of the international arena of the 1950s and contrasts them with their counterparts today. He vividly recreates the polarized East-West political and strategic parameters within which postwar American policy was framed, and which also shaped the unprecedented array of international security, economic, and dispute resolution institutions that were conceived and launched during that period. He maps the main features of the policy environment that then prevailed, from the collapse of Western colonialism, to the economic dominance of the United States, to the brimming confidence with which Americans viewed themselves and the American role in the world. He identifies not only the concerns that were perceived as paramount, but also those (e.g., international drug trafficking, environmental degradation, human rights violations in the less developed world) that were not. Briefly, but with care not to reduce complexity to simplistic stereotype, Bundy proceeds, issue by issue and region by region, to steep the reader in the overriding postwar realities in response to which the main objectives and principles of U.S. policy were born.

Bundy then turns to the current world scene. His brush captures the full spectrum of intervening change, from the relatively predictable economic evolution of Europe, to the startling transformations of Japan and China. He muses skeptically on the significance of the Gorbachev phenomenon as a practical guide to current or future Soviet behavior, particularly in the Third World, but assigns great weight to it as a symbol of Russian acknowledgment of the failure of their system to measure up to the demands set by the Western example. He contrasts the resulting unpredictability of future internal evolution within the Soviet Union—and the related and perhaps even more fateful uncertainty vis-à-vis Eastern Europe—with the bleak certainty of the Stalinist era. Identifying the change in Sino-Soviet relations as probably the most important single geopolitical event of the past forty years, he also notes the general economic distress and dependency of the "outer ring" of non-European countries allied with the Soviets. On the American side of the East-West ledger, Bundy traces the decline and fall of the "intermediate ring" of 1950s-vintage foreign bases and other security arrangements outside Europe, as well as the erosion of U.S. economic dominance and, eventually, some of its competitiveness in the face of European recovery and the mercurial growth of the Japanese economy.

By tracing these developments in specific terms, Bundy gives substance to such oft-mouthed phrases as "diffusion of power" and "reduced centrality of the East-West struggle." He also places in perspective such important changes as the transformation of East Asia from cockpit into bustling marketplace and the rise of Muslim fundamentalism in the wake of the Iranian revolution. He sketches not only the ups and downs of nations and regions, but of issues, whether old (arms control, terrorism, the role of international law), or new (universal human rights, U.S. competitiveness, world demography, and planetary resources). At the end of his odyssey, he concludes that, although some aspects of the security-related challenges faced by current U.S. policy makers are basically familiar, the overlay of much more complex economic problems, as well as newly appreciated global concerns, combines with an eroded national consensus on central issues to create a very different bill of fare for the American policy maker of the 1990s, as compared with his or her counterpart four decades earlier.

In the second chapter, Fred Bergsten, director of the Institute for International Economics and former assistant secretary of the treasury for international affairs, homes in on the historic economic policy choices that he believes face the Bush administration and Congress. His primary focus is on the twin deficits in the federal budget and in America's trade account with the rest of the world, which have become chronic features of the nation's economic picture in recent years. His thesis is that the massive borrowing required to finance deficits of this scale is not sustainable without decisive moves to eliminate them over time, and that, unlike the situation in former years, circumstances have now developed in which international and domestic economic policy concerns argue for the same basic package of policies and actions by the United States and the other principal actors involved.

Bergsten sketches the sharp contrast between apparent American prosperity in late 1988 and the conditions that he foresees if, and to the extent that, the foreigners who have lent the United States $700 billion to finance these deficits over the past six years lose their enthusiasm for holding American debt, or begin any substantial withdrawal of the $1.5 trillion in liquid assets that they now hold in this country. For both economic and political reasons, he argues, the president should set as his goal the elimination of both the trade deficit (now $130 billion to $140 billion per year) and the structural deficit in the federal budget (about $150 billion per year) in the course of the four years 1989–1993. Bergsten believes that this goal can be met through a combination of federal tax increases and expenditure cuts, reorientation of the U.S. economy toward more investment and the production of exports, and limitation of the expansion of total domestic demand to 1 to 1.5 percentage points below the growth of potential output of goods and services (which he forecasts to grow at about 2.5 percent per year). He sees these policies as responsive both to current domestic worries, which center on renewed surges in inflation and interest rates as the economy approaches full employment, and to international concerns, which focus on the decline in American competitiveness because of a productivity lag born of a very low national rate of saving to support investment. In order for the policy package to work, however, Bergsten emphasizes the need to avoid any move toward protectionism in American trade policy, and counsels an end to existing voluntary restrictions on imports into the United States.

Bergsten makes clear that his approach would require important and sometimes painful cooperative moves by other nations and international institutions in order to accommodate "the American correction." These steps range from a concerted program, led by multilateral lenders, to solve the debt crisis in fifteen Third World countries; to changes in the domestic economic policies of trade surplus countries, notably West Germany, the smaller European Economic Community (EEC) members, and Japan; to the agreement of America's allies to accept a significantly greater share of the defense cost burden. Meanwhile, the success of the entire program would, in Bergsten's view, require a 15 to 20 percent reduction in the late 1988 relative value of the dollar, accompanied by concerted international action to assure that the bulk of the adjustment comes vis-à-vis the currencies of the countries with the largest trade surpluses, and that the dollar neither falls further nor soon begins rising again, thereby discouraging the new investment in export production that American firms would be encouraged by the program to make. This, in turn, would require abandoning the system of floating international exchange rates that began in 1973, and replacing it with a system of "target zones" of currency fluctuations that, in Bergsten's judgment, would both place a firm foundation under the adjustment of the imbalance in American trade accounts and provide a much improved basis for cooperation in the complementary management of national economies.

Bergsten dubs this full package a strategy of "competitive interdependence." It represents an explicit attempt to act on what he perceives as the two insights that must be understood and accepted if the United States is to deal effectively with the economic realities of today: that American economic health is inextricably linked with world economic health and with a strong U.S. position in the world economy and that America can still pursue its global interests, but in ways that differ from the past. He believes that we ignore these new facts of life, and their implications, at our considerable peril.

To say that the two commentaries that follow Bergsten's view disagree with it is to beggar the language. Characteristic of both the breadth and the heat of the current debate about the state of the American economy, the gap between Bergsten and his critics extends far beyond current facts and trends to basic questions of legitimacy of opposing frameworks for analyzing and interpreting the present future state of national economic health.

The first commentary, authored by Paul Craig Roberts, the holder of a chair in political economy at the Center for Strategic and International Studies and another former assistant secretary of the treasury, argues that Bergsten fears a phantom "boogeyman" because he misconceives both the nature and the causes of the budget deficit and the trade deficit. The former deficit, says Roberts, is not the red ink spilt to finance a national consumption binge, but the result of a revenue shortfall that traces directly to the combined effects of the 1981–1982 recession and the accompanying sudden fall in the inflation rate. Together, Roberts argues, these events wiped out $2.5 trillion in taxable income during the years 1981–1986. Since this income was not there to be taxed, federal expenditures exceeded revenues for reasons that Roberts asserts to be quite unrelated to consumption-fueled demand. Similarly, Roberts avers that the trade deficit does not result from foreign capital rushing in to finance the U.S. budget deficit, but rather from American money staying home in the form of investments in a domestic economy where such investments had been made more attractive by the simultaneous reductions in U.S. tax burdens and decline in the attractiveness of competing investments abroad, especially those in the Third World.

Roberts pooh-poohs what he regards as hysterics about the shift of the United States from creditor to debtor nation, arguing that the proper measure of net position is the ratio of a nation's earnings on its foreign investments as against its payments to its foreign creditors—a calculation which registered a net yield of $21 billion in America's favor in 1987. And reviewing the comparative growth of U.S. budget deficits and public debt since 1970, Roberts concludes that, as a share of GNP, U.S. ratios have run half or less of the ratios of such countries as Canada, Italy, and the Netherlands. As against larger economies, Roberts observes that the share of the U.S. GNP comprised of federal debt has grown only a fraction as fast as the corresponding shares of the Japanese and West German GNPs; yet he detects no international concern about debt crises in those countries.

Finally, Roberts dismisses both the charge that U.S. prosperity is built on a shaky footing of excessive borrowing and the allegation that the American rate of saving is falling. Rather, he argues that Bergsten mistakes differences in the composition of the post–1981 tax cut investment profile for basic changes in the propensity to invest and overlooks what Roberts sees as sturdy resistance of the private saving rate to demographic forces exerting pressure to reduce it. While Roberts would not oppose policy measures designed to encourage other countries to improve their investment climates or to achieve a decline in the U.S. budget deficit, his analysis of the urgency of these matters is clearly on a different intellectual planet from that inhabited by economists of Bergsten's persuasion.

While advancing some of the same arguments, the second commentary proceeds from a different dominant premise. In it, Arthur Laffer, chairman of A.B. Laffer & Associates and a member of President Reagan's Economic Policy Advisory Board, asserts that a trade deficit is the necessary price of attracting the influx of foreign capital that he sees as required to finance healthy growth in the United States. For Laffer, the genuine barometer of economic well-being is a surplus of capital flowing abroad. Such a surplus can only be maintained, he argues, if the United States is prepared to buy more in imports than it sells in exports, thereby providing foreign investors with the cash to invest in the United States. The fact that these investors see fit to use their export proceeds to invest in this country Laffer views as symbolic of American success in creating the most attractive major investment arena in the world. This success, he maintains, has permitted the United States to harness foreign assets to the creation of a net total of 15 million American jobs since 1983. The threat that Laffer sees is not that the red ink on the trade account will continue, but that Americans will erroneously interpret trade deficits as problems rather than as success indicators, and take "corrective" actions that will lessen the attractiveness of the U.S. investment climate, spurring a flight from American holdings by U.S. and foreign investors alike. Most worrisome to Laffer in this regard is Bergsten's inclusion of a tax increase in his recommended package of measures to eliminate the U.S. budget deficit.

The most striking aspect of this exchange on economic realities and prospects is the looking glass quality of the opposing measures of success and danger. What Bergsten sees as ominous, his critics rejoice in. What they see as self-defeating, he sees as imperative. The difference is not one of degree, but of fundamentally incompatible views of the driving forces of the economy and of the factual indicators of economic health and progress. Viewed as a whole, the Bergsten chapter and the commentaries nicely illustrate the immense differences in professional theory and perception that have been among the most notable outgrowths of the increasing complexity and international linkage of the world economy.

In the third chapter, former secretary of defense Harold Brown, who is now chairman of the Johns Hopkins Foreign Policy Institute, examines the implications of what he sees as the primary changes of the past decade—economic stagnation and political evolution in the Soviet Union and diffusion of economic power formerly centered in the United States—together with future trends that can now be foreseen, as these factors affect possible amendment of the definition of U.S. political and military security interests that has largely prevailed for the past four decades. Brown conducts his inquiry along two axes of change. The first is possible movement of U.S. policy along a spectrum ranging from a "minimalist" security policy, which would provide for reduction of the actual or potential American military role to the irreducible minimum required to preserve the physical security of U.S. territory, to what might be termed a "gradualist" policy, in which existing alliances and other defense arrangements would be largely maintained, but the United States would take steps to encourage roles for its allies in cost burden sharing and joint decision making that more closely approximate their current relative economic capacities.

The second axis of Brown's analysis is the relative degree and pace of change in the world picture that may develop in the years leading up to the millennium. He examines two scenarios. The first, which he thinks the more likely, is basically an extrapolation of current trends, though involving certain extremely important wrinkles, such as reversion to traditional internal policy by the Soviet Union in the wake of a flattening out of economic progress after four or five years of only modest results from Gorbachev's initiatives. The alternative scenario features one or more major discontinuities, which, if they should occur, he sees as likely to take the form of acceleration of current trends. He provides a daunting roster of candidates for such acceleration, from festering situations within certain countries and regions, to the burgeoning potential of key scientific and weapons developments, to planetary changes such as the greenhouse effect. Since it is impossible on current evidence to assign a probability to any or all of these jolts—beyond the certainty that some forms of "alarums and excursions" will in fact occur, as they always have in previous decades—he concludes that the continuity scenario is the proper basis for prudent security planning.

Having explored these axes in general terms, Brown then turns to the major issues that he believes will need to be faced, and the options available for dealing with each. As to the U.S.–Soviet strategic balance, he considers a spectrum of policy choice ranging from attempts to restore American strategic superiority (or even dominance), to reduction in strategic forces down to the bare minimum number of survivable warheads necessary to deter attack against the United States, to an effort to transform the whole strategic equation by placing maximum reliance on developing defensive techniques against nuclear assault. In the end, he favors continuation of current strategic policy, which seeks stabilization at lower levels of nuclear armament. Brown then examines a similarly broad range of policy options with respect to conventional forces, concluding that the optimal policy in and around Europe is to seek very asymmetrical reductions and large-scale redeployments of Soviet forces, perhaps stimulated by modest upgrading of allied conventional strength (which is all that he believes the West Europeans can be persuaded to pay for). Outside Europe, he finds that both prospects and options vary greatly between regions and types of confrontations.

Brown then reviews the choices available to deal with a further series of pressing issues—economic relations, particularly those with the USSR; relations with America's allies, with a special focus on sharing the burden of Western defense costs; and problems in the Third World, especially the criteria and weight the United States should attach to local human rights policies, whether economic development in these countries will much affect U.S. security, and the evolution of regional powers. Finally, he addresses the main issues of defense budgeting and of strategic, conventional, and geographic military doctrine, as they will present themselves in the 1990s, and the optional approaches that the United States could take toward each. He ends with a judgment on the currently fashionable assertion that America is suffering from "imperial overstretch," a malady said to afflict world powers that permit their overseas commitments to outstrip their economic capacity to support them. Citing comparative shares of gross national product (GNP) devoted to defense and international affairs by the United States and other countries in previous eras, Brown finds that the issue is not one of overextension, but of the balance that Americans elect to draw among the responsibili-

ties, the risks, and the burdens that will present themselves, at
home and abroad, in the years ahead.

In the chapter that then follows, Seyom Brown, chair of the
department of politics at Brandeis University, steps back a bit
from the hurly-burly of immediate policy choices and assesses
whether the traditional geopolitical doctrine that has informed
most Western strategic thinking over the past century continues to be relevant in the world that is now emerging. He starts
with the fundamental premise of the insular powers and those
outside the Eurasian land mass that the rimland of that mass
must be kept out of the hands of the power that controlled the
heartland, lest that power dominate the world. He then ana-
lyzes the application of this principle to the postwar situation
and concludes that American inheritance of Britain's role as
chief protector of the rimlands exerted powerful incentives to
form a global alliance against the reigning heartland power,
the USSR, just as similar incentives operated on the Russians.

However, in his view, the subsequent failure of much of the
world to coalesce into two tight, mutually hostile blocs has
now combined with the impact of advances in military technology, communication, and transportation to substantially de-
value the utility of worldwide alliances to both superpowers as
a means of preventing global dominance by the other. Simultaneous with this erosion, in Brown's view, both Communist
and anti-Communist ideological glue began to fail as the Soviets recognized that the coming of nuclear arms in capitalist
countries nullified the official Marxist vision of capitalism
stamped out through a series of mop-up wars, and the Americans receded from the conviction that the success of Commu-
nist-like movements anywhere in the world represented a clear
and intolerable threat to survival of the American way of life by
a monolithic campaign for world domination controlled by the
Kremlin. These lessons were reinforced and the East-West
axis of world affairs was further compromised, according to
Brown, by the difficulties and frustrations that both superpowers encountered in their attempts to enlist, influence, ally with,
help, placate, or otherwise cope with the less developed countries.

Spurred by technological developments, Brown sees these trends as creating major new fault lines within the traditional nation-state as well as between nations. He believes that the revolution in human capacity to move people, things, diseases, effluents, and, most particularly, money is putting great stress on the efficacy of nations and blocs of nations to perform the functions for which they were created. Riven by the mismatch between modern conditions and the capacity of traditional national and international organizing principles to deal with them effectively, and increasingly freed of the galvanizing fears of the cold war, Brown sees the world drifting toward what he calls "polyarchy"—a many-communitied globe host to multiple "spheres of influence; hegemonic imperiums; interdependencies; nationalisms; and transstate religious, ethnic, and ideological affinities," some overlapping, some concentric, and some in conflict with each other. For Brown, the question of whether humanity will emerge from the twenty-first century in reasonable shape depends in large part on whether steps are taken in the relatively near term to steer this drift in what he regards as a benign, rather than a dangerous, direction.

Brown sees the benign variant of a polyarchic world as one in which the multiple bargaining activities that would characterize relations between so many power centers would tend to reinforce the incentives upon each center to moderate its exertion of coercive influence—most importantly, of violence—upon others so as to avoid losing chips that will be needed in other, simultaneous bargaining situations where the object of the influence may be needed as an ally. (Anyone who has ever attempted to manage a multifaceted legislative program through the labyrinth of functionally organized power centers represented by a legislative committee system will readily recognize this constraint.) On the other hand, the dangerous variant of polyarchy, for Brown, is what might be termed the warlord phenomenon, where independent capacity for physical coercion becomes the sole measure of power center efficacy, and the incentives to acquire advanced arms and engage in lawless behavior (e.g., state terrorism) become irresistible. He sees the benign and dangerous variants as about equally plausible, but regards the dangerous alternative as too threatening to risk.

Brown examines three U.S. policy options for dealing with this new challenge: passive, pragmatic adaptation as polyarchy pulls apart postwar alliances and institutions; an attempt to restore the cold war consensus; and what he calls "creative adaptation," which is his preferred course. The third option would attempt to exploit polyarchic trends to shape a new world order to replace the postwar version. This would, as Brown sees it, require the United States to adopt a strategy of "deliberate depolarization," the overt object of which would be to reduce the degree to which the planet is divided into two opposing military camps, and increase the scope of territory in which the United States and the Soviet Union have formally agreed upon military disengagement. This agreement should not be to refrain from competition for influence, in his view, but to maintain free access to compete, subject to regulation only by the host country's tolerance of outside involvement. He asserts that such a step would need to be accompanied by extensive further nuclear arms reduction agreements between the superpowers (in order to lessen incentives for nuclear proliferation that might accompany U.S.–Soviet disengagement), by much greater superpower equanimity with respect to the ideological leanings of indigenous governments, and by the evolution of new, transnational arrangements that require those who substantially affect the way that others live to be politically and legally accountable to those affected, and normally act only with their consent. Brown emphasizes that his favored option would not forego containment of aggressive Soviet expansion, should it reemerge, nor would it involve any unilateral treaty abandonments or U.S. concessions on nuclear or other arms. His intent is simply to adapt postwar institutions and national roles to the new geopolitical realities that he believes have made many of our traditional definitions and reflexes obsolete.

In the following chapter, Graham Allison, dean of the Kennedy School of Government at Harvard University, provides a comprehensive review of essential U.S. foreign policy objectives, microstrategies, and performance in the setting offered by the postwar international arena, and proposes goals and strategies suited to what he anticipates will be the global setting through the year 2000. Looking backward, Allison asserts that an objective observer would adjudge the expansion in American influence—military, political, economic, and cultural—as the main feature that has distinguished the last half century of international affairs. He presents a four-part analysis of U.S. postwar international strategy, setting forth U.S. objectives, the policy environment in which they were formulated and to which they were directed, the microstrategies by which America sought to achieve its goals, and his assessment of U.S. performance to date.

To remind us of what the United States set out to do in the postwar era, Allison brings us back to perhaps the most seminal single policy document of that period, National Security Council (NSC) document #68 (originally top secret, but long since declassified). Having set forth the military, economic, and political objectives stated in NSC-68, he delineates the specific strategies that were developed to accomplish them, ranging from containment of the Soviet Union by nuclear deterrence and other measures, through unprecedentedly generous help in the economic reconstruction of both allies and vanquished, through establishment of new international financial and monetary institutions. Measured against the fondest contemporary American hopes for the future at the time that the basic lines of postwar U.S. policy were laid down, or against the record of prior victor nations following other wars, Allison concludes that the American postwar performance must be declared a striking success.

Looking forward, much of Allison's analysis, like much of that presented by both Harold Brown and Seyom Brown, puts one in mind of the ancient adage that those whom the gods would torment find their fondest prayers answered. All three chapters emphasize that it is the very success of U.S. postwar policy that has created the new challenges we face today. Had that policy failed, the authors seem agreed, today's problems would be much worse. Nevertheless, the fact that most of our

current dilemmas are outgrowths of a basically successful U.S.
response to postwar conditions and opportunities does not
make them any less formidable. By Allison's lights, the main
problem areas that have in part survived and in part arisen
from the general success of U.S. policy are three: the fact that
for the first time in history another nation has the discretionary
capacity, at whatever cost to itself, to destroy the United States
as a functioning society; the fact that one-fourth of the inhabi-
tants of a drastically shrunken globe must survive on an income of less than $200 per year; and the fact that the interde-
pendent world economy now both severely penalizes such
national mistakes in economic management as those of which
the United States has recently been guilty and makes the cooperation of other key nations a necessary condition for the success of any American domestic economic strategy.

For Allison, the first challenge to Americans posed by the
altered world of the 1990s is to manage a conceptual stretch
beyond the goals and concepts with which they have under-
standably become familiar and comfortable. The problem he
describes comes down to summoning the wit and vision to
determine what kind of world we want, in an affirmative sense,
in addition to what kind we want to avoid. Although the depth
and duration of the current flux in the Soviet Union remain to
be determined with certainty, he reminds us that such certainty is unlikely to arrive before the opportunity to realize
maximum advantage from the change is long past.

Allison believes that the most fundamental American objectives set forth in NSC-68 remain valid, but that the policy environment in which they are pursued has evolved sufficiently to
require U.S. policy makers to stretch their thinking to new or
refined versions of at least six basic postwar concepts: from
containment to the terms on which we are prepared to see the
USSR admitted to the international system created by the
Western democracies; from solely defensive alliances of Western powers to arrangements that recognize the new and very
important status of a more integrated Western Europe and of
Japan; from bipolarity to multipolarity; from nuclear deterrence based on what he sees as an increasingly noncredible

threat to commit national suicide to a more cogent theory of strategic defense and the role of nuclear weapons therein; from a concept of the Third World as primarily a cold war frontier to one that differentiates among its component nations according to their circumstances and desires; and from complacency about the U.S. economic base to recognition that it must be strengthened and weaned away from productivity decline and excessive borrowing. Allison further stresses that in the arguably revolutionary policy environment of the 1990s, all of the answers to these questions must, to a much larger degree than ever before, be developed in consultation with others, not, as in the past, solely "made in America."

Allison stakes out four areas in which he thinks new microstrategies are needed if the United States is to adjust successfully to the evolving realities of the 1990s. The first is reconstruction of the American economic base, which he believes requires eliminating the federal budget deficit, increasing the savings rate, and, hardest of the three, reviving the productivity growth rate. The second area is an aggressive effort to settle the cold war essentially on Western terms, which first involves determining just what those terms are. Pointing out that actual Soviet behavior to date is far removed from the forthcoming tone of Gorbachev's rhetoric, Allison proposes the development and application of a series of specific tests to see whether Gorbachev actually means what he says about normalizing Soviet relations with the West, and whether he is capable of carrying out steps that are both implied by his stated positions and would further U.S. interests. As examples of the latter, he cites reduced Soviet defense spending, less Soviet troublemaking in the Third World (e.g., Central America), more arms limitation agreements and less Soviet secrecy in military matters, greater concessions on internal human rights, and similar tests of Soviet intentions in other realms. The overall aim of these tests, in Allison's view, should be to determine how far the Soviets are prepared to move toward a world safe for peaceful competition between the Western and Communist systems, which, he points out, is the world aspired to in 1950 by NSC-68.

The third area where Allison believes that new approaches are needed concerns America's relations with her Western allies. The first imperative here, as he sees it, is to prepare for the inevitable strains that will occur within these alliances if and as Gorbachev relaxes the perception of the Soviet threat—a perception that is already in some disrepair in many European countries. Another and related requirement is to develop concepts—he suggests adaptation of the Japanese idea of "comprehensive security," which defines security to include its economic and political as well as its military components—under which it is possible both to make more equal partners of the allies and to persuade them to bear an equitable financial share of the costs of building a safe and stable world. A further need in this area, as seen by Allison, is progress on the host of major bilateral and other issues that now exist between the United States and each of the allies taken individually, most particularly Japan. And perhaps both most important and most difficult, Allison believes that efforts in this area must eventually involve a coherent articulation of the world order that the commonwealth of industrial democracies seeks to create as a long-term goal.

The final area for new strategizing discussed by Allison concerns the treatment of nuclear weapons. Here, his counsel is that such weapons are and should remain integral to American defense strategy, although efforts should be made to reduce their number through further agreements with the Russians. He does not reject attempts to create new nuclear defense technologies, though he does not believe that they can ever be fully protective against nuclear attack. And Allison urges that U.S. policy makers return to the drawing board to think through the fundamental elements of nuclear credibility in a world of mutual superpower capacity to destroy each other after absorbing a first strike.

In the essay that succeeds Allison's, Lawrence Eagleburger, president of Kissinger & Associates and former under secretary of state, portrays the United States and its democratic allies as entering a period of transition from a postwar era of relatively successful avoidance of the horrors that pervaded the globe in the first half of the twentieth century to a new era characterized by multipolarity among nations. This multipolar state of affairs, he points out, is more typical in history and now seems unfamiliar only because of the aberrational bipolarity of the past four decades. He believes that America must make peace with a shift in its role from "overwhelming predominance to a position more akin to 'first among equals,'" while Western Europe and Japan must avoid intoxication by the potent elixir of new found independence from the American writ. These adjustments are made more complex, he observes, by the fact that the old bipolar adversary, the Soviet Union, is undergoing an even more stressful adjustment that is necessary to avoid its deletion from the world's list of highly developed economies. For Eagleburger, the key test faced by the Western powers is whether each now reverts to what he considers a myopic, unilateral pursuit of its own narrow interests, or, taking heed of lessons so hard learned in the first half of this century, they move to a collective mode of action that realizes the powerful synergies that he believes they can achieve in pursuit of the basic goals that they hold in common.

Despite its diminished predominance, Eagleburger believes that America's unique status as the only nation in the West that both acts and thinks as a global power entails a similarly unique capacity to comprehend the challenge and lead its confreres to a similar understanding. He discerns an ebbing of intimacy in the Western alliance over the last decade that, beyond sheer generational evolution, he attributes to differences in European and American perspectives on issues of mutual defense, the utility of nuclear weapons, the nature and distribution of international responsibilities and attendant costs, the requirements of proper consultation and joint strategizing, and the significance of the Gorbachev phenomenon. He foresees no rupture in the alliance, but suggests that chronic U.S.–European differences on how to respond to Soviet overtures—the U.S. wishing to go slow, the Europeans preferring rapid movement on the economic front and schizoid about movement on defense issues—could generate languid drift toward more unilateral action by both. Eagleburger identifies the market unification of Western Europe, now scheduled to occur in 1992, as the primary regulator of the direction and speed of this drift, depending upon whether the new European market becomes a protectionist bloc that impedes trade with the U.S. or a facilitator of North Atlantic commerce.

Eagleburger believes that the *sine qua non* for avoidance of negative impact on the alliance is for both the U.S. and Europe to recognize that the major decisions connected with unification of the West European market are political, not just economic, in nature, and must be addressed in the higher reaches of national capitals. From the American standpoint, he argues, the process must include recognition that any outcome of the European market unification—which he believes will inevitably lead to greater political and defense unification if the market meld proceeds on schedule—will necessarily reduce the role of the United States, as compared with the role this country has played in previous decades.

Turning his attention to other key players on the world stage, Eagleburger notes the dramatic but still embryonic character of the Gorbachev initiative. He argues that what is most clear is that the Soviet leader is a formidable figure and that his driving motive is to strengthen the Soviet Union, not to do the West any favors. Wary of the implications of a stronger Russia, Eagleburger says that the verdict is still out on the authenticity and durability of the Gorbachev move, pending evidence that realities are being reshaped to match rhetoric. In Eastern Europe, however, Eagleburger does see signs of change, though in different directions in different countries. Plagued by economic troubles and unpopular governments and never in postwar history capable of accommodating major reform without reaching the point of military repression, these countries face, in Eagleburger's view, a quite novel challenge in circumstances where their residual mailed fist, the Soviet Union, is itself pressing for reform. Whatever their response, he expects important changes in the relationship between Moscow and its allies, and stresses the significance of a united Western response to these changes.

Eagleburger attaches great significance to the question whether the qualities that so quickly transformed Japan into an economic colossus can be harnessed to the international responsibilities that come with that status. He sees U.S.–Japanese relations as inherently more difficult than their North Atlantic counterpart because of the vast and still largely unbridged gap between the Japanese and Euro-American cultures. His prescription is a process for much closer and more regular trilateral consultation on political, economic, and military issues.

Finally, Eagleburger directs our attention to the problem of Third World debt, which he cites as living proof of the fact that solutions to contemporary world problems are instrinsically multilateral in nature. Fearing that debt pressures will lead to default or even violence, he calls for abandonment of what he sees as preoccupation with "band-aid" measures in favor of a comprehensive multilateral approach aimed at reducing debt to the point where growth can be restored and, with it, popular stakes in political stability. To illustrate what he believes hangs in the balance, he cites the case of Mexico, where he sees a level of restiveness that threatens "civil unrest bordering on revolution" within the next decade. Eagleburger maintains that only a truly multilateral debt relief program can forestall this deterioration—he doubts that the legacy of U.S.–Mexican history will permit a tenable bilateral program—and return Mexico to economic progress and relative political stability.

Eagleburger's provocative essay completes a series of six thoughtful chapters which, though differing quite significantly in substance and emphasis, are united in the expectation that American policy must adapt to important changes in the world that are already asserting themselves and are likely to become more prominent in the 1990s. No matter how clear this need may be from the standpoint of American international interests, however, there remains the critical matter of the willingness of American voters to support change. This question occasions the final chapter, authored by John Marttila, a partner in the public opinion polling firm of Marttila & Kiley, which reports the relevant findings of a penetrating series of eleven

polls of registered voters in the United States, exclusively on
foreign policy and national security issues, which were carried
out under bipartisan auspices throughout 1988.

By beginning with a replication of probably the most powerful single foreign policy related television campaign commercial of the 1980s, Marttila forcefully reminds us of the enduring themes that undergird majority American public opinion
about the Soviet Union and U.S. relations with it. He also
dramatizes the resonance in the electorate that adroit use of
this increasingly dominant medium can generate when it
strikes these underlying chords. There is, he says, a "truly unshakable national consensus" that the United States should be
involved in negotiations to reduce the threat of nuclear war,
but that, because of deep suspicion of the Soviets and their
leadership, such negotiations should be carried on very cautiously and from a position of American strength. The feat
required of successful foreign policy leadership, he implies, is
to keep this fundamental fact in mind while simultaneously
understanding the strong currents of change in the American
mind-set that are also under way.

Marttila demonstrates the shape of these changes in majority perceptions with wave upon wave of revealing polling data.
He shows that most Americans believe that the requirements
of national security are changing, and that new threats—international drug trafficking, nuclear proliferation, terrorism, environmental degradation—are seen to pose greater danger in
the early 1990s than most expect to arise from Soviet expansionism. He also reveals the depth of popular concern about
the American economy, where only about one American in five
believes that the United States ranks first among world economic powers, and one in three ranks the United States behind
Japan and West Germany in this respect. And he documents
the singular personal popularity that Gorbachev has achieved
in the United States, ranking him behind only British Prime
Minister Margaret Thatcher and the Pope among twenty world
leaders tested for favorability of impression among Americans. Yet he contrasts Gorbachev's personal popularity with

the continuing suspicion that most Americans evidence with respect to the genuineness of Soviet peaceful intentions, and with the majority conviction that the United States should maintain a strong defense establishment and that American leaders should "go slow" in negotiating any major changes with the Soviet leader.

Marttila also reports trends and temperatures of U.S. public opinion on a broad array of specific issues—the significance of Soviet withdrawal from Afghanistan, the Reagan Strategic Defense Initiative, the U.S.–Soviet balance of nuclear and conventional forces, the intermediate nuclear forces (INF) treaty and the basic U.S. negotiating position in renewed Strategic Arms Reduction Talks (START), the most likely cause of a nuclear war, the proper priority of U.S. defense spending to protect various parts of the world, the topic areas of acceptable and unacceptable U.S.–Soviet cooperation in addressing world problems, the incidence of isolationism, the perceived value of foreign aid, and several other critical issue areas. These data include any number of intriguing findings, such as the fact that only one American in ten believes the most likely cause of nuclear war to be Soviet surprise attack, whereas about one in three identifies the act of a madman, a terrorist, or a nonsuperpower involved in a regional conflict as the most likely cause. The data also include some fascinating minority views, such as the 41 percent of those polled who thought it likely that the United States and the Soviet Union would enter into a long-term military alliance.

The poll results reported by Marttila also spotlight important fissures in the structure of American public opinion, of which the most striking is probably the pronounced relative conservatism on U.S.–Soviet and nuclear matters that is consistently demonstrated by female voters without college educations. Marttila's very recent data also reconfirm the already established fact that there are critical, longstanding elements of postwar U.S. policy that most Americans do not believe are in fact official government policy, or, when so informed, do not believe that any American government would actually carry out. Most notable among these is the "first use" doctrine providing that the United States will respond with nuclear weapons to a successful Soviet attack upon Western Europe that solely employs conventional weapons. The margin by which those polled considered such a U.S. response an improper use of nuclear arms was eleven-to-one. Indeed, only a bare majority of 57 percent of poll respondents found it proper for the United States to make a nuclear response to a limited nuclear attack on American military forces engaged in combat. With these and other examples, Marttila drives home the subtlety of the complex relation between prevailing public opinion and the range of policy choice which, filtered through the dynamics of political representation and the influence of special interests and other organized advocacy, is actually available to the makers of American foreign policy.

Marttila leaves no doubt as to which issue is making Americans most apprehensive, and which they believe will increasingly dominate the U.S. foreign policy agenda in the 1990s. This is the state of the American economy and its place among competitive national economies. Fully half of those polled recorded the belief that the U.S. economy is "slipping dangerously" as compared to its industrialized competitors, and about twice as large a share of the respondents ranked Japan as a "very strong" competitor in the world economy as rated the United States in that category. Moreover, those polled split almost evenly as to whether economic competition from Japan and West Germany did or did not represent a greater threat to America's future than Communist expansion ever did. Although of relatively recent origin and still tinged with the exaggerated pigments that often attend current obsessions, these convictions now seem strong and deeply set. They may be seen as the other bookend in an opinion structure, masterfully mapped by Marttila, that is bounded by deeply entrenched cold war instincts and suspicions of Soviet behavior, on the one hand, and recognition of the need to cope with pressing new international economic challenges and other opportunities, on the other. Marttila's work suggests that the challenge to the U.S. leadership of the 1990s is to recognize and successfully negotiate these shoals of public opinion while neither losing its popular mandate nor failing to adapt to the new conditions that will require important course corrections.

In the end, it is the reader who must weave these strands of analysis and prescription into a coherent fabric of perception and conviction. In doing so, it is important to reintroduce the real world element of simultaneity, which can easily be lost in the sequential reading of analyses such as these. Life is seldom so convenient as to offer its challenges in neat sequence. The same nation that is addressing the pressing economic problems that Bergsten describes is likely to be simultaneously faced with the need to adjust to Soviet changes, to redefine its relations with its key allies, to cope with as yet unknown upheavals in the Third World, to monitor and address planetary phenomena from the greenhouse effect to depletion of the ozone layer, to understand and exploit an unprecedentedly promising prospect of scientific breakthroughs of bewildering variety, and to deal with a humbling array of domestic problems. Thinking about any particular foreign policy problem as though it will occur in a vacuum free of these simultaneous concerns is likely to be at best unproductive and at worst quite dangerous.

Thus the task of integration is left to all of us fortunate enough to be exposed to this rich store of knowledge and projection. It falls to each of us to piece together, in the light of these chapters, the assessments, expectations, priorities, and aspirations that add up to our own perception of the world of the 1990s and the appropriate American response to it. Some will see the need for fundamental adjustments in postwar concepts. Others will not. At the very least, however, these essays make a powerful case for explicit debate of the question and its implications. It is to stimulate and inform this debate that this volume was prepared. It is impossible to capture the full sweep and power of any of the essays in a brief overview. Only a full reading of each will yield the rich dividends of factual information and reasoned argument that each provides. In the end, I believe that the reader who attends carefully to these chapters, whatever the directions of his or her own thought, will be far better equipped to take an active and constructive role in what looms as the most critical reappraisal of American purpose that has taken place since 1945.

1

The 1950s Versus the 1990s

WILLIAM P. BUNDY

Introduction

T his is an essay on how the world, and American perceptions of it and of their own situation and role, have
changed since the main lines of U.S. postwar foreign policy
were laid down. My aim is to set a foundation for other chapters in this volume, which propose policies for the 1990s.

WILLIAM P. BUNDY, most recently a visiting lecturer at Princeton
University in 1985–1987, was from 1972 to mid–1984 the editor of
Foreign Affairs. As editor, Mr. Bundy also wrote a number of articles
for *Foreign Affairs*. Between his graduation from Yale in 1939 and from
Harvard Law School in 1947, he was from 1941 to 1946 in the U.S.
Army, rising from private to major commanding a small Signal Corps
unit that worked with the British in the ULTRA operation that broke
high-level German ciphers. After four years of law practice in Washington, in 1951 Mr. Bundy joined the Office of National Estimates in
the Central Intelligence Agency, where he served until 1961. He then
served in the Kennedy administration as assistant secretary of defense for international security affairs, and under President Johnson
as assistant secretary of state for East Asian and Pacific affairs, a post
he held until 1969. Mr. Bundy is currently writing on U.S. foreign
policy since 1972.

The title is, of course, neater than life. Resistance to Soviet expansion in Iran, Greece, and Turkey dated from 1946–1947, as did George Kennan's seminal cables and "X" article; the Marshall Plan from 1947–1948; the North Atlantic Treaty Organization (NATO) as a formal structure from 1949. Yet it is clear that the first Soviet nuclear test in late 1949, and above all the onset of the Korean War in June 1950, galvanized the nation and its policy makers to transform framework into institutionalized substance, rapidly and on a worldwide scale.

At the other end of this policy-creating period, 1958 saw the first serious arms control talks (over nuclear tests), and it was in 1958–1959 that the concept of large-scale development aid to poorer countries began to take hold, and that Latin America became again (as in prewar decades) a major focus of American policy. In short, "the 1950s" might more accurately be defined as running from about 1947 to about 1959.

As the examples just cited suggest, neither policy perceptions nor the objective situation remained fixed and immutable during this period. Even the Khrushchev who banged his shoe on the table at the United Nations in 1960 was, and seemed, a big change from Joseph Stalin. By then, too, it was clear that continental Western Europe and Japan, flat on their backs in 1947, were moving ahead solidly. Decolonization and the decline of European influence came in stages, starting with India and Indonesia and at an accelerating pace in Indochina and North Africa, with the 1956 Suez fiasco both a practical and psychological signal of great consequence.

Notably, too, the degree of national consensus on foreign policy within the United States—often described nostalgically as if it had been monolithic—fluctuated greatly, solidifying only after the middle of the decade as acute early differences over China, Korean War strategy, and the activities of Senator Joseph McCarthy tended to recede. By 1960, when I worked on the report of President Eisenhower's Commission on National Goals (an American Assembly project, incidentally), the areas of broad agreement among those who seriously followed foreign policy seemed greater than in any previous time of peace. To be sure, the political campaign that year was vigorous, but John Kennedy's real theme was, in effect, "anything you can do, we can do better." The tone of debate that year seemed cool indeed to those who had lived through the 1950 and 1952 campaigns.

Thus it is possible to speak of a mind-set among informed Americans that took shape in this span of a decade-plus and lay at the root of American foreign policy. It is the world, and the role of the United States in that world, as it was then perceived, that we shall first discuss. As we move to describe, in section II of the chapter, the contrasting "facts" and perceptions of today, we can pause occasionally to note where events have modified or confounded what was seen or judged earlier.

I.

Any listing of the key perceptions of the 1950s is bound to be somewhat arbitrary. This one is designed to highlight judgments and assumptions that stand in contrast to the perceptions of the present. We start with the salient elements in the strategic and political setting of foreign policy, move to the economic setting, and conclude with brief notes on some factors within or directly relating to the United States.

The Strategic and Political Setting in the 1950s

Concentration of Power

It is hard to exaggerate the degree to which the United States and the Soviet Union dominated the international scene in the first fifteen years after the end of World War II. In power terms alone, the way each had emerged from that war would have virtually assured its preeminence. The fact that the two shortly became implacable adversaries made their dominance much more acutely felt, contributing greatly to what is accurately thought of as a bipolar era.

Their bases of power differed substantially. Soviet power derived largely from its military strength, its victory over Nazi

Germany in campaigns far bloodier than any in other theaters, and its conquest of a new empire in Eastern Europe. Benefiting from the prestige thus gained was an international apparatus of long standing, trained and equipped to influence, subvert, and spy, with loyal Communists who identified Soviet interests with their own. Moreover, the impression of implacable power and will was fortified by the ability of the Soviet leadership to control public opinion and to marshal resources for military production and heavy industry.

Confronted by this newly menacing and highly secretive adversary, other nations, including the United States, tended to exaggerate Soviet strengths and minimize the exhaustion and damage of the war. As the Soviets tested their first nuclear weapons in 1949, moved to thermonuclear tests in 1953, and then to missile and space tests in the late 1950s, each step renewed and fortified the impression of immense strength. The result, in the absence of technological intelligence capabilities, was a consistent overestimating of Soviet conventional military capabilities throughout this period, as well as some exaggeration of Soviet economic performance, where high growth rates came in larger part than was recognized simply from reconstructing a shattered economy.

Most important, not only to American but to European eyes, Soviet postwar policy created a strong impression of unrelenting pressure and probing for possible gains. After Poland, Iran/Greece/Turkey, Czechoslovakia, and the Berlin blockade, key countries in Western Europe were at least as eager as American policy makers for a formal North Atlantic alliance and, after Korea, for giving NATO real military muscle and an integrated command structure. Other nations too felt threatened, and the alignments of the cold war rapidly took shape around the Soviet Union and the United States as leaders of the rival camps.

In contrast to Soviet power, the tangible base of U.S. power was both military and economic. The United States controlled the Western nuclear posture and supplied most of the conventional arms for years, even to its sophisticated allies, and its economic hegemony was unquestioned, based not only on statistical supremacy (in GNP and just about all key sectors of production) but on what other nations considered to be coherent, wise, and generous policies, exemplified above all by the Marshall Plan and the Bretton Woods framework of international organizations.

Throughout the 1950s, America's power to help other nations gave it enormous practical influence, extending not only to members of what I shall call the Inner Alliance but to many other nations outside the Communist sphere. Shared perceptions of the Soviet threat would perhaps have led the Inner Alliance in any event to accept, for example, the early introduction of fairly severe controls on any trade with the Sino-Soviet bloc with the slightest strategic implications: American power removed all question, and gave the operation teeth. America also had the power to hurt, in practice seldom invoked: its classic demonstration, perhaps, was against the closest U.S. ally, Britain, in the refusal to support the pound at the time of the Suez expedition, a move quickly decisive in bringing the campaign to a halt and forcing early British withdrawal. Earlier, the dependent and second-level power status of France had been demonstrated by its inability to conduct the first Indochina War without massive U.S. support.

American dominance of the Inner Alliance largely explains why NATO settled rapidly into a strategic mold that has largely endured, with the threat of first use of nuclear weapons at the core of deterrence. Part of the reason was the overestimate of Soviet conventional capabilities just mentioned, with a strong psychological undertow to boot: how could one hope to counter the juggernaut that had just dealt with the Nazi colossus? Part was simple cost: in the years after 1952 Western Europe would have been terribly hard pressed to meet the NATO conventional force goals set in that year. Part was the change from the conventional arms oriented Truman to Eisenhower's "massive retaliation" strategy—which did seem feasible and sensible in Europe.

Finally, it was the almost instinctive belief of many Americans, not least in the military, that America could retain clear-cut nuclear superiority indefinitely. Closely associated with this was confidence that ways could be found to make nuclear weapons tactically effective, even perhaps to use nuclear weapons in such discriminate fashion that a local encounter would not spread to general war. Reflecting such views, the basic statement of national policy under Eisenhower actually laid down that nuclear weapons should be regarded, for military planning purposes, as just as available as conventional weapons.

Yet such beliefs were never uncontested. Others, especially scientists and those close to them, supposed from the first that the Soviets would readily achieve whatever the United States did, without long delay. Moreover, many even in the military contested the arguments that nuclear war could be controlled. The result was much greater tension of belief and policy than later interpretations of the period have sometimes suggested. For example, while a succession of projects in the NATO context stressed the nuclear role (tactical weapons, VISTA, railborne medium-range weapons), only the tactical weapons were actually deployed, and these without any clear doctrine for use.

All in all, nevertheless, primarily but not solely in the United States and other NATO countries, nuclear weapons in superpower hands were widely accepted not only as inevitable but also as tending to keep the peace. In 1953, at the time of the armistice in Korea, fifteen other nations joined with the United States in a declaration suggesting, in unmistakable terms, that any renewal of aggression there would be met by unified action that might not be confined to Korea itself or to the use of conventional weapons—in effect a threat of nuclear attack on China or even the Soviet Union. In the United States certainly, as Daniel Yankelovich and Sidney Harman reminded us in 1988 in *Starting with the People,* only a quarter of the public, in a 1955 sampling, thought that even all-out nuclear war would truly destroy mankind. As they rightly note, the nuclear strategy and American dominance in NATO went hand in hand from the start. Leaving it to Uncle Sam was congenial both to a Western Europe struggling to its feet and to an America tending to relish its new role.

On the Communist side, the Soviet Union was, of course, even more dominant, controlling its Eastern European satellites in every key respect. From the start, the Warsaw Pact was Soviet *dictat,* only nominally similar to the consent and popular support that bound the NATO members and the other core Western alliances.

China, however, was a different case—even, it may be argued, an exception to the picture of bipolarity. Its 1950 treaty of alliance with the Soviet Union and then, late that year, its massive intervention in Korea created an image of enormous power for a time in American policy circles as well as in East Asia. Throughout the 1950s American policy papers, as well as public rhetoric, spoke in alarming terms of the threat of "Communist China" and of a "Sino-Soviet Bloc."

Toward the close of the decade, however, as American analysts, official and private, perceived before most top leaders, China was getting only lukewarm support from the Soviet Union on many fronts—notably in the second Offshore Islands crisis, in 1958—while responding to its own backwardness by the disastrous Great Leap Forward. After public breaks with the Soviet Union in 1960 and 1961, China was to reemerge in 1962–1967 as a perceived regional threat of grave dimensions, on its own, but the monolithic "Sino-Soviet" image of the 1950s no longer existed in any influential quarter.

Arms Sources, Arms Races, and Arms Control

Two final aspects of Soviet/American dominance deserve special mention. One was their position as overwhelmingly the most important producers and suppliers of military equipment. Britain and France had their own limited capacities, including a few sophisticated items, and there was embryonic competition for arms sales to countries outside the NATO sphere, also a 1950 tripartite pact to consult on and limit sales in the Middle East. But by and large it was to the United States or the USSR that any nation wishing to have a substantial military capability had to turn, an important element in the power of each.

The second was the near-duopoly in nuclear weapons that prevailed throughout the 1950s, broken only by the small British capability and, at the very end of the decade, the first French tests. While giving nuclear ambitions a peaceful outlet was part of the motive for Eisenhower's "Atoms for Peace" initiative boosting nuclear power, the cost and technology barriers to nuclear weapons development on an effective scale were still just high enough so that weapons proliferation had not become an acute issue.

Regional arms races did exist (notably between India and Pakistan), but limited local resources, plus a certain amount of supplier restraint and control, kept them from running rampant. The arms race that really counted was that between the superpowers, predominantly in the nuclear area, and the part of that race that most bothered the rest of the world, and a great many Americans, was the fallout from atmospheric thermonuclear tests. In concentrating on this subject, from 1958 to 1963, arms control efforts—despite bouts of high-flown rhetoric on both sides—never came to grips with the problems of capping or reducing numbers of weapons, or of limiting new technologies or weapons categories.

The Centrality of the East-West Struggle

At its height in the 1950s, the cold war was almost all-pervasive in the orientation and status of national governments, and often shaped political conflict within nations, in such functional structures as labor unions, and in international organizations, both political and functional.

On the Soviet side were the East European "satellites" and other nations under Communist regimes aligned with the Soviet Union. Although the possibility of a "national Communist" regime breaking with the Soviet Union had been demonstrated by Yugoslavia, conclusively in the eyes of most informed Americans (so that Yugoslavia received substantial U.S. aid from 1949 on), to many other Americans (and the FBI) any regime professing to be guided by Marxist tenets was ipso facto hostile.

Communist parties in most countries were in fact under tight Soviet control, and communism was a lively force in trade union movements in many countries, industrialized or less so. On the international front, the change from Comintern to Cominform hardly affected the reality of a network of international organizations ostensibly private but in fact guided by Moscow.

To meet these challenges, and to back anti-Communist political forces in threatened countries, became very early (in 1948, on the recommendation of George Kennan) a significant facet of American covert activity. In the 1950s both perceived need and capability extended rapidly from political action and paramilitary actions auxiliary to the Korean War to peacetime covert paramilitary operations, all becoming big parts of the work of the fledgling CIA.

Communist ideology then had considerable appeal in Western countries as well as in the Third World (a term little used till the 1970s). This was largely due to Russian performance during the war, with an assist from Allied refusal to criticize the Soviet system while the Russians were war partners. Moreover, for a time Soviet economic growth seemed to show that the system could be productive: Khrushchev's boast that "we will bury you," coming on top of the pioneer launching of Sputnik in 1957, seemed to many in the world a credible claim that in less than another generation the Soviets would have caught up across the board, and even drawn ahead in key categories, especially those directly tied to military power.

The U.S. "bloc"—soon called "the West"—was much more variegated. Its core was the Inner Alliance structure, NATO and the defense treaties embracing Japan, Australia and New Zealand (ANZUS), South Korea, the Philippines and the Republic of China, with the Southeast Asian Treaty Organization (SEATO) initially at a lower level of U.S. commitment or involvement. In the Western Hemisphere the Organization of American States (OAS) Treaty had comparable security provisions, and the organization was dominated by the United States, but the relationship with its members was in fact less close in key respects than with other treaty nations, or than the

U.S. relationship with Iran. (Ties with Israel were nowhere near so close as they later became. It had a variety of ties at this time, notably with pre-Gaullist France.)

The sweep of U.S. military and economic aid programs deserves special mention. Initially grounded in security concerns but taking on more of a developmental thrust toward the end of the decade, these extended to a whole "intermediate ring" of non-Communist nations, some allied, some not, who depended on the United States to support their military postures.

In many cases these ties related to U.S. base rights. At its height, the U.S. overseas base structure ran into the hundreds of installations, in Spain and North Africa, Libya, Ethiopia, Saudi Arabia, and Liberia, for example, as well as several in each allied country.

Semantic arguments about whether this structure amounted to an American "imperium" miss its essential distinguishing feature: nations all over the world genuinely wanted U.S. help and protection (committed or implied). To this end they accepted a high degree of U.S. influence, as well as U.S. aid programs designed in accordance with American views of need, not just as "rent" for base rights or other concessions.

The structure already involved one problem that was to bulk large in later years, that of the friendly but failing regime and whether the United States should intervene. It did so substantially in the selection of Ramon Magsaysay rather than Elpidio Quirino in the Philippines in 1953, but for the most part took regimes as they were, provided only that they governed effectively. In general, geopolitics at this time came well ahead of human rights—American public opinion, except for a vocal liberal segment, was little concerned at being in bed with General Franco in Spain, or with traditional monarchs in a host of cases.

American missions came to pervade the Third World, except in the nonaligned countries. In many capitals, especially in East Asia, American officials were a dominant presence, far outnumbering the missions of other nations—and, not incidentally, the representatives of American private concerns. Revisionists to the contrary notwithstanding, if Pax Americana was a fair description of much of the world at this time, it was a hegemony driven much more by strategic and anti-Communist concerns than by economic interests in any narrow sense. Even the concern for Middle Eastern oil ran parallel, and often subordinate, to concern for the security of nations there, notably Iran and Israel.

While the American government, especially under Eisenhower, laid great stress on strengthening threatened non-Communist nations, it never reached a satisfactory answer to the problem of strategy to deter or deal with either direct or indirect aggression outside the NATO area. For the former, one lesson of Korea was thought to be that the other side may have believed (from Dean Acheson's Press Club speech of January 1950) that the United States would not respond even to an invasion: hence Dulles's "pactomania," the thrust to create alliances on sometimes shaky or ambiguous foundations. Militarily, the stated strategy of massive retaliation was never regarded as satisfactory when any case actually loomed (e.g., the Offshore Islands crisis of 1958, when the Navy had to scramble madly upon being told it might have to go into action using only conventional weapons). Yet an opposite strategy of responding with conventional ground and air forces, as in Korea, tended to be dismissed in the Pentagon by the slogan "never again!"

Hence, as historian Stephen Ambrose rightly notes, Eisenhower went to great lengths to use the CIA's covert action capabilities in order to avoid having to make bigger choices, and because he believed the public would not support a sustained conventional conflict. There remained an unresolved tension between proponents of large conventional forces for all purposes, like General Maxwell Taylor, and those who clung to the nuclear emphasis, at one end of the scale of force, and to covert action at the other.

The result by 1960 was a paradox from which the nation was to suffer greatly: on the one hand, wide consensus that Communist aggression in the Third World must be resisted even though its location might not be in itself vital; on the other, neither a clear-cut overall strategy nor coherent plans in individual cases if the balloon went up. The dilemmas of the Bay of Pigs and, repeatedly, the Vietnam War did *not* (contrary to legends in some quarters) have clear answers at this earlier time, as one who was in the policy circle both then and later can testify.

Strong security ties, either to the United States or to the USSR, were by no means universal, however. A major feature of the period was the formation, at Bandung in 1955, of the nonaligned grouping. Its founding leaders—Nehru, Tito, and Sukarno, notably—flaunted their independence to considerable effect, and for a time did live up to their label, both accepting U.S. aid and welcoming the courtship of China's Zhou en-Lai. But the very formation of such a group suggested how pervasive the urge to alignment was, as well as how little power each of the participants felt itself to have individually. The power and appeal of the Bandung group, its reason for being, came straight from the centrality of the East-West struggle.

Perhaps, for a time, cleavages behind aligned and non-aligned nations tended to limit the formation of groupings of a more regional character, or the emergence of regionally dominant nations. In another way, the fact that so many nations were caught up in the East-West struggle may also have dampened urges to reopen local quarrels or bring them to the point of conflict. Certainly this was true of the historic conflict between Greece and Turkey over Cyprus. In other cases as well, American influence operated to inhibit resort to force against a local opponent, in part through explicit conditions attached to American military aid that recipients were reluctant to challenge. (Ethiopia and Pakistan were examples.)

A bigger factor may have been the limited sources of arms, especially of a sophisticated nature. With the major arms suppliers preoccupied by the cold war and unsympathetic to any other conflict that might spill over in unforeseen ways, such local conflicts as did break out were limited in scope and duration.

Areas of Concern and Conflict

On what both Moscow and Washington always considered the main front, namely Europe, the 1950s are framed by the bookends of the 1948–1949 Berlin blockade and the renewed Berlin crisis that began in late 1958 and simmered till late 1962. Revolt in East Berlin, Poland, and Hungary also briefly flared up, only to be put down ruthlessly by Moscow—with the West declining to act despite Republican election rhetoric about "rolling back communism." The result was to confirm the solidity of the divisions of Europe and Germany. Reunification of Germany remained a rhetorical platform in the Federal Republic and in official American statements: the underlying reality was growing tacit acceptance that the division would probably continue for many decades.

Although the cold war had started over Europe, its most active theater of conflict and confrontation, year in and year out through the 1950s, was East Asia. From the Chinese civil war to the Korean War, to the first Indochina War, the Offshore Islands crises, the Sumatra rebellion (abetted by the United States through the CIA), to the early moves in the second Indochina War at the end of the decade, crisis was endemic. By 1960 U.S. forces were programed on the basis of a potential two and a half wars, one in Europe, the others in East Asia (one major, on the Korean model, and one lesser conflict).

Third in degree of concern was the Middle East, embracing Egypt. The Suez fiasco was not an East-West event, nor was the Lebanon crisis of 1958. But the latter reflected the main source of pressure, Nasserite Egypt operating with Soviet support, as well as the radicalization of Iraq and its alienation from the West, which left the British organized Central Treaty Organization (CENTO) Alliance little more than a shell. (The United States had already limited itself to observer status in CENTO.) The threat of Arab nationalism, stimulated by

Nasser, tended to dominate U.S. thinking, as well as driving Israel first into the Suez venture and then into growing dependence on the United States.

Iran quickly became a special concern. Always the most important nation in the area and a historic target of Russian ambition, it was the scene of the first outright cold war confrontation, over Azerbaijan in 1946, and its shaky regime led in 1951 to concerns over a possible takeover by the Soviet oriented and supported Tudeh party, not only in London and Washington but in the bazaars, mosques, and military headquarters of Iran itself. Thus in 1953 after Eisenhower had come to power, Anglo-American support, through a small CIA covert team, played a limited but crucial role in a coup against Mohammed Mosadeq's National Front government, restoring the shah to power. The result was to solidify Iran's status as an American client, heavily dependent but not equally influenced by U.S. advice at this period.

In all, the Middle East and North Africa were a fluid semibattleground, with few clear lines and a marked visible reduction in British and French influence, including the independence of Tunisia and Morocco. The United States assumed a much larger role, with a 1954 commitment to Pakistan, strong influence in Turkey and Iran, and bases scattered through the area, but only limited ties in the Arab world and the Horn of Africa.

The Pakistan commitment was a particularly fateful move in South Asian terms. India's determined nonalignment would always have precluded close U.S. security ties with it, although by the end of the 1950s careful diplomacy and large-scale economic aid had made the relationship a reasonably relaxed one. But the tie with Pakistan, because of the latter's conflict with Afghanistan over claims to Pushtunistan, did limit the U.S. role in Afghanistan, where both America and Russia had limited aid programs in different parts of the country. In considerable measure, U.S. policy in South Asia rested on a high estimate of Pakistan's unity and potential and a less sanguine one of India's—judgments that both turned out to be wrong.

Closer to home, U.S. policy toward Latin America in the

1950s lacked any clear thrust, other than the reflexive sensitivity to Communist-leaning regimes that led to the semicovert overthrow of the Arbenz regime in Guatemala in 1954. In 1959, however, Castro's coming to power in Cuba—after an initial period of ambiguity—seemed a much more formidable threat. It raised the specter of successful subversion, and at the same time highlighted the economic needs of the area and the possibility of U.S. aid contributing constructively on this front, with side security benefits.

In the latter respect, the impetus contributed to what later became the Alliance for Progress. Cuba itself was a different story. What Castro represented, above all, was the problem of whether the United States could accept a Communist regime in any Latin American country, a problem with Monroe Doctrine overtones but in essentially new form. In the Cuba case, the U.S. response was almost a prototype of others to come: feeble anticipation, little preventive action, slow assessment of the change, and then a hostile posture strong enough to strengthen the new regime's appeal to the Cuban people, but not strong enough to damage it. It was a weak policy that suggested the depth of the dilemma and an unresolved tension of views that was to recur in other cases, right to the present.

Finally, Africa south of the Sahara was in the 1950s virtually *terra incognita* to American policy makers. (I recall being drafted in about 1957, from a near-zero base of knowledge, to write a comprehensive national intelligence estimate on the area, using the inputs of a literal handful of African hands.) The area was, until the end of the decade, the notable exception to a central feature of the period, namely the demise of Western colonialism.

The Ebbing of Western Colonialism

World War II doomed the Western colonial structure. More clearly than most European metropole countries, American leaders foresaw this, though not always the rapidity of the change. As most of the former colonies, including the largest and most important, gained their independence, either through agreement or force, a few, notably Indochina, became battlegrounds in the East-West struggle. In others, such as Indonesia, American policy had to make painful choices between its ties to the metropole country and its support, in principle, of an end to colonialism. Then, whether their births (or rebirths) were peaceful or traumatic, the newly independent nations usually were precarious economically and unsure politically, presenting special and individual problems for American policy—as indeed did the colony the United States itself set free, the Philippines.

In most areas, the process of decolonization was virtually complete by the late 1950s. One of the most hotly contested cases, Algeria, was after the advent of de Gaulle in 1958 visibly headed for the French withdrawal of 1962. The exceptions were a few small Portuguese holdings and enclaves (Timor, Goa), and above all, as just noted, Africa south of the Sahara.

As of the mid–1950s, most in the West, including Washington, supposed that decolonization in Black Africa, while inevitable and in the American view to be accepted and supported, would come only very gradually over a period of another decade or two. Instead, it came precipitously at the end of the decade, except in the Portuguese and British territories in southern Africa. Only then did the U.S. State Department set up an African Bureau.

In policy terms, the rapidity of the release cut both ways. For the most part, with the notable exception of Belgium in the Congo, ugly choices between metropole and former colony were unnecessary. On the other hand, the new nations of Black Africa came into their own after only the most cursory preparations or transition measures; their resulting difficulties were from the first far greater than most American or Western observers or officials had even dimly foreseen.

The U.N. Charter, Multilateral Organizations, and International Law

Almost before the cold war was truly under way, the earlier belief of some Americans that the United Nations itself could be a vehicle for controlling conflict or organizing collective security on a global basis had disappeared, blown away by the first Soviet veto in the Security Council. Fairly quickly it became clear that the Security Council could not act in any situation affecting significant Soviet or American interests, in a manner to which the affected superpower objected. (Only a temporary Soviet boycott, for other reasons, made possible the key Council resolution supporting military action in Korea in mid–1950.) Accordingly, the United States turned in 1948 to regional alliances, framed to operate in accordance with Article 51 of the Charter permitting such collective action for self-defense.

The Charter did remain a basic point of reference in U.S. policy throughout the period, notably in the U.S. organized response to Korea and even more strikingly in Eisenhower's less predictable response to Suez. While a cynic could say that it was easy to stand up for principle when the West controlled the Assembly and usually a large majority in the Security Council as well, belief in the Charter and in international law generally did run deep in key individuals and in a large segment of American public opinion. Eisenhower's and the public's reactions to Suez rested substantially on this belief.

Behind this was a perception that accepted norms were not only in line with American faith in the domestic rule of law but would work in practice in favor of American interests more often than the reverse. Basic to American policy, though never put in so many words in internal papers, was that America generally stood for the status quo, subject only to peaceful change.

Regard for the United Nations was likewise generally high at this time. At the end of the decade, a big influx of Third World members foreshadowed a new era, but the change had not made itself acutely felt by 1960.

In the functional international organizations, the International Bank for Reconstruction and Development (World Bank) and International Monetary Fund (IMF) were dominated by the United States and its close allies (with no Communist voice at all). Such bodies as the International Labor Organization (ILO) and the United Nations Educational, Scientific, and Cultural Organization (UNESCO) generally responded to Western influence, and there was constructive cooperation among many nations in the Food and Agriculture Organization (FAO). (Yet to be introduced, of course, were organizations aimed at environmental, energy, or population concerns, while the successful Law of the Sea Conference of 1958 covered only a fraction of the issues that later emerged on this front.)

Broadly speaking, the United States and the West did try in this period to keep the cold war out of international organizations, with fair success most of the time. By 1960 the United Nations, under Dag Hammarskjold, its strongest secretary-general, was reaching further into peacekeeping operations sensitive to the superpowers than ever before, in the Congo; his death and the negative Soviet reactions to his role tended thereafter to nail down the proposition that the U.N. could act only where both superpowers at least acquiesced, or where neither was closely involved.

Concern for Human Rights and Democratic Practices

We have noted that in the U.S. "imperium" at this time, concern for a regime's internal behavior usually took a back seat to geopolitical need. In the world as a whole, other factors contributed to the same tendency not to press on issues of human rights or degrees of democracy and popular participation.

Thus the newly independent nations, by and large, either adopted the systems they had been taught by the colonial power (India notably), drew on traditional precolonial patterns of rule, or adopted what seemed needed to get started—which in practice often meant turning to the military as the most experienced administrators as well as holders of ultimate coercive power. Even Latin America, long independent, presented an uneven picture, with many military regimes.

Perhaps repression, at this period, seemed to have a less

ugly face than it displayed on many later occasions. Perhaps worldwide communications were not spreading the word as they came to do later—television in particular became widespread only in the late 1950s even in the West, and was rarely even present in the Third World. Certainly there were almost no private organizations, and only rare U.N. debates, to agitate even cases of torture and extreme mistreatment.

In short, concern in this area was at only a tepid level. Perhaps the most striking evidence of this was the general acceptance of South Africa, launched on the course of apartheid in 1948 but cased out of the British Commonwealth (on its own motion) only in 1960 and then still present in other organizations.

The Economic Setting of the 1950s

The Western Economic System

The story of events from Bretton Woods to the Marshall Plan and reconstruction of Japan, to the formation of the Common Market in 1957—with the growing role of the Organization for Economic Cooperation and Development (OECD) along the way—is broadly familiar to most Americans who follow economics at all. Linked in its early stages to the East-West struggle, and never wholly separable from it, the development of a Western trading, financial, and commercial system rapidly took on a life of its own. By the mid–1950s, it had become the foremost economic feature of the international structure, growing and flourishing even as its Communist counterpart remained isolated and without significant economic impact on other areas.

In this system, the United States held unquestioned hegemony. It was the banker of last, and very often first, resort. Its currency was the standard medium for all dealings. And it was the leader in promoting freer trade, in setting and modifying the rules and customs on which the system operated, and in the transfer of official resources to aid other nations.

What may be most striking, in retrospect, is that the United States held this leading position while playing only a relatively small role in world commercial trade (except with Canada and Mexico). Financially, U.S. private investment in other industrialized countries was a major force contributing to progress and American profits alike; production facilities were set up abroad on a large scale, for convenient access to markets and in time to get behind Common Market restrictions. Yet the United States was not a dominant player in the international movement of goods.

Western Europe emerged from reconstruction and the West German "miracle" as an increasingly active force in the international economy. However, Japan up to 1960 had a totally subordinate role, just coming to the point of full domestic recovery but with little impact on world or U.S. markets, only small competitive effect, an insignificant role in foreign assistance, and only limited links to other East Asian countries. (It is perhaps symptomatic that as late as the mid–1960s its main export to South Korea was seaweed.)

There were no "newly industrializing countries" at this stage. Top candidates such as Brazil were still largely turned inward, and the later "tigers" of East Asia were far from that state—South Korea, in fact, nearly flat on its back, Taiwan just shedding U.S. bilateral aid, Hong Kong and Singapore frail and politically uncertain.

In general, the poorer countries were engaged in the system primarily as suppliers of resources and raw materials, thriving when the terms of trade were in their favor (as in the Korean War period), tending to lag at other times.

The U.S. Competitive Position

The U.S. position was extremely strong throughout the 1950s. Powered by a thriving domestic economy tripled in size by the war and its aftermath, the United States held a clear competitive advantage in nearly every market for industrial goods in which it cared to compete. Indeed, the primary challenge to American foreign economic policy was to keep the combination of U.S. financial and productive power from stifling the recovery of the other potentially major players in the world economic system.

Likewise, American science and technology led the world by a large margin, with an only less marked margin in terms of bringing inventions into production. American management and production organization were world models. Labor mobility was much greater than it had been before the war, and labor relations were relatively calm (except at intervals in a few industries such as coal and steel). The quality of American goods was, in most areas, superior.

All in all, the United States was in an apparently unchallenged competitive position. This was so even though the dollar was, by any general measure, overvalued throughout the period. Keeping it high, even at the price of some adverse impact on the balance of payments, was regarded, in effect, as the necessary concomitant of American hegemony in the system as a whole, and to some extent as a matter of national pride. The result, of course, was to promote high American investment abroad, while keeping levels of foreign investment in the United States very low.

Signs and Thoughts of Change

The picture was never, of course, as static as the above description of its highlights might suggest. With the advent of the Common Market and general progress, Europe loomed as a growing competitor. So did Japan to a few, though not remotely on the scale that actually emerged even in the 1960s.

A big question toward the end of the 1950s was whether the less developed countries (as they were called by then) could "take off" and follow the path blazed by Europe and America. That this could be done, with the aid of some jump-starting by Western capital and other resource transfers on a large scale, was urged strongly and influentially by Walt Rostow, Max Millikan, and an articulate new worldwide corps of development economists. India stood high among their candidates for such potential progress, and there was for a time a perception that

its progress, as compared with China's, was an important test
of the two systems.

One way or another, the feeling was strong that with the
right policies of aid and technical assistance, very substantial
rates of growth could be achieved in these countries, with industrialization a higher priority, generally, than agriculture.
That the countries were often pursuing state oriented policies
was not, in this analysis, regarded as a serious drawback to
their prospects.

Little Worry about Global Shortages
or Other Problems

Concern about global and national population growth became significant toward the end of the 1950s—given a shove in
a seminal report by William H. Draper to President Eisenhower (shoehorned into discussion of his assigned topic of
U.S. military assistance programs, of all things). If this reflected what serious professionals were by then arguing, the
popular temper was equally reflected by Eisenhower's prompt
pigeonholing of this section of the report, in the belief that it
would stir up an unproductive controversy and not be accepted by Congress.

In other respects, concern for "global issues" was almost
dormant even as late as 1960. Framing the appropriate subjects for the National Goals report that year, I consulted with a
flock of deep thinkers and got an almost unanimous view that
the adequacy of natural resources (subject of a big Paley Report in the late 1940s) was not a concern warranting a chapter
in our report. (The main potential concerns were thought to
be key minerals; I do not recall anyone mentioning oil!) As for
environmental disruption, narcotics, or special and exotic diseases, none was even high in the agendas of forward-thinking
professionals.

To this general picture there were, however, two striking
exceptions. One was the near-conquest of key diseases such as
smallpox and malaria, a field where the World Health Organi-

zation (WHO) and U.S. aid programs were both active. The other was the onset of the "green revolution," through the development under private U.S. auspices of new strains of rice and other crops that were already, by 1960, giving promise of the sensational gains that later emerged.

America's Own Situation in the 1950s

Here three brief points, dogmatically stated. Each was mostly taken for granted at the time, as part of the air one breathed.

The first was the favorable image of America, and of American policy, held by most key countries and peoples. To this there were, naturally, some exceptions (for example, horror at McCarthyism and some resentment of American preeminence in top-layer Europe). But by and large American policy, at least from the Marshall Plan onward, drew on a big reservoir of respect and good will, and managed to keep that reservoir replenished well into the 1960s. At a different level, to be an American abroad at the time was (again with obvious exceptions, usually reflecting insensitive behavior by Americans themselves) to be treated with respect, consideration, and often affection by most foreigners. Hostile incidents directed against Americans were, in my perhaps frail recollection, almost unknown: Richard Nixon's treatment in Caracas in 1958 being the exception that proves the rule.

How much this mattered is, of course, debatable. My view is that it was a large assist to American national influence.

Second, Americans at the time had a strongly positive image of themselves, pretty much across the board, from moral quality to political capacity and participation, to economic success, to military power. To be sure, there were bouts of self-criticism and controversy, but the existence of a high, and historically exceptional, level of national self-confidence cannot, I think, be challenged. Exhibit A for its flavor would be John Kennedy's inaugural address in January 1961, and the way that the nation received it.

Third, and with more direct practical effect on foreign policy, was the high prestige and credibility Americans accorded to authority generally, and in particular to the national executive in the conduct of foreign policy. Even during the hurricane of the "loss" of China and of Joseph McCarthy, Truman got Congress to approve virtually all of his main initiatives, while Eisenhower after him had more trouble with his own party (Knowland, Bricker) than with the Democrats who, in a fashion incredible today, truly controlled not only their own partisans but, through respected committee chairmen (no women), a disciplined Congress.

The corollary to this, and to the national focus on the cold war's main theaters, was that special ethnic groups, as well as special economic interests, had only very limited impact on foreign policy. An exception, of course, was the strong influence wielded throughout this period by the notorious "China lobby" (a grouping far more ideological than ethnic). Public opinion, also, had very definite likes and dislikes among foreign nations, not always in tune with executive branch calculations of national interest, but the resulting frictions were minor.

What all three points added up to was an American government with greater freedom of action, greater credibility and acceptance, and greater ability to enlist support in the public and in Congress than at any other peacetime period in the country's history. This is a basic and central conclusion to this catalogue. In itself, it was neither good nor bad; any student of history or classical drama would have seen in it the potential for grave contemporary and future error and tragedy. But it was the fact.

II.

Such was the setting in which the main lines of postwar American policy were laid down and, over time, mostly institutionalized. The contrast with the present and prospective future is, of course, enormous—especially in "The American Situation" as just described. Three decades of turmoil, above all the traumatic national experience of the Vietnam War, have dealt harshly with the national self-confidence and faith in executive leadership that prevailed in the 1950s.

How have those decades affected the external situation and the power and role of the United States? In stressing the points of difference between the 1950s and the 1990s, it is also important to underline certain perceptions and facts that have *not* changed, and are not likely to change, all that much.

The analysis below leaves out, or scants, many "hard" changes in the world setting—in technology and basic science, notably—as well as those "soft" changes in thought, habit, and religious belief that have often remade interstate relations over a period of time. No short summary could do justice to these changes, which have been in historical terms very great indeed. I will highlight a few instances in which they have impinged most directly on international affairs and the conduct of U.S. policy.

The Current Strategic and Political Setting

Diffusion of Power and Reduced Centrality of the East-West Struggle

The United States and the USSR no longer tower over the world scene as they did in the 1950s. They do remain considerably the strongest military powers, particularly in nuclear capability, as well as the only nations with the assets to assert themselves almost anywhere. And they remain at the center of major alliance structures, held together as before by consent and *dictat,* respectively.

In that broad sense, there are still two key poles in the world power structure, East and West. But the sweep of this bipolarity and its impact on other nations have been reduced by the independence and greater power of several other individual nations and regional groupings, as well as by the substantially greater comparative economic power, and in many cases, military capacity, of nations and areas once almost powerless.

Start with *the Soviet Union* itself. Secretary General Mikhail Gorbachev's *perestroika* is above all a response to the lagging performance of the Soviet economy for more than a decade. Economic distress and lack of capacity are fundamental today, with a key question whether the present degree of reform can truly improve matters.

At the same time, Gorbachev's foreign policy has been far more sophisticated and appealing than that of any predecessor. In Europe, in other areas, and for the most part in America, Gorbachev's Soviet Union is perceived as substantially less threatening than that of Stalin or even Khrushchev. While its external links have hardly made it a significant force in the international economic system, it is a vastly more open society than in the 1950s, and its population has a growing sense of the outside world, and thus of the shortcomings of its own system. Meanwhile, the nationality problem shows itself on occasion, the population will be more than 50 percent non-Russian shortly, and the large Muslim sectors could become vulnerable to convulsions in the Islamic world.

With all its failures and present problems, Soviet Russia remains a powerful and strongly directed state. Its assets no longer include ideological persuasiveness or prestige as an economic system, but its capacity to engineer the Leninist overthrow of vulnerable governments, and then to secure their Communist successors, is perhaps greater than in the 1950s. Militarily, in addition to nuclear parity and very strong conventional forces sited mainly against Europe, it has major outreach capabilities and a big league navy, as it did not in the 1950s, and its intelligence capabilities are still great, especially concerning Western technology, both military and civilian (money having replaced ideological sympathy as the recruiting attraction).

Conversely, the technological intelligence capabilities of the West make the estimating of Soviet military strength much more exact than it was in the 1950s. The recent intermediate nuclear force (INF) treaty is an important breakthrough in Western exposure and presence. While opinion remains sharply divided on the extent of Soviet violations of arms control agreements, there has certainly been no violation of truly major practical significance. The technological superiority of Western, especially U.S., weapons is far less than it was in the 1950s, but it still exists in most areas and certainly at the level of invention.

All in all, the Soviet Union and Soviet policy present a vastly more complex picture than in the 1950s. While this observer doubts that the changes yet point clearly to a real letup in exploitation of Third World opportunities, Soviet policy makers are sensitive to limited trade pressures, widespread world disapproval, and their own public opinion in ways unthinkable in the 1950s: the latter two, surely, were major factors in the landmark decision to pull out of Afghanistan.

Moreover, U.S. policy must take account of the fact that many abroad, and some at home, see recent Soviet behavior in a clearly favorable light: the polls in Western Europe that for a time rated Gorbachev higher than Reagan are surely an important signal. Yet hard-line views do continue to be prevalent in France and in conservative circles in Britain, and the thesis that the present phase is merely a tactical breather from which the Soviet Union will emerge far more powerful and threatening has many takers on both sides of the Atlantic (for example, Richard Nixon).

The main point is simply that whereas the Soviet Union of the 1950s clung to an internal system and external policies with a high inertia factor and predictability (with rare periods of exception), the Soviet Union of today and tomorrow is in flux to the point where its own rulers almost certainly do not know what sort of shape they will be in a decade from now. Communism as a system of social and economic organization has lost prestige enormously, not least with its own adherents; yet as engines of naked power, the Soviet version and a few others continue powerful. In the political and diplomatic arena, greater worldliness and sophistication make Russia somewhat less difficult to deal with, but also, on occasion,

more threatening to U.S. and Western interests. The unevenness of the combinations of factors make confident analysis or
prediction extremely difficult.

In Eastern Europe, Soviet control remains strong and outright revolt unlikely. Yet national feeling remains totally un-
subdued, and the relationship to the Soviet Union is more
edgy deep down than at any time since World War II. For the
short term, eruptions going beyond Poland do not seem likely;
in the longer term, however, depending in part on what happens within the USSR and the possible ripple effect of reform
there, instability in Eastern Europe looms as the biggest
source of trouble and potential conflict in the world, perhaps
by the end of the century.

In the "outer circle" of other countries that call themselves
Communist (some with real conviction, others not) and look to
the Soviet Union, almost all are heavily dependent and in terrible economic shape, e.g., Vietnam, Cuba, Ethiopia, Angola.
True, Cuba continues to play the role of Soviet proxy (as in
Africa), but the costs of distant ventures are getting more bur-
densome, one surmises. Central America is a different proposition—there Cuban leaders really care.

In geopolitical terms, this "outer circle" is bigger than it was
in the 1950s, and each of these Soviet wards presents a regional problem of varying dimensions—perhaps most potentially significant at the moment in the Soviet base facilities in
Vietnam. Yet neither individually nor in the aggregate do they
add much to Soviet power, or affect the East-West balance
nearly as much as appeared to be the case from the mid–1970s
to the mid–1980s.

China and Sino-Soviet relations have changed beyond recognition from the 1950s, in what is probably the most important
single set of developments in these decades. In his book *1999*,
Richard Nixon has described the Sino-Soviet split as the most
"significant" geopolitical event of the postwar era, noting that
China's concern about Soviet threats in the early 1970s "gave
it no choice but to reach out to the U.S."—accurate (if belated)
judgments that put the sequence as well as the initiative for the
Sino-American rapprochement of 1972 where they belong.

Having broken with the Soviets in the early 1960s and passed through a phase of total hostility, China's foreign policy today is utterly self-centered and pragmatic, with almost no sentimental or ideological attachments, communicating with the Soviets but still wary of former adversaries and foreign influence generally. On occasion China has been impelled by financial factors into unwise military sales (notably to Iran), but it seems little disposed to direct interventions—in sum, a power not to be meddled with in East Asia, but an active player only on a very few fronts, notably Kampuchea.

The reason, of course, lies in its absorption with internal reforms of the most profound potential importance, for its own stability and power and for the future of Communist precepts. So far these reforms have shown more momentum and lasting power than their Soviet counterparts, and led to much greater foreign ties and exposure. But the convulsions and distractions of the 1960s and 1970s have left China still far below its demographic and skill-capable potential. Those who assume its straight-line progress at a rapid rate (e.g., Paul Kennedy) can point to enormous potential gains there for the taking—even more than in Russia in the 1950s; yet the imponderable of political stability must make any student of recent Chinese history hesitate.

At any rate, in any future projection of world developments, or any U.S. policy that aims at the long-term future, China is by far the biggest variable. It has shed the behavior patterns of the 1950s, but not yet shown what it will really be like even by the end of the century, let alone beyond.

Western Europe, by contrast, is much closer to where it appeared to be headed in the 1950s. The Common Market has been a success (and will be more integrated in 1992), but the vision of a Europe truly drawn together remains elusive. Key nations, notably the Federal Republic of Germany, have developed their own lines of thought on relations with the East, with rapidly growing ties of all sorts between the two Germanies a big force and factor. Others, notably France, are prone to assert their independence of judgment and action in Third World situations. Since 1973 in particular, Europe has frequently been at odds with American perceptions, and affected by different specific interests, above all in the Middle East, and on occasion over strategic trade controls with the Soviet bloc.

The economic ties that bind the West have become even more extensive since the 1950s, and these, together with essentially common views and concerns on most European security issues (France now included), and the success of the intermediate missile deployment, have limited the endemic frictions within NATO in recent years. Today, however, American pressure for a greater European contribution in some (often unspecified) way could come hard up against the European desire for only continued slow and limited change in the division of labor and burdens that arose in the 1950s. Moreover, the tendency in many European quarters toward unquestioningly benign views of Soviet policy, plus Europe's limited economic progress in recent years, make it reluctant to sacrifice for the sake of the improved conventional balance on the Central Front that most American leaders see as fundamental to long-term stability.

Next to China, the greatest change since the 1950s has been in *Japan,* which has made a quantum jump in economic status while still adhering to the fundamental lines of security policy that had developed by 1960. To state the obvious, Japan is today rapidly becoming the world's greatest investor and aid donor, the largest force in financial markets, and the strongest player in world trade, with enormous (and hard to reduce) trade surpluses with the United States, Europe, and other areas. It has adapted to economic change far more effectively than the United States or Europe, and its capacity for invention is moving up steadily. Moreover, Japan now has sophisticated conventional military forces, presently geared to local missions only.

What is not obvious is where such a Japan goes from here. Its essential dependence on other nations for markets and resources will continue to inhibit activism in foreign policy. Yet it is hard to see Japan refraining, for another generation, from a more active role where its interests are directly affected, above all in East Asia.

What is clear, above all, is that Japan is becoming more and more independent in its thinking, and more and more sure of itself (with more than faint signs of contempt for others, including Americans). It has come into the world in ways that hardly seemed conceivable in the 1950s, but it remains an intensely self-centered society at the core.

Arms Races and Arms Control

The two key features of the 1950s situation relating to military weapons—superpower control of sophisticated arms supplies and nuclear duopoly—have both been modified considerably. Arms production is now widely diffused, including a lot within the Third World, and control of the arms trade is almost nonexistent. The result has been a marked spread and intensification of regional arms races, even at the conventional level only, along with much higher levels of fighting and supply consumption in local wars, and much greater ability of small nations to resist larger ones, even superpowers.

In the nuclear area, the two superpowers still have far more destructive arsenals than the three other declared nuclear powers. Negotiations on strategic arms have remained bilateral, between the United States and the USSR, and those on nuclear weapons in Europe largely so. The results so far, despite enormous effort and attention, have been limited: some numerical ceilings in the 1970s (tending to accentuate the competition in areas not covered by the agreements) and now the removal of intermediate-range missiles from Europe and the Soviet Union.

In political terms, however, arms control remains very much at the forefront it assumed in the early 1970s, in the United States and perhaps especially in Europe. Polling data (notably by Daniel Yankelovich) seem to confirm that Americans' concern over the possible use of nuclear weapons is far higher than it was in the 1950s, and the sense of their cataclysmic impact more acute.

At the same time, the increasing cost and sophistication of conventional weapons systems raises serious problems for any shift to more total reliance on them. No longer, as in the 1950s, can large quantities of the most advanced weapons be bought even within the most generous defense budgets, and no longer, as then, is the capacity of personnel to handle equipment a relatively manageable problem. The implications of this trend (highlighted, for example, by Paul Kennedy) have yet to sink in.

Change among Intermediate
and Regional Powers

Here an obvious point is the almost total dismantling of the U.S. "intermediate ring" of foreign defense arrangements constructed in the 1950s. Partly for technological reasons (e.g., missiles replacing aircraft for key missions), but largely because other countries no longer felt so threatened, the U.S. worldwide base structure of the 1950s is now a thing of the past. With Western Europe also sensitive to its ties in the Middle East, and to its oil dependence, the experience of resupply of Israel in the 1973 Middle East War showed dramatically how difficult it may now be for the United States to get to key areas of conflict. In Spain, Greece, Turkey, and now the Philippines, a reduced sense of threat and common purpose is surely a major factor in the now-established custom of demanding exorbitant aid commitments as "rent" for U.S. bases.

In the danger levels of particular regional areas, the changes have been as striking as among the great powers. East Asia is no longer the area of dominant security concern, but instead the scene of bustling economic progress and, in general, a political settling down. The Middle East, on the other hand, has more than fulfilled the dire predictions voiced by a few in the 1950s: its surge in oil power in the 1970s interacted with greater and more intractable conflict on the Arab-Israeli front, contributing directly to the excesses that led to the Iranian Revolution and helped to set off smoldering fires of Islamic fundamentalism. With dashes of Soviet opportunism and desire for position, the result is a witches' brew.

Both areas, in different ways, illustrate clearly the point that the East-West struggle is nowhere near as central as it was in the 1950s. Perhaps the Soviet Union will play a part in getting Vietnam out of Kampuchea; certainly, its base structure in Vietnam adds a potentially serious complication for the policies of the United States and the Association of Southeast Asian Nations (ASEAN), as does its increased naval strength in the area more generally. But there are no signs of a repetition of the encouragement and support given to North Korea in 1949–1953, or even of a repeat of the Ussuri River incidents with China in 1969.

On its side, the U.S. alliance structure of the 1950s has been curtailed, with the effective demise of the SEATO treaty and that with Taiwan. While South Korea remains dependent on its U.S. security ties, the United States has much less influence now than earlier. In the Philippines, likewise, the large U.S. role of 1985–1986 will be increasingly hard to replicate: serious internal problems there are essentially home-grown, and much more resistant to an effective U.S. contribution than in the 1950s.

In the Middle East, both the United States and the USSR have strong and direct links to key nations: the Soviets to Syria and Iraq most notably, the United States to Israel and Egypt. That the United States should now be the patron and key helper of Egypt is a total change from the 1950s, while the scale and totality of Israel's dependence on the United States have raised it to a different order of concern and involvement than existed at that earlier time. It would be extraordinarily hard for an American president today to put on Israel the kind of pressure Eisenhower used in 1957 to get Israeli forces away from the Gulf of Aqaba; moreover, the closeness of ties with Israel and the power of the pro-Israel lobby in Congress greatly complicate U.S. relations with moderate Arab states.

Not since 1967, however, has any phase of the Arab-Israel conflict been triggered in any direct way by either superpower: each has responded with an eye to long-term ties and influence, but not to the point of rekindling that phase, or the conflict generally. Moreover, the Iranian Revolution—perhaps the most important change in the area since the 1950s, as well as a heavy blow to U.S. policy and influence—arose essentially from indigenous forces, as did the Iran-Iraq war that followed. In that war each superpower played a role, but in their respective balancing acts neither was decisive or emerged in a new position with either belligerent.

An important outgrowth of the Iranian Revolution has been a surge in messianic Islamic fundamentalism. For the moment the acute concern of the early 1980s appears to have receded, but the sentiment behind the surge could be rekindled in a time when, all over the world, rapidity of change contends with established frameworks of belief and custom, perhaps especially in Muslim societies. At any rate, such religious forces cut right across the ideological lines of the East-West struggle.

As the Iran-Iraq War and the 1973 war before it have shown, the weaponry available to combatants in the Middle East is now sophisticated, devastating, and available from many sources. Control of supply and resupply has become extremely difficult to achieve, even if a serious effort were made. In particular, missiles able to attack cities could at any time change the effect of local conflict drastically and dangerously—with the additional possibility, as Iraq has shown, of their being equipped with chemical warheads. (Nuclear proliferation is addressed separately below.)

Available weaponry is an element, also, in another key change, namely the ability of determined local forces to resist even superpower military action. The United States in Vietnam, and now the Soviet Union in Afghanistan, were each forced to levels of military action in local wars that entailed serious costs (in differing combinations in the two cases). Each case demonstrated, too, a weakness in the national "will to empire"—a feature of long standing in the United States, but more recent and noteworthy in the USSR.

The Soviet withdrawal from Afghanistan must be seen as an extremely important change from the perceptions of the 1950s, or for that matter those of the mid-1980s—even though it leaves Afghanistan itself in a wholly uncertain situation and does little to resolve the intractable problems of Pakistan. Whether the Soviet Union now has closet Caspar Weinbergers arguing that the military must never be sent into action without the clear prospect of early success, as well as solid popular backing, one can only speculate. What is less speculative is that the image of an implacable and ruthless Soviet juggernaut must have been much reduced in key parts of the Third World, with accompanying effects on Soviet diplomacy and pressure tactics.

It may be, of course, that the willingness of the Soviet Russian to sacrifice for his country was exaggerated in the 1950s. Were the Soviets, even then, prepared to face substantial casualties in any cause less than the defense of the homeland? Were they, too, already subject to that neglected trend, toward ever-decreasing acceptance of loss of life, that ran so clearly in Britain from the Somme in 1916 to the planning of D-Day in 1944, and can readily be traced in America from the Civil War to Korea to Vietnam and now to Lebanon? We will never know, but there seems little question that popular resistance to losing lives for any cause not clearly vital is today a big factor in decisions on both sides of the East-West divide.

None of this suggests, at least to this observer, that the cold war is clearly over in the Third World, its main theater for more than two decades. Signs of Soviet restraint are present in the behavior of Angola and Cuba, perhaps marginally in Central America. Yet threats to any Soviet-backed Communist regime, or a case of large opportunity, maximum embarrassment to the West, and minimum risk to the USSR could well lead again to Soviet action. Such a case, for example, could be presented by civil war in South Africa, with the Soviet Union going all out to arm the blacks through their ties to the African National Congress.

To continue with our area assessments, *Latin America* today is from every standpoint, security included, both more important and a greater source of potential conflict and difficulty than it appeared in the 1950s. Cuba, apparently passive in the late 1960s, moved in the 1970s to high activity outside Latin America, becoming an important Soviet surrogate in Africa (acting for its own reasons as well). The issue it posed in the 1950s, whether the United States could tolerate a Communist regime in Latin America, remains unresolved after unpleasant experiences in Chile and Nicaragua. Central America today reflects both that old problem and a new question, whether nations within the region can set norms on their own and thus further reduce the U.S. role. The continuing crisis there also seems to confirm the judgment that Latin Americans are much more resistant to a strong U.S. role than was the case in the 1950s.

Politically, Latin America has generally progressed toward more responsive and democratic regimes, with a considerable assist from the example of Spain and Portugal, in the 1970s, replacing their authoritarian rulers by democratic systems that seem to be settling down solidly. On a "correlation of forces" scorecard, such as one imagines the Kremlin to keep handy, this and the failure of Eurocommunism must rank as outstanding negative entries for the past twenty years.

The two main features of Latin America today, however, are the emergence of Brazil and Mexico as major actors and as problems for U.S. policy and the grave overall economic problem of the area, symbolized in the "debt crisis." Each presents complex and multiple issues, with tremendous long-term security implications, but still best addressed, in this chapter, under the "Economic and Social" heading.

To conclude this area survey, *Africa* south of the Sahara has been, since independence, a constant source of conflict and maneuver involving France, Libya, and on important occasions the superpowers (in Angola most notably, as well as the activist Soviet role in Ethiopia). The area's political and economic progress has fallen well below the hopes of the late 1950s, confounding, for many, the very hope that Western aid can be effective there. In geopolitical terms, Black Africa counts for little more than it did three decades ago.

To this, Southern Africa is a striking exception. World and American sensitivity to the barbarities of apartheid in South Africa is at a much higher level than it was in the 1950s, and black nationalism has grown slowly but steadily through the past fifteen years. Majority black rule seems, even to many Afrikaners, the inevitable outcome; how and whether it can be achieved without chaotic disruption and massive bloodshed remain terribly hard to see. Mozambique and Angola, grim as their situations are, may be able to dig out of their present civil wars. As to South Africa itself, however, one is moved to turn Lincoln on his head: "With little confidence in the future, no prediction in regard to it is ventured."

Terrorism and Its Targets

As noted earlier, there was plenty of what would today be called terrorism in the 1950s. Usually it was auxiliary to anticolonial struggles (as in Palestine before the creation of Israel), or in Algeria (on both sides). Seldom was it directed at Americans.

In recent decades terrorist tactics have been adopted by domestic extremists (Red Guards and the like), and used much more extensively by nationalist movements (Palestinians, the IRA), and more recently by Islamic fundamentalist groups, many tied to revolutionary Iran. Many terrorist groups have close state ties, notably with Libya and Iran, as well as equipment and training from the Soviet Union. In recent years Americans have often been preferred targets, so far outside the United States itself.

This diversity of origin and motive makes it hard to generalize about "terrorism" now or into the future. Clearly it is quantitatively different from similar actions in the 1950s, calling for intense international concern and cooperative action. Where it is tied to political causes, however, these are almost by definition of long standing and highly resistant to negotiated resolution.

The U.N. Charter, Multilateral Organizations, and International Law

Here too there has been enormous change, both in fact and perception. With the enlargement of U.N. membership—159 members in 1987, versus 99 in 1960 and 60 in 1950—has come a total shift in the power balance within its constituent bodies. The dominant Afro-Asian bloc tends to be much more critical

of the United States than of the USSR (Afghanistan a conspic-
uous exception, the victims being Muslim). To some extent,
on the other hand, the sounding board and emotional outlet of
U.N. debates and critical resolutions have drained steam from
the role played by the nonaligned group in the 1950s. Although that group too has become more tilted toward the
Communist side of issues, it has tended to fragment and
become powerless.

By its anti–U.S. tendencies and especially by its sharp criticism of Israel since 1973, the Assembly in particular has alienated important sectors of moderate and liberal American public opinion that were formerly the U.N.'s stoutest supporters.
Sloppy and ideological management of U.N. agencies (notably
UNESCO) has led latterly to U.S. withdrawal and withholding
of dues—leaving the way open for the Soviets to appear com-
paratively forthcoming.

The picture of U.N. practical action, however, is much less
bleak. Recently, its mediation over Afghanistan was effective,
and it has shown itself able to handle many tough peacekeeping missions, an activity recognized by the Nobel Peace Prize
for 1988. Moreover, Security Council resolutions have had important impact on several conflicts, such as the Iran-Iraq War,
and set benchmarks for diplomacy. In response, the U.S. funding in 1988 of part of its arrears may indicate that relations,
and the U.N. situation generally, are improving.

As a norm of international behavior, the U.N. Charter has
receded a great deal since the 1950s, as majorities have taken,
in case after case, positions guided by self-interest rather than
principle. In recent years, the United States itself has joined in
derogating the Charter on occasion, and belittling international law generally. As forces in international affairs, both
stand well below where they were in the 1950s.

Nuclear Proliferation and Attitudes
toward Nuclear Weapons

An embryonic threat in the 1950s, this has gone through
stages of acute concern—the Non-Proliferation Treaty of the

1960s and various moves in the mid–1970s by the Carter administration—and other periods when it got little attention. Remarkably, the nations that admit to having a nuclear weapons capability are still only the five of 1964 (France, China, the United Kingdom, and the two superpowers), although it is universally believed that Israel and South Africa have such weapons, and the probabilities seem high for others such as India and Pakistan. Certainly the technology and cost barriers are now far lower than earlier, such that many nations could have weapons very quickly if they chose, and their possession by terrorist groups seems increasingly feasible.

The factors that have deterred outright weapons capabilities in individual countries are too various to summarize. For some, perhaps, a major factor has been a growing world awareness of their destructiveness and consequent revulsion at any thought of their actual use, and even on occasion at their being held for deterrent purposes. New Zealand's unwillingness to accept U.S. naval vessels unless assured they do not carry nuclear weapons (thus, in effect, challenging longstanding U.S. policy not to confirm or deny the presence of nuclear weapons at any location) symbolizes a popular movement very different from sentiments of the 1950s, with important implications for U.S. deployments and bases. In NATO, such sentiments have been overborne, for the time being, by belief in the nuclear-reliant deterrence strategy.

Overall, including the United States itself, concern and outright rejection both seem to be increasing. Public discussions of the late 1980s, stimulated in part by President Reagan's impulsive (and quickly withdrawn) acceptance of a Gorbachev suggestion at Reykjavik in 1986 that the complete abolition of nuclear weapons should be a goal, have moved debate into areas inconceivable in the 1950s.

Concern for Human Rights and Democratic Practices

Speaking impressionistically, this observer notes three points. First, concern on this subject remains selective, in U.S.

opinion but also abroad: conservatives highlight the flaws of
Communist or leftist regimes; liberals, those of regimes with
the label or flavor of the right or of military domination. Few
keep the same scorecards for all.

Second, the trend line of concern is slowly but steadily upward, again not just in the United States. Lawless Argentina
did become a pariah in Latin America; Marcos in the Philippines and Chun in South Korea were ousted; democracy as a
goal is more and more a rallying appeal. The "third basket"
concerning human rights, in the Helsinki Accords of 1975, has
served to keep the subject to the fore and to highlight Soviet
practices, some now being modified in marginal ways.

Third, however, performance has not kept pace with concern. Sophisticated security measures solidify the power of
non-Communist as well as Communist rulers more effectively
than in the past. In East Asia, democracy is often "guided"—as
Lee Kuan Yew is doing even in once-exemplary Singapore.
Africa is almost entirely authoritarian and not apologetic
about it.

The Current Economic and Social Setting

In the 1950s economic concerns came far behind those of
security and international politics, in the minds of American
policy makers and the American public alike. Today the shoe is
emphatically on the other foot. A hypothetical Rip Van Win-
kle, involved in policy in the 1950s and then asleep for thirty
years, would find the security situation not all that surprising.
The economic transformation would startle him, particularly
and above all the change in the status and role of the United
States itself.

In rarely vivid statistical terms, America's share of world
GNP has gone from nearly 50 percent at its peak, in that earlier
period, to just over 20 percent today. Such calculations have to
be taken with a grain of salt, dependent as they are on the
exchange rates of the moment. (This one is a bit distorted by
the overvaluation of the dollar earlier, just as its precipitous
drop in recent years exaggerates the trend line in favor above

all of Japan with its immensely strong yen.) Yet currencies themselves mirror underlying reality. Part of the solution to almost every economic problem in the 1950s, the dollar is now, in acute degree, part of the problem. And the yen's strength reflects the new status of Japan as the steadiest and most effective member of the international economic community, the one to whom others turn, as they used to do to the United States, when it comes to new measures to help the Third World, as well as being a key player in maneuvers affecting exchange rates.

The Western economic system as a whole continues to dominate the world economy, perhaps even more than it did in the 1950s. India and China are being drawn into it, the Soviet bloc gets loans from it and trades more with Western Europe, it has impressive new recruits and centers of production in the newly industrializing countries, especially the "tigers" of East Asia, and its attractions have on several occasions drawn potentially Communist situations in the Third World back to relative moderation.

To say that the United States is no longer the hegemon in that system is true in some ways, but may tend to exaggerate the degree of change. America is still at least *primus inter pares,* first among equals, deferred to and able in recent years to resist the pressures of other governments to change fiscal policies widely regarded as terribly mistaken. It is the convener of important subgroups on key problems that usually bite deeper than the annual formal meetings of the seven most prominent industrialized countries—though these summits are themselves an important change from the 1950s. It remains the bellwether nation on trade restrictions and can still lead when it chooses.

But the weight of the United States is far less than it was earlier. This is in part because of the relative drop in the status of its economy—a drop largely inevitable given American postwar support for Europe and Japan. But it also reflects avoidable vulnerabilities: in particular, with the U.S. savings rate the lowest of any major country, not only the dollar but American financial markets can now be drastically affected by the actions of others, both public and private. And it reflects also an important change in the intangible but significant factor of respect for U.S. policy. From the high level that prevailed virtually throughout the 1950s, such respect sank in the early 1980s era of Donald Regan to the head-shaking level in virtually every important capital and business center, and remains heavily burdened by the twin budget and trade deficits that dominate informed discussion around the world, much more than they do the American political debate.

In the system as a whole, currencies float in increasingly narrow ranges, the policies of the major nations tend to move in some sort of rough harmony much of the time, and the financial system showed itself remarkably resilient as oil prices went up, less so when they went down. The advent of genuine worldwide financial markets—perhaps in the long run the most important economic change of these three decades—has added to the flow of resources and, very greatly, to the pace and competitiveness of change.

With these recent trends has come a strong impetus to contract and accept debt, of all sorts. Whether this is more risky than constructive, and how to keep its benefits and control its risks, are questions best left to the other chapters of this book. What is clear and inescapable is that the whole "Western economic system" in the 1990s will be more and more truly global, more integrated, more interdependent, more competitive and fast-changing—and with all this more risky and harder to manage—than that of any previous period, notably the relatively controlled and straight-line 1950s.

The U.S. Competitive Position and Capacity to Support Security Commitments

The drop in the American competitive position vis-à-vis Japan has been dramatic. Japanese efficiency and adaptability (and latterly inventiveness) have been like a searchlight, exposing all the weaknesses that had crept into American practices, many of them since the 1950s. By comparison with Western Europe, on the other hand, America has been flexible and effective in creating jobs, and it has kept a reasonable competitive position vis-à-vis other nations and areas, with the rise of the NICs heavily due to their much lower average wages. Japan is the competitor that cannot be explained away, and eats at the American public and its government.

Japan's new status and the more predictable growth in European economic capacity would in themselves raise serious questions about the disproportionate U.S. share in the security costs of the Inner Alliance, a share that dates basically from the 1950s although it has been chipped away to some extent since then. In addition, to a significant number of informed Americans, the decline in America's relative economic capacity suggests that the whole set of American commitments, assumed largely in the 1950s, may now exceed America's economic capacities, and that the discrepancy could accelerate a decline in America's relative power overall.

Part of what this thesis reflects—a tendency to see power more explicitly in economic terms than before—seems likely to be a solid and enduring change in perceptions of international affairs, both in America and abroad. As the Japanese have shown that a nation can be at the great power level with only local military capabilities, so the experience of the Soviet Union has highlighted the limitations of great and growing military strength that is not backed by parallel economic improvement.

This chapter must note this thesis—if only because it contrasts so strongly with the unquestioning confidence of Americans in the 1950s—but space permits only two glancing comments on it. First, statistically speaking, it is open to attack: the percentage of American GNP going to defense, and to foreign policy as a whole, is substantially less today than it was in the 1950s (roughly 7 percent today, versus 10–11 percent in the steady-state late 1950s). If Americans felt as strongly about external threats and the importance of military posture in countering them as they did then, the economic capacity exists to support a higher percentage than today. On this point, neoconservative critics of Paul Kennedy are right: it is a question, ultimately, of national will, of motivation.

Second, as the discussion then turns to national will, it is at once obvious that American politics today reflect the growth in these three decades of concerns and claims for social spending that have greatly expanded this part of the federal budget (though it remains far less than in Europe). Less obvious, perhaps, save to those who recall the 1940s and 1950s, is the growth in recent years of an assumption that the entrepreneurial initiative and investment that drive the economy upward can only be enlisted at much higher levels of individual reward and lower levels of tax than prevailed through the first three postwar decades. Those who saw those driving forces operate at peak in periods of accepted sacrifice and high taxes must see such an assumption as in itself a commentary on the present state of national will, and in a sense contrary to the domestic arguments of neoconservatives and their allies.

The result of these self-contradictory sets of views (and their counterparts among liberals, in lesser degree) is a budget bind yet to be loosened by some coherent expression of genuine national will. That bind could persist into the 1990s, and be made even more acute by an economic downturn. If so, American capacity to carry even a somewhat reduced share of the overall cost of the military and foreign policies it shares with the Inner Alliance could indeed become doubtful, and the resulting strains would be very serious matters indeed.

The Condition of the Less Developed Countries

As we have noted, a few key Latin American countries, notably Brazil, and the East Asian "tigers" have become in effect part of the industrialized core of the Western economic system. Others have progressed in very uneven ways since the 1950s.

India remains of great importance and outside any category. Since 1965 it has been clearly the dominant power in South Asia, and in some respects, notably agricultural production, it has made remarkable gains. Yet it remains immensely varied and unwieldy, with its politics uncertain and tending to fall back into historic patterns of corruption and self-seeking.

In Southeast Asia, the ASEAN countries have generally advanced, save for the Philippines, from a diversified resource base and making good use of foreign investment. Burma remains backward and now convulsed, but the other non-Communist countries of the area, as already noted, are incomparably better off than they were, or seemed likely to be, in the 1950s. Conversely, united Vietnam has lagged, with the added burden of the occupation of Kampuchea—another example of the decline of communism as a model.

As the population of Latin America grows apace, its economies are marked by glaring contrasts between wealth and poverty. Nowhere is this more striking than in Mexico, which is now inevitably a much more pressing and involved neighbor to the United States and a much greater focus of policy attention than in the immediate postwar period. It is the largest contributor to the important Hispanic migration to the United States (both legal and illegal), and the interaction along the border is pervasive. Less active and influential in Central America than its size and location might suggest, it remains the geopolitical linchpin of its area, and its problems—debt, a weak economy, a political system in transition—defy even general prognosis.

There, and in Colombia and other countries to the south, drug production and distribution to the United States raise problems undreamed of in the 1950s. Once focused on Turkey and Southeast Asia, drug supply is now worldwide, fluctuating from area to area, with Latin America now in the lead. Drugs will surely be one of the biggest policy problems of the 1990s, as well as an important factor in interstate relations in the hemisphere.

If the development theories of the late 1950s have been helpful in such skilled and high-energy countries as Korea, and had a mixed impact in India, their area of greatest failure has surely been Black Africa. Rapid population growth, economic stagnation, neglect of agriculture, and political convulsions have made the life of the individual citizen worse in many countries than at the time of independence. There are few bright spots (such as Botswana) to lend hope that the next decades may see more progress.

The transfer of resources from the industrialized to the transitional and developing world moved in the 1970s much more to the private sector, as the financial reserves of the oil producing countries were recycled by the banking system as loans to countries in these categories. The result, when oil prices collapsed and worldwide recession appeared, was of course the "debt crisis" of recent years. In one sense this is a big change from the 1950s, in another the reappearance in new form of questions much to the fore even then, whether developing nations can be effectively assisted by wealthier nations and whether economic difficulties and failure to keep pace with population growth in those countries may in turn precipitate internal convulsion and external conflict. While the evidence from Latin America has not yet reached a clear-cut alarm level, such indicators as the growth of opposition parties in the recent Mexican elections could point to serious political trouble in the next few years.

In all this, the multilateral economic organizations, notably the World Bank and International Monetary Fund, play a much more active part than in the 1950s. U.S. influence in both is much less than it was then, and there is now Communist membership though not yet significant influence. Japan is much more to the fore here as elsewhere in this sphere. Not surprisingly, the control and behavior of multilateral organizations reflect the new diffusion of international economic power.

Demographic Change in the World

This subject might have been put at the very head of section II, or indeed of the whole chapter. It is, of course, basic to understanding many differences between the 1950s and the 1990s. Yet it also lends itself to excessive conclusions, in particular the idea that population growth must fairly rapidly show some clear correlation with power status. Though usually true among nations of similar culture and background (e.g., Britain and then Germany as European powers in the nineteenth century), any such correlation breaks down badly as between vastly different areas and cultures.

Population in these decades has grown rapidly pretty much throughout the Third World, most strikingly in Latin America and Africa. The Soviet Union, Japan, and the United States have seen low to medium growth, while Western Europe has grown very little and parts of Eastern Europe not at all, with decline in prospect.

The resulting trends will undoubtedly have enormous significance in the long run. Within the time frame of this chapter, however, it is hard to point to a country that has gained significantly in status or influence because of population growth, and easy to name countries that have become more and more concerned to restrain growth (China the foremost example) or that have seemed to outsiders to have suffered from too rapid growth (Central America, the Philippines, Kenya).

As for cooperative international efforts in the field, the record has been mixed—a far cry from the passivity of the 1950s but less than appeared for a time likely in the early 1970s, and marked most recently by reserve and restriction on the part of the United States itself. Each nation makes its own policy, and the trend is generally toward greater control and restraint. Almost nowhere, however, can such policies materially alter the projections of high population growth in many Third World areas and countries over the next forty years or so.

Environment, Resources, and Health

In the key area of energy, the concern for adequate oil supplies at reasonable prices that dominated the 1970s has receded for the time being, as demand growth has been slowed by conservation and (to a lesser extent) new energy sources have been developed. The mix has become somewhat more diversified, with coal and natural gas moving up, while nuclear power, after a period of growth, went dramatically downward in future planning even before the hammer blows of Three Mile Island and Chernobyl.

Yet at this point, future energy sources and practices raise new and potentially intense issues, to add to those debated in the 1970s but still not firmly resolved. In particular, growing scientific acceptance of the "greenhouse effect"—that fossil fuels are operating to raise atmospheric temperatures and change climate significantly, often adversely—adds a major complication and potential source of disagreement. The rapidly growing rate of tropical forest destruction relates both to the greenhouse effect and to preserving varieties of life. Present international pressures on Brazil and Indonesia to control tree cutting could be the precursors of pressures in the opposite direction, on the United States and other major nations to reduce their use of fossil fuels.

Similarly, recent evidence of the impact of chlorofluorocarbons (CFCs) on the ozone layer, threatening much increased skin cancer, raises worldwide questions in which the United States, as a major CFC producer, may find itself in a difficult position. Acid rain, too, is a major problem, not only in North America but more acutely in Central and Eastern Europe.

Finally, there are the great epidemic problems, headed today by acquired immune deficiency syndrome (AIDS). Technically much more difficult to address than most diseases that were thought menacing in the 1950s, AIDS could under some conditions become a major interstate problem.

Concerns in these areas (relatively low in the 1950s) fluctuated greatly from the mid-1960s to the mid-1980s. For the decade of the 1990s, the threats appear larger and more solidly founded than ever before. They are challenges not only to effective national management but to international cooperation.

America's Own Situation Today

In the economic sphere, the image of the United States in the world is a striking paradox. On the one hand, in the relatively small circle of informed opinion, the reputation for sound and constructive government policies that existed in the 1950s has declined since the mid-1960s, more or less steadily and through many administrations, to a nadir in the last few years. On the other, market forces and private initiative as the engines of economic growth have become, in recent years particularly, more appealing worldwide and also more directly associated with the United States. America has the image not of outstanding success in these years—that palm clearly goes to Japan—but of having a better basic economic system (as well as exceptional political stability), as compared to more state oriented economic systems and especially to Communist systems.

As for the level of national self-confidence, this is clearly lower than in the 1950s and early 1960s. The impact of the Vietnam War still lingers, notably in the response to Central America, and the mixed record of recent years has built back confidence only to limited degree.

Finally, the process of making national foreign policy has obviously changed out of recognition from that which generally prevailed in the 1950s. Through fluctuations in the prestige of individual presidents, Congress has steadily consolidated a major role for itself in all but the briefest special periods. Lacking the cohesion and centralized control that made for effective coordination with the executive at that earlier time, it is far more affected by groups concerned with particular nations, issues, or economic interests. The tendency to assert views based on historical or ethnic ties can be expected to increase as a result of the heavy immigration of the past fifteen years.

Conclusion

In sum, the America that is entering the 1990s is a very different country from the one of the 1950s. Its leaders face challenges and problems similar in some security aspects to those of the earlier time, but vastly more complex in the economic sphere and with new global problems of potentially formidable character. And they do so with the necessity to marshal support from a country much more diverse and with far less consensus on key issues than was the case when the main lines of postwar American foreign policy were laid down.

2

America in the World Economy: A Strategy for the 1990s

C. FRED BERGSTEN

The Issues

The new administration and Congress that took office in early 1989 immediately faced a series of major international economic challenges. First, they confronted a current account deficit that remains well over $100 billion, and that will probably never fall below $100 billion on the basis of present policies and exchange rates. They have to attract several hundred billion dollars of additional foreign financing for

C. FRED BERGSTEN, director of the Institute for International Economics, was assistant secretary of the treasury for international affairs during 1977–1981 and under secretary for monetary affairs during 1980–1981. From 1969–1971 Dr. Bergsten served on the senior staff of the National Security Council, as assistant for international affairs to Henry Kissinger. He has been a senior fellow at the Brookings Institution, the Carnegie Endowment for International Peace, and the Council on Foreign Relations. Dr. Bergsten is the author of numerous books and articles on international economic issues. This chapter is adapted from a book of the same title released by the Institute for International Economics in 1988.

these deficits during the Bush term of office, even if a transition to a sustainable external position is successfully launched. They are the first administration and Congress in almost eighty years to govern a United States that is a net debtor country—indeed, a United States that is for the first time in modern history the world's largest debtor, with a net foreign debt that could rise to $1 trillion in the early 1990s in the absence of corrective action.

The Bush administration will have to decide whether to continue, abandon, or accelerate the efforts of the world's major economies during recent years to achieve more active management of exchange rates and better coordination of national policies, as exemplified by the Plaza Agreement of 1985 and the Louvre Accord of February 1987. It will have to avoid a precipitous fall in the dollar, as in 1987 (and 1978), which would push up inflation and interest rates. But it will also have to avoid a premature strengthening of the dollar, as in 1988, which would produce a renewed deterioration in the current account and heighten the risk of a future crash of both the currency and the economy.

The Bush administration also confronts a number of important trade policy questions. Should it try to speed the reduction of the trade deficit and protect America's industry and jobs by restricting imports, at least those from countries with "unfair" trading practices? Should it provide direct federal assistance to boost exports further? How can it strengthen America's competitive position, especially in high-technology sectors?

The Congress and the key domestic constituency groups—notably agriculture, business, and labor—will look for early signs of whether the Bush administration "can be trusted to defend American interests." They will watch closely its responses to the numerous stipulations in the Omnibus Trade and Competitiveness Act of 1988 (henceforth referred to as the Omnibus Trade Act), which was signed into law in August 1988. Early decisions also have to be taken on a wide range of sectoral problems, including agriculture, aircraft, semiconductors, steel, and textiles.

A third set of issues relates to specific international financial questions. Total Third World debt now exceeds $1.2 trillion and continues to hamper world growth, to threaten financial disruption, and to jeopardize political stability in a number of countries in Latin America and elsewhere. There is growing pressure on some of America's chief allies to assume larger shares of the costs of maintaining global peace and prosperity. In light of these and related questions, important decisions must be made concerning the roles of the International Bank for Reconstruction and Development (World Bank), the International Monetary Fund (IMF), and the Inter-American Development Bank (IDB), and the size of future U.S. financial contributions to these institutions.

Underlying these pressing issues are fundamental questions concerning the role of the United States in the world economy of the 1990s. America has become increasingly dependent on events occurring outside its borders. Its earlier ability to dominate global economic outcomes has eroded with the rising capabilities of other countries. Yet the United States remains by far the most powerful individual nation, with substantial leverage to pursue its international economic interests and a central role in determining the course of the world economy. America can neither dominate nor abdicate.

The rest of the world will be watching closely U.S. decisions on all of these issues, knowing that every newly elected administration of the past twenty years (Nixon, Carter, Reagan) has begun its tenure with sharp departures from the course set by its predecessor. Will the United States maintain a basically cooperative approach, or will it veer toward unilateralism—of either a "benign neglect" or aggressively mercantilist nature? Will the United States pursue an open trade policy, turn inward toward protection, or fall somewhere in between? Will it push for a successful Uruguay Round of multilateral trade negotiations and try to halt the erosion of the GATT (General Agreement on Tariffs and Trade) system, follow a primarily bilateral route, or try to do both? How will it respond to the charge that "foreigners are buying up America" and need to be stopped?

This array of international economic challenges presents an

extraordinarily difficult agenda for the Bush administration and Congress. Reducing the domestic budget deficit, which lies at the heart of an effective program to reduce the external deficit, seems to have become an intractable domestic political problem. Maintaining economic growth and cutting the trade gap have seemed to demand incompatible policies. Coordinating national policies to achieve satisfactory international outcomes raises delicate issues of sovereignty in each country. Japan, Germany, and other key countries abroad are far less anxious to reduce their surpluses than they were to build them up. There are sharp differences of view, both within the United States and around the world, on how economies respond to particular policy changes, and there is disagreement on some of the key economic variables, such as the correct level of exchange rates.

The apparent absence of immediate threats to the current prosperity, both in the United States and in most of the other industrial countries, may make it difficult to muster the political determination to implement substantial policy changes. The American economy indeed appeared to be in good shape as 1989 began. The longest peacetime expansion was continuing. Unemployment was near its lowest level in fifteen years. Inflation remained relatively subdued. Exports were booming. The trade deficit had started to come down. The dollar, far from collapsing, had risen through much of 1988.

The Urgency of Policy Action

This prosperity, however, has a precarious foundation. It is based to a very large extent on borrowing—both from America's own future and from the rest of the world. In particular, the external financial position of the United States represents an enormous threat to future prosperity, both in the short run and over time.

No respectable analysis shows the account deficit at this writing, given present policies and exchange rates, ever falling much below $100 billion. It could begin rising again by 1990. Without a significant shift in policy, the United States would thus have to continue borrowing indefinitely about $10 billion each month from the rest of the world. Its net foreign debt would continue to rise at breathtaking speed.

If foreign investors and central banks finally stop lending in such quantities to the United States, recognizing the unsustainability of the situation, the dollar will plunge and interest rates will soar. The result could be a revival of both double-digit inflation and sharp recession. There would be enormous disruption to a financial system that is already quite fragile. U.S. income distribution would be skewed further because the poorest groups are hit hardest by inflation and are the first to lose their jobs in a recession. Neither fiscal nor monetary policy would be available to respond to the crisis. The outcome would be even worse if foreigners were to withdraw some of the $1.5 trillion in liquid assets that they already hold in the United States.

These risks are not theoretical: the first steps of this scenario, and related international developments, triggered the sharp falls in the bond market in early 1987 and in the stock market later that year. Rapid and massive intervention was required by the world's monetary authorities to avoid a "hard landing" for the economy. The United States was able to borrow the amounts needed in 1988 with little difficulty, but this may have been due largely to the market's recognition that the major central banks would do whatever was necessary to support the dollar during an American election year, when serious adjustment measures could not be expected.

The risks are greater now than in any recent period. Foreigners lent $700 billion to the United States in the years 1982–1988, and their appetite for additional dollar assets could wane at any moment—especially if the U.S. trade deficit stops improving. With the U.S. economy near full employment and domestic demand growing rapidly, however, continued improvement of the trade balance at anything like the recent pace would generate heavy pressure on resources and ignite a sharp rise in inflation. So a sharp fall of the dollar is now quite possible whether or not the trade deficit continues to fall, unless the growth of domestic demand drops simultaneously.

With concerns about inflation already emerging, such a fall of the dollar could trigger rapid price rises and a quick move by the markets to higher interest rates. The U.S. Federal Reserve Bank (Fed) would have to tighten monetary policy to counter the inflationary pressure, producing increases in real interest rates that could turn the economy downward. Such a combination of higher interest rates and economic turndown would trigger more bankruptcies within the country and threaten defaults abroad.

Alternatively, the loss of foreign confidence could build up over time, as large trade deficits persisted and the ratio of U.S. foreign debt to exports and gross national product (GNP) continued to rise, rather than explode over some short period of time. In this case, interest rates would have to remain high to attract the required foreign funds and avoid withdrawals. Growth would slow. Investment would be discouraged. Productivity would suffer. Periodic market disruptions, like those in 1987, could be expected.

But the crisis could not be averted forever. Indeed, it could erupt when the condition of the economy was much less favorable. If growth had already slowed, a sharp rise in interest rates would be far more painful. The need to tighten fiscal policy would come at a much worse moment. The time for strong remedial action could arrive long after the Bush administration's "honeymoon" period is over, making it far more difficult to forge an effective political response.

In political terms as well, it would seem far better for the president to move preemptively early in the new term rather than be forced to react to a crisis later. President Reagan's deep recession of 1982 was old news by 1984. By contrast, President Carter tried to prolong an expansion, in the face of rising inflation and external deficits, and had to seek adjustment at the worst possible time—just prior to the next election.

On both economic and political grounds, it would therefore be extremely risky for the Bush administration to try to skate through four more years of massive borrowing from the rest of the world. One of the central goals of its economic policy should therefore be to eliminate the current account deficit during its first term, reducing it at an average annual pace of about $35 billion from the expected 1988 level of $130 billion to $140 billion. Early adoption of a credible program to achieve this ambitious goal is essential to avoid a crisis (sooner or later); to ensure market confidence in the dollar; to attract the sizable financing that will be needed during the extended adjustment period; and to provide a solid foundation for a sensible trade policy, an adequate response to Third World debt, and other key U.S. policy objectives.

A credible program to eliminate the external deficit, while maintaining economic growth and financial stability, must include three components. Significant changes in macroeconomic policy in the United States and complementary macroeconomic measures in the major surplus countries (mainly Japan and Germany, but also Taiwan and Korea) to keep their markets growing, along with some further changes in exchange rates, lie at the heart of the effort. An aggressive trade policy is essential to promote American exports and open markets abroad, and to counter the powerful domestic pressures for more import protection, which would undermine the effort to boost American competitiveness. More effective strategies are needed to resolve the debt crisis in the Third World, to restore growth and expand markets in those countries, and to improve the sharing of the international costs of maintaining global stability among America and its allies, mainly by using the international financial institutions in more ambitious and innovative ways.

Eliminating the Twin Deficits

To eliminate its external deficit during the first Bush term, the United States must reorient its economy toward exports and private investment (to boost export capacity and overall productivity), and away from consumption and government spending. Exports have been rising at annual rates of 20 to 30 percent since the middle of 1987, primarily because of the sharp fall in the exchange rate of the dollar since early 1985.

This indicates an impressive restoration of American competitiveness in world markets. The United States should thus be capable of achieving export-led growth in the early 1990s, as it did in the late 1970s. The annual expansion of total domestic demand must be held 1 to 1.5 percentage points below the growth of potential output (about 2.5 percent annually) to permit a transfer of resources of the requisite magnitude into the improvement in the trade balance.

The only assured and constructive means to achieve these results is for the United States to eliminate the federal government's structural budget deficit (about $150 billion) during Bush's four-year term. The Gramm-Rudman-Hollings schedule already sets such a course, mandating cumulative annual reductions in the deficit of about $36 billion, which would bring it to zero in fiscal year 1993 (ending September 1993). The president and Congress should follow this prescription by promptly adopting a balanced package of cuts in government programs and tax increases, designed to slow the rise of public spending and private consumption, that will phase in irrevocably during the adjustment period.

Such a program would increase national savings by eliminating the drain of government dissaving through the budget deficit. It would dampen inflation and calm fears of a new spiral. It would reduce interest rates, perhaps considerably, in both nominal and real terms. One result should be an increase in private investment, while simultaneously reducing and in time halting the build-up of foreign debt. Such a program would build a firm foundation for eliminating the external deficit and reinforcing the confidence of the markets, because it would free resources for export (instead of for domestic consumption by individuals or the government) and spur investment in new capacity to produce the needed goods and services.

Growth would be sustained by steady improvement in the trade balance, by increases in private investment induced by the fall in interest rates, and by the continued expansion of interest-sensitive components of consumption. The main threat to the economy in the short run, a collapse of the dollar and a return of inflationary recession, would be preempted. Fiscal policy would again become a flexible policy instrument, available to respond to future slowdowns. The prospects for higher levels of national savings, private investment, and productivity, and hence improved living standards over the long run, would be greatly enhanced. The main cost of such a program would be a slowdown in the growth of consumption, to less than 1 percent annually per capita during the adjustment period, after it had risen by about 3 to 3.5 percent per year during the initial phase of the expansion.

Purely domestic considerations call for similar policies. The economy neared full employment in 1988 following the creation of over 17 million jobs since the deep recession of 1982. Renewed inflation and higher interest rates have become the primary domestic concerns in the short run. There is no economic theory that justifies budget deficits near 3 percent of GNP in the United States when the economy is so close to full employment. As they address economic policy, the Bush administration and Congress should face no contradiction between the country's domestic and international priorities.

The longer-term goals of the U.S. economy point in the same direction. The American standard of living has grown very modestly since the early 1970s. Other countries, especially Japan and the newly industrializing countries (NICs) of East Asia, are catching (or passing) the United States in global competition. The underlying source of both problems is the modest rate of American productivity growth, which is caused in large part by the low and declining rate of national saving to support productive investment. The economy's expansion during the years 1982–1988 was made possible only by the importation of $700 billion of capital from abroad, which turned the United States into the world's largest debtor nation and mortgages its future increasingly to the actions of foreign creditors.

It is thus essential that the United States, for long-term structural as well as for immediate reasons, sharply raise its levels of domestic savings and investment. There is no conflict between the short and long runs. The international dimension plays a central role in both, because trade deficits and a continued dependence on foreign capital could jeopardize the country's ability to achieve its fundamental objectives over both time dimensions.

The need to avoid a protectionist relapse, and further severe erosion of the trading system, adds strongly to the case for the adoption of the program proposed here to eliminate the current account deficit. If the decline in the external deficit were to stall at or above $100 billion, and especially if it were to start rising again, the political message would be that the effort to solve the problem primarily through macroeconomic measures had failed. The proponents of this approach—former Treasury Secretary James A. Baker III, who launched the strategy in 1985 in large part to head off the threat of rampant protectionism; Federal Reserve Chairmen Paul Volcker and Alan Greenspan; officials in the other key countries; and virtually all economists around the world—would be discredited. Even if the real problem were a failure to implement the macroeconomic approach effectively, because of inadequate U.S. budget deficit cuts or insufficient growth abroad, the entire strategy could be jettisoned.

Given the absence of feasible alternatives, a major swing to protectionism might ensue. An American import surcharge would become a distinct possibility, as in the similar—but far less extreme—circumstances of 1971. Widespread foreign retaliation and emulation would be certain. The entire trading system could be shattered. Both the United States and its major partners abroad have compelling reasons, arising from considerations of trade policy as well as from those of growth and financial stability, to take the necessary steps to complete the adjustment of the current imbalances.

An Activist Trade Policy

These macroeconomic steps by the United States will have to be supported by macroeconomic steps abroad, which are described below, to achieve the full international adjustment. The United States itself, however, should also take a series of microeconomic measures to exploit its restored price competitiveness, transfer resources into the external sector, and bolster its international competitive position over the long run.

Active export promotion is particularly critical to overcome the marketing re-entry problem faced by many firms that were priced out of global competition in the early 1980s by the overvalued dollar. A new "Export Expansion and Removal of Disincentives Act" could sharply expand the direct lending and guaranty programs of the Export-Import Bank and eliminate or reduce many of the self-imposed constraints on American sales abroad.

Trade policy must assure that foreign markets remain open to U.S. exports and exert continuing pressure on other countries to reduce existing import restraints. Successful negotiation of multilateral cuts in barriers in the Uruguay Round will be the most effective way to rebuild global momentum for trade liberalization, opening markets for the American export drive. To help achieve maximum liberalization in the industrial countries, the Bush administration should propose that they eliminate all tariffs on their trade in industrial products by the year 2000. To obtain maximum concessions from both industrialized and developing countries, the United States should offer to reduce its own key barriers (including those for agriculture and textiles) on a fully reciprocal basis.

With exports booming and American price competitiveness restored, and with macroeconomic policy geared to export-led growth for several years, it would be folly for the United States to take protectionist steps that would be emulated abroad. As other countries' trade balances shrink and accommodate the American improvement, any new U.S. controls—against direct investment as well as imports—would encourage and justify reciprocal actions by other countries at the worst possible time for the United States.

Developments in Europe add a particular urgency to this component of the proposed strategy. The member countries of the European Community (EC) have made a firm commitment to "complete the internal market" by 1992, and are already moving in that direction. This intra-European integration could have major positive effects for the United States and the rest of the world economy, by increasing growth in the world's largest market and providing a stronger European partner to help share international responsibilities.

There is considerable concern outside the European Community, however, that the adjustment costs of internal liberalization will be passed on to outside countries in the form of new external barriers and discrimination (including measures against firms based in non-EC countries). Pressures in this direction could be significant since Europe, especially Germany, must simultaneously accept a considerable reduction in its external surplus as part of the global adjustment. If the world economy were to turn down, as a result of a collapse of the dollar or for any other reason, these pressures would be even more acute.

The United States thus has a major interest in pursuing initiatives that engage Europe externally while it is uniting further internally. The most important is the Uruguay Round, which aims to reduce trade barriers on a global basis and to write new rules to govern trade in agriculture and other potential areas of U.S.–European contention. It might in fact be desirable to aim for a two-stage outcome for the Round: an initial package in 1990 could center on short-term measures and a framework agreement for agriculture that would influence the U.S. farm legislation scheduled for 1990; the final deal in 1992 would coincide with Europe's target date and would maintain external pressure on the European Community. Conversely, the erection of new barriers by the United States would be extremely risky because it would add to protectionist pressures in Europe that may already be formidable. New American efforts to negotiate bilateral or regional free trade areas, modeled after the agreement with Canada, could also induce Europe to concentrate on deepening its "bloc" rather than cooperating on a global basis.

The United States should adopt several other trade policy changes. It should reject any future use of so-called voluntary restraint agreements (VRAs) to limit imports, largely because they enable the foreign competitors of American companies to reap billions of dollars of windfall profits that ultimately enhance their competitive positions, and offer to convert existing VRAs to less noxious forms of restraint (tariffs or auction quotas). The United States should substantially improve the adjustment assistance program, especially for workers in trade-impacted industries. It should require all industries seeking import relief to apply through designated legal channels, and offer a comprehensive plan for fundamental adjustment. These changes would promote the competitiveness of the U.S. economy and should be adopted primarily for domestic reasons. However, they could also strengthen the country's international negotiating position and enhance the prospects for a successful Uruguay Round.

The United States will also need to adopt a number of microeconomic measures ranging beyond trade policy to support its international economic position. Private investment might be stimulated through a revival of a modified investment tax credit and permanent status for the research and development credit (as well as by the lower interest rates resulting from budget correction). A refurbishing of the entire educational system, which is responsible for developing the nation's human capital, is clearly required. The country should designate a new institution, perhaps the Council on Competitiveness created by the Omnibus Trade Act, to develop projections for the future of key American industries and to assess the impact on them of the policies of foreign governments. These analyses would provide baselines against which to judge industry requests for import relief or other governmental assistance and the need for U.S. responses to other countries' trade and industrial policies.

On all these issues, it is essential that future U.S. policy take full account of the need to support the country's international economic and financial position. Historically, most American economic (and other) policies have been determined on strictly domestic grounds. The external dimension was ignored, or the country tried to export its internal preferences to the rest of the world. With the increase in America's dependence on world markets and the decline in its ability to dictate global outcomes, that approach is no longer viable. From this point forward, both macroeconomic policy and microeconomic measures will have to be adopted with full cognizance of their implications for the country's external position—the "competitive" component of the strategy of competitive interdependence suggested in this chapter.

The Foreign Dimension

The United States cannot do all this alone. The necessary improvement of about $150 billion in America's current account will require an equivalent reduction in the aggregate current account position of other countries. Management of the dollar and trade liberalization require cooperation from many countries. More effective responses to Third World debt and a range of other financial issues must be addressed multilaterally. Any comprehensive American strategy must contain an "interdependence" component as well.

Many countries are experiencing their own external deficit or debt problems, however, and thus cannot accept much, if any, current account decline. Canada and some of the European nations (including France, Italy, and the United Kingdom) are in this position. One group of countries that can paradoxically contribute to the global adjustment because of its current weakness is the Third World debtors. The fifteen largest debtors (listed in Table 1) are now paying about $30 billion more in annual debt service than they are receiving in new loans. This "negative financial transfer" requires them to run sizable trade surpluses, in contrast to the deficits that they have traditionally run and that are far more appropriate for countries at their stage of development. The shift in these countries' trade balances made a significant contribution (perhaps $15 billion to $20 billion) to the deterioration of the U.S. trade balance in the early 1980s.

These countries would clearly like to grow faster and stop running such large trade surpluses, but they must experience a sustained reduction in their net financial outflow to be able to do so. A four-part response to their problems, which would

TABLE 1 Proposed Program for Eliminating the "Negative Financial Transfer" from the Fifteen Heavily Indebted Developing Countries[a] by 1992 (billions of dollars)

Instrument	Impact by 1992	Comment
Reduced interest payments resulting from elimination of U.S. budget deficit and correction of imbalances among industrial countries.[b]	5–10	Each 1 percent decline in U.S. interest rates reduces interest payments by about $5 billion.
Increase in World Bank lending and speed-up of disbursements.	5–10	Contingent on adoption of effective adjustment program by borrowers. Facilitated by greater emphasis on structural adjustment loans. Supported by General Capital Increase (GCI).
Increase in Inter-American Development Bank lending and speed-up of disbursements.	5	Same as above. Requires new capital increase of about $25 billion (with U.S. share of about $9 billion).

also reduce the risk of financial instability triggered by further interruptions of debt servicing, could eliminate the "negative financial transfer" over the proposed four-year adjustment period and contribute at least $20 billion to the international correction (see Table 1).

The first component of the effort would be the reduction in dollar (and probably world) interest rates and other beneficial results of the U.S. budget correction and the reduction of imbalances among the industrial countries. Each one percentage point decline in interest rates reduces the annual debt service of the debtor countries by about $5 billion. The macroeconomic policy changes proposed here would probably cut interest rates by at least one to two percentage points, and there-

TABLE 1 *(Continued)*

Instrument	Impact by 1992	Comment
Increase in IMF lending.	5	Same as above. Facilitated by using "enlarged access" limits fully and doubling country quotas.
Voluntary debt relief.	5–10	Facilitated by World Bank guarantees of exit bonds for countries with effective adjustment programs. Includes buybacks, debt-equity swaps, and other devices.
Additional flows of private capital and officially supported export credits.	5–10	Especially direct investment and purchases of equities, but perhaps including modest amounts of new bank lending.
Total	30–50	

[a]The countries included are Argentina, Bolivia, Brazil, Chile, Colombia, Ecuador, Ivory Coast, Mexico, Morocco, Nigeria, Peru, Philippines, Uruguay, Venezuela, and Yugoslavia.
[b]This would reduce the interest earnings of industrial countries (including the United States) and thus does not contribute to the global current account adjustment addressed in the text and summarized in Table 2.

fore reduce the annual debt service costs of the poorer countries by $5 billion to $10 billion. Continued world growth and renewed trade liberalization would also boost debtor export growth, providing a further improvement in their external positions (though no additional decline in their debt service payments).

This part of the proposed package for the debtors would have no net impact on the global current account imbalances, even if fully offset by a reduction in their trade surpluses, because of the reduction in interest earnings of the industrial countries. However, it would reduce the extent of trade balance deterioration in the rest of the world needed to accommodate the American correction. Moreover, by reducing the "negative financial transfer," it would limit the financial risks emanating from Third World debt, and thus further support the case for the industrial countries to adopt the proposed economic adjustment program.

Second, the key international financial institutions should be prepared to increase significantly their lending to the debtor countries in support of more effective growth and adjustment policies. The World Bank should, as rapidly as possible, raise its available commitments from the present annual level of about $15 billion to about $25 billion, instead of the $21 billion now planned, and it should speed its disbursements by placing greater emphasis on structural adjustment loans. The Inter-American Development Bank should double its annual lending capability from the current level of about $3 billion. The IMF should immediately transfer considerably larger amounts to countries with effective stabilization programs, by utilizing the full "enlarged access" limits of 90 percent of quota rather than the considerably smaller amounts applied in most cases. Later, it should double the quotas of all members to permit even larger transfers.

Each of these three institutions is now contributing to the "negative financial transfer" by withdrawing funds from the large debtors rather than providing them with net inflows. The United States should support the proposed changes in these institutions, to further its broad interest in faster less developed country (LDC) growth (and thus political stability in Latin America, the Philippines, and elsewhere) and an easing of the global financial risks as well as for their direct impact on the U.S. external adjustment. This will require the United States, and other donor countries, to provide its full subscription to the new capital increase in the World Bank immediately, following the recent British example and along with other donor countries, rather than staging its payments over six years, as now planned, to provide the capital base for the acceleration in lending (and for a new guarantee program described below); agreement on a capital increase for the Inter-American Development Bank; and support for a doubling of quotas at the IMF. The budget costs of these measures are minuscule: because only a small portion of capital in the development banks is paid in and no outlays at all are required for the IMF, the United States can support an increase of about $200 billion in the combined resources of the three institutions with budget outlays of only $645 million (of which $50 million for the World Bank was already appropriated in 1988).

The third element of the strategy for Third World debtors is a broadening of the mechanisms available for the voluntary extension of debt relief by commercial banks. Comprehensive debt relief plans are impractical because there is no way to force banks to participate, no way to limit the relief to countries with effective adjustment programs, and no prospect of providing large amounts of public funds to support them. But schemes in which banks voluntarily write off part of their claims have already been worked out for Bolivia, Chile, and Mexico. Further innovation in relief techniques will add to the menu of possibilities, and a major expansion of this approach would be possible with the issuance of World Bank guarantees for exit bonds sold by debtor countries with approved adjustment programs. Depending on their maturity and terms, such bonds could substantially reduce the level of outstanding debt over time and provide at least modest cash flow relief in the short run.

Finally, every effort should be made to increase the flows of direct investment, equity capital, and other forms of nonbank private capital to the debtor countries. The capital-exporting countries and, in particular, the debtor countries themselves will need to make a number of policy changes to induce these flows. It will probably be some time before the flows become sizable, given the adverse environment created by the debt crisis itself. But the potential for significant increases is clearly demonstrated by the record of less debt burdened developing countries. More immediately, the export credit agencies of the industrial countries (including the Export-Import Bank of the United States) should restore and expand their programs in debtor countries with effective adjustment programs.

About $30 billion of the foreign counterpart of the American external adjustment can thus be generated by the largest

Third World debtors, with adequate support from the industrial countries. The rest of the correction must come primarily from changes in the small number of countries with large surpluses. (One other group of countries that might "contribute" to the global adjustment is the Organization of Petroleum Exporting Countries [OPEC], if the oil price were to fall substantially and they were able to borrow enough externally to avoid a corresponding cutback in imports. The magnitude of any such effort would depend on the extent of the price decline and the countries' creditworthiness. The group's current account deteriorated from rough balance in 1984–1985 to a deficit of about $30 billion when the price of oil plunged in 1986, and leveled off by 1988 at a deficit of about $15 billion.) Japan is the world's largest surplus country, by far, and it will need to accept an adjustment of about $60 billion. Germany is the key to Western Europe, the world's largest market and largest trading entity, and it is running a surplus that is second largest in absolute terms and larger than Japan's relative to the size of its economy; Germany needs a correction of about $40 billion, and the three smaller surplus countries in Europe (Belgium, the Netherlands, and Switzerland) should add another $10 billion. The Asian NICs, mainly Taiwan and Korea, have by far the largest external surpluses relative to GNP—about 13 percent and 8 percent, respectively, compared with 3 to 4 percent for Germany and Japan—and should adjust by about $20 billion (see Table 2).

Some of the reduction in these countries' surpluses will follow automatically from the proposed policy changes in the United States. But they will need to make efforts in three areas: achieving and maintaining sufficient growth of domestic demand in their own economies; keeping their markets open and reducing their trade barriers; and cooperating to reach and sustain equilibrium exchange rates among the dollar and the other key currencies. Fortunately, such steps would meet the most pressing internal needs of the countries themselves: a sharp cut in Europe's continuing double-digit unemployment and growing intraregional imbalances, and a steady rise in living standards and domestic welfare in Japan and the Asian NICs.

TABLE 2 Proposed International Allocation of the Adjustment of National Current Account Positions, 1987 to 1992 (billions of dollars)

Country	1980–81 average	1987	Proposed[a] 1992	Proposed[a] Change from 1987
United States	5	−155	−5	150
Japan	0	90	30	−60
Germany	−10	45	5	−40
Smaller Europeans[b]	−5	15	5	−10
15 Heavily Indebted Developing Countries[c]	−30	−10	−40	−30
Taiwan and Korea	−5	30	10	−20

[a]A significant fall in the world price of oil, if sustained through this period, could produce a further increase in the current account deficit of OPEC countries and reduce the needed adjustment in countries other than the United States. On the other hand, some allowance is made for reductions in the deficits of countries other than the United States (such as the United Kingdom).
[b]Belgium, the Netherlands, Switzerland.
[c]See Table 1.

There is considerable debate among economists about the benefits to the American trade effort of faster growth abroad and the liberalization of foreign trade barriers. Some analyses show very modest gains from one or the other, while others show substantial payoffs. The importance of achieving the full correction is so great and the required magnitude is so large, however, that the message for policy is straightforward: maximize the effort on all fronts. Domestic demand is already expanding vigorously in Japan, rising by more than 7 percent in 1988, and needs to be maintained at about 6 percent per year throughout the adjustment period. The large European countries other than Germany are all running deficits and cannot expand on a sustained basis alone, but Europe as a whole (and Canada) can and should expand domestic demand by about 4 percent annually through 1992. Since the external surpluses of Japan and Europe would be declining (in real terms) at about 1 percent of GNP annually through the four-year adjustment period to achieve the international adjustment, the resulting growth of GNP would be about 5 percent in Japan and 3 percent in Europe. Such growth rates could expand U.S. exports by about $50 billion annually after they had worked their way through fully to the trade flows.

Another key international consideration, beyond these macroeconomic policy changes and the trade negotiations addressed earlier, is burden sharing among the allies. The security arrangements that were developed in the early postwar period have worked exceedingly well, as has the compartmentalization of security and economic relations among the allies that has prevailed for most of the period. With the rise of General Secretary Mikhail Gorbachev in the Soviet Union and the possibility of new progress toward lasting peace, it will be especially crucial to maintain (and even strengthen) alliance solidarity into the 1990s and avoid any destabilizing interaction between these two sets of issues.

Alliance security arrangements were developed, however, at a time when the relative economic capabilities of the allies were considerably different than they are today. In the United States, there is rising domestic political pressure for a change in distribution of the costs of maintaining global security, including its economic components, such as foreign assistance and debt relief. The stability of the security system can be assured only if there is a substantial reallocation of responsibilities according to economic capacity—carrying with it, of course, a corresponding reallocation of economic rights.

It is noteworthy that some of the major surplus countries—especially Japan, Germany, and Korea—are also among America's most important allies and are in fact linchpins of its most important collective security systems. When they respond to U.S. adjustment needs—whether this involves growth rates, exchange rates, trade liberalization, or financial contributions to the relief of Third World debt and poverty—these countries need to have these broader considerations very much in mind. The most promising venue for formal changes in burden sharing is the international financial institutions. Japan and the others should sharply increase their funding for these organizations through an early selective capital increase (SCI) in the

World Bank and perhaps similar steps in the regional development banks; a possible new facility at the World Bank to back exit bond guarantees; and further adjustment of quotas in the IMF. The United States and the allies, particularly Japan, should discuss these issues explicitly and reach an early agreement on the methods by which better burden sharing will be achieved, and on the concomitant shifts in leadership roles within the institutions.

The Dollar and the Monetary System

The final component of the adjustment package is exchange rate policy. The decline of the dollar has restored much of America's price competitiveness. By late 1987 the dollar had roughly reversed the appreciation of 1980–1985. However, this was probably not quite enough to restore balance in the current account, even if macroeconomic policies both at home and abroad were altered, because the United States had shifted to debtor status in the interim and because other structural changes had occurred.

Several steps will therefore be needed in this area. First, if the other macroeconomic policies proposed here for the United States and the other key countries are put into place, a depreciation averaging about 15 percent in real terms from the level of the fourth quarter of 1987 should be sufficient to eliminate the current account deficit by 1992. (If the surplus countries abroad failed to maintain the growth rates proposed above, the additional dollar depreciation would have to be closer to 20 percent.)

Second, these further currency movements will have to fall primarily on the surplus countries. As noted above, a substantial portion of across-the-board changes would affect weaker countries that could not accept them and would therefore take offsetting measures, aborting the adjustment and prompting a series of iterations until the bulk of the impact ultimately fell on the stronger countries in any event. Above average appreciations will thus be required for the surplus countries, taking their currencies to perhaps 100:1 for the yen, 1.25:1 for the

DM, 23:1 for the New Taiwan dollar, and 675:1 for the Korean won. Such a DM appreciation implies a realignment of about 20 percent within the European Monetary System (EMS), which will clearly be needed in light of the growing trade imbalances between Germany and its European partners.

Fourth, it will be essential to avoid any premature renewed appreciation of the dollar. The necessary expansion of U.S. exports will take place only if American firms substantially increase their export capacity, and many are reluctant to do so because they fear being priced out of foreign markets by a rising dollar again before their new plants come on stream. The dollar might fall on its own if the United States enacts the budget policies proposed here and interest rates decline in response. But it could also surge, given an improved trade outlook and the sense that America was finally "fixing the only thing that is broke." The authorities will have to resist any such appreciation until full correction of the external deficit is achieved and maintained for some time. To this end, they might announce an agreed ceiling for the exchange rate of the dollar and defend it vigorously.

(An alternative scenario would be for the dollar to depreciate by the needed amount, either due to spontaneous market developments or with some encouragement from the authorities prior to the coming together of the proposed budget policies. Announcement of those policies should then arrest the dollar's slide and provide the internal transfer of resources needed to translate the further depreciation into sustained improvement in the trade balance. The authorities would still have to agree to resist firmly any resulting upside pressures on the dollar, but under this scenario might have better prospects for maintaining an equilibrium level.)

Fifth, the major countries should work out the details of a system of target zones for their currencies and install it as soon as the required adjustment policies are in place and the currencies have reached levels that are likely to be sustainable. This would help avoid any premature rise of the dollar. Over time, it should promote the orderly achievement of required currency changes as needed (such as a steady appreciation of the yen in response to Japan's lower inflation, its higher productivity, and its rapidly rising investment income as the world's largest creditor country). Target zones should also provide a strong foundation for improving international coordination of national economic policies (and thereby helping to maintain a global orientation for the European countries even if they deepen their internal arrangements through the EMS). Again, short-term and longer-term considerations point to the same policy approach.

The nonsystem of floating exchange rates that has been in place since 1973 has permitted (or even fostered) huge currency misalignments, generating major economic distortions and protectionist trade pressures. The governments of the world's leading economies, the so-called Group of Five (the U.S., the U.K., France, Germany, and Japan) and Group of Seven (the previous five plus Canada and Italy), have been groping toward a new system since the Plaza Agreement of September 1985. They installed "reference ranges" for most of their currencies in February 1987. Completing of the process with a full target zone system should provide greater monetary stability and an effective mechanism for forging closer policy coordination. The IMF, supported by a doubling of its quotas, should ultimately manage the system and again assume a central role in global financial affairs.

We noted at the outset that a precipitous fall of the dollar could have devastating effects on the U.S. and world economies. Indeed, a central goal of the entire strategy proposed here is to avoid such an event. But we have just suggested that the dollar must come down by another 10 to 15 percent to achieve the needed adjustment, even if the major countries abroad maintain domestic demand growth at the recommended rates. How are these two views to be reconciled?

The critical distinction is whether the dollar falls because of the absence of a comprehensive adjustment program or in the context of such a program. In the former case, with the United States near full employment and domestic demand rising rapidly, and with foreign growth at moderate levels, the main effect of a sizable and rapid dollar decline would be faster U.S.

inflation (and thus little depreciation of the exchange rate in real terms). Interest rates would rise and the "hard landing" scenario set forth above could ensue. The trade deficit might decline, but it would do so mainly because of a U.S. recession (unless other countries experienced recessions of similar magnitudes, in which case there would be little or no improvement in the U.S. trade balance). The size of the dollar decline could also turn out to be far greater than the average of 10 to 15 percent (in real terms) that is needed, because it would be caused by a lack of confidence in the dollar, or even a widespread flight from it, that was in turn the consequence of a widespread belief that the United States was never going to "get its house in order" by dealing with the twin deficits.

In contrast, a depreciation of the dollar in tandem with the proposed macroeconomic changes in the United States and abroad would achieve effective adjustment and thereby enhance the prospects for an orderly completion of the currency realignment. Such a package would simultaneously expand the supply of American goods available for export, at more competitive prices, and increase demand for those products around the world (see summary in Table 3). The U.S. fiscal program and companion steps abroad should assure confidence in the underlying strength and stability of the dollar. Further dollar depreciation as part of the package proposed here should enhance stability, whereas a depreciation of similar magnitude in the absence of such a program could be destabilizing and counterproductive. As noted earlier, however, the immediate problem may in fact be to keep the dollar from soaring prematurely.

Implementing the Strategy

The United States can best pursue its national interests in the context of an essentially cooperative, but vigorously competitive, world economy through a strategy of "competitive interdependence." The "competitive" component of the proposed strategy would be implemented largely through three new legislative packages, worked out by the Bush administra-

TABLE 3 Proposed Program for Adjustment of U.S. Current Account
Deficit by 1992 (billions of dollars)

Instrument	Impact by 1992	Comment
Elimination of U.S. budget deficit and 15 percent decline of trade-weighted dollar from average level of fourth quarter 1987.	90[a]	Depreciation targeted largely against currencies of surplus countries (yen, DM, Swiss franc, Dutch guilder, Belgian franc, NT$, won). Also requires reversal of dollar rise in 1988 (3 percent from fourth quarter 1987, as of 1 October 1988).
Increase of about 1 percent above expected baseline in annual growth of domestic demand in other industrial countries during 1989–92.	50	Requires GNP growth of about 5 percent in Japan and 3.5 percent in Germany, 2.5 percent to 3 percent in rest of Europe and Canada.
Increased capital transfers (including through voluntary debt relief) to 15 heavily indebted countries of Third World (see Table 1).	10	Enables Third World debtors to reduce debt constraint, grow faster, and import more.
Total	150	

[a]This impact would be greater ($15 billion per percentage point per year) if the U.S. budget correction produced a slowdown in U.S. economic growth. The analysis in the text suggests, however, that GNP growth would be maintained because the induced improvements in the trade balance and, because of lower interest rates, in private investment and other interest on sensitive expenditures would offset the cutbacks in government spending and other private consumption.

tion in full consultation with Congress: one aimed at reducing the budget deficit, another to promote export expansion (including some related microeconomic measures), and a third intended to strengthen the ability of the international financial institutions to address Third World debt and alliance burden sharing. The "interdependence" component would encompass a series of major international negotiations: to coordinate national economic policies among the industrial countries and reduce the impact of Third World debt, in order to eliminate the present imbalances and ensure continuing growth; to achieve equilibrium among the key currencies and maintain it with a reformed international monetary system; to renew the process of trade liberalization through a successful Uruguay Round of negotiations under the General Agreement on Tariffs and Trade and bilateral talks where necessary; to improve and expand substantially the programs of the international financial institutions; and to better redistribute the allies' contributions to the maintenance of a stable world economy according to their ability to pay.

The United States would gain significantly from the proposed strategy, most crucially by eliminating its external deficit and thus the constant financial threat to its prosperity and stability. The risks of financial instability would also be reduced, over both the short run and the long run, by an improved response to Third World debt and by the new system of target zones. The United States would also benefit from the relative increase in the contributions of other countries to shared international economic goals, and from the renewed liberalization of world trade. It would contribute substantially to world adjustment by bringing its budget deficit under control, agreeing to stabilize the dollar once equilibrium levels were reached, liberalizing its own trade barriers (including those in sensitive sectors), and providing more financial resources to the international financial institutions (with very modest budget outlays).

Japan, Germany and the smaller European surplus countries, and the Asian NICs (notably Taiwan and Korea) would need to ensure continuing rapid growth of domestic demand throughout the adjustment period, further liberalize their import restraints, accept additional appreciation of their currencies, and increase their shares of funding for the international financial institutions. In return, these countries could resolve their most pressing internal economic problems: unemployment and regional imbalances (which could impede further economic integration) in Europe and low standards of living (including poor housing and inadequate social infrastructure) in Japan and the Asian NICs.

These countries would also share in the enhanced prosperity and stability that would result from an orderly correction of the global imbalances, the creation of a more effective monetary regime, renewed liberalization of trade, and a resolution of the Third World debt problem. Particularly for Japan, larger contributions to the system of economic management would mean greater influence. Their security positions would be confirmed, and the prospects for successful negotiations with the Soviet Union enhanced, by the cooperative response to these enormous economic problems.

At this juncture, there are no fundamental contradictions between the internal and external policy objectives of the major countries that could impede the implementation of this program. Nor are there conflicts between the countries' immediate and longer-term goals. The United States must become much more outward-oriented, both because of its permanently increased dependence on the world economy and to correct its current imbalances. The surplus countries must rely much more heavily on expanding domestic demand, rather than exports both for their own long-term growth and to correct the present imbalances. Both the domestic and international political dimensions of the situation suggest that the proposed program is necessary and quite feasible.

The new package could be unveiled at a special international summit meeting. Such a launching would have a dramatic positive effect on market confidence around the world. It would greatly strengthen credibility of the process of international policy coordination. Targeting such an agreement for an international summit, with full contributions by all the major countries, could help galvanize political support for the needed policy changes within each of them.

It will be vitally important for the Bush administration and Congress to adopt, launch, and begin to implement such a strategy early in the first term of office. Their action on the U.S. budget is the centerpiece of the program; without it, little else may be possible. The markets and foreign officials may not wait long before rendering a judgment, via their attitudes toward the dollar, on the Bush administration. The Third World debt crisis could erupt at any time. The Omnibus Trade Act requires early action on a number of components of trade policy.

It is also true that there are only a few windows of opportunity within which American governments can adopt major policy initiatives. The checks and balances of the constitutional system, particularly those between the executive branch and Congress, usually preclude dramatic change except in response to crises. The greatest opportunity tends to come in the initial stages, or "honeymoon period," of a new administration. The popular mandate from the election enables it to launch new initiatives, and the Congress will tend to give it the benefit of the doubt. Rapid action is thus necessary for both substantive and political reasons.

America in the World Economy of the 1990s

The proposed strategy of competitive interdependence rests on two central premises: American prosperity has become inextricably linked to the health of the world economy and to the maintenance of a strong American position in that world economy, and the United States retains the ability to pursue its interests effectively on the global scene, albeit in different ways than in the past. The strategy attempts to provide a cohesive framework for the decisions by the U.S. government on specific international economic issues. Internally, it calls for a reorientation of America's economic policies, especially at the macroeconomic level but also in some microeconomic areas, much more heavily in the direction of achieving and sustaining a strong international economic and financial position. In this era of heightened dependence on the external environment and reduced (though still substantial) unilateral clout, the United States must tailor its "domestic" policies increasingly to the realities of the world economy. This is the "competitive" component of the proposed strategy. Internationally, this strategy advocates negotiating actively to promote immediate U.S. interests and to improve the global systems of trade and finance—the "interdependence" element of the approach.

The strategy of competitive interdependence thus views any return to the "benign neglect" of the first Reagan administration (and the early years of the first Nixon administration) as extremely dangerous. It holds that a continuation of the policy coordination efforts of the second Reagan administration offers considerable potential advantages to the United States, and thus rejects economist Martin Feldstein's suggestion that "the United States should now explicitly but amicably abandon the policy of international coordination of macroeconomic policy." It rejects protectionism or more subtle versions of "managed trade," which would undermine America's central needs for a more competitive economy at home and more effective policy cooperation abroad.

The United States must be prepared to deploy its considerable leverage—arising from the appeal of its market, the role of the dollars, and its security guarantees—to pursue its goals, as all countries do. It can probably use these sources of leverage more successfully as inducements than as threats, given the specific nature of each. It can clearly do so with the greatest prospect of success within an essentially cooperative international framework, rather than in an institutional vacuum or in an environment of hostility triggered by unilateral steps of its own. The United States can also achieve its goals far more effectively if it puts its own house in order and keeps it that way by bringing its budget deficit under control, avoiding protectionist steps that close its own markets, and making its fair contributions to the financial institutions.

Explicit adoption of this strategy, and widespread communication of its premises and policy implications, are needed to produce an American foreign economic policy that is consistent across issues and over time. It is also essential to provide clear guidance to the numerous domestic actors involved—including the business community, labor, farm groups, the bureaucracy, and the media—and to other countries. If the Bush administration and Congress fail consciously and publicly to adopt a coherent strategic approach and stick to it, the different constellations of political actors that revolve around individual issues will inevitably produce an incoherent pattern of outcomes—some protectionist, some ignoring the external dimension, some lashing out internationally in a counterproductive manner. At a minimum, the result would be a further erosion of both U.S. interests and U.S. influence in the world economy. At worst, the fundamental American objectives of prosperity and stability would go unrealized, and America's economy and foreign policy would both be at risk.

Commentary:

PAUL CRAIG ROBERTS

O ne of the most striking things about our country is that its intellectual class has no confidence in it. Fred Bergsten's paper reminds me of the hysterical papers written in the 1970s about the "energy crisis" and America's "dependence on foreign oil." The story is always the same. Only the villain changes.

Today the boogeyman is the "deficit crisis" and America's "dependence on foreign money." This boogeyman comes alive for Bergsten because he believes that the "twin deficits"

PAUL CRAIG ROBERTS holds the William E. Simon Chair in Political Economy at the Center for Strategic and International Studies in Washington, D.C., and he is a senior research fellow in the Hoover Institution at Stanford University. A former editor and columnist for the *Wall Street Journal,* he is currently a columnist for several business publications, including *Business Week,* the *Financial Post, Liberation,* and the *Washington Times.* During 1981–1982, Dr. Roberts served as assistant secretary of the treasury for economic policy, and from 1975 to 1978 he served on the congressional staff, where he drafted the Kemp-Roth bill and played a leading role in developing bipartisan support for a supply-side economic policy. Dr. Roberts has published several books on economic theory and policy.

are results of a deficit spending policy to fuel a consumption boom with tax cuts. Excessive consumption has forced us to borrow "both from America's own future and from the rest of the world," undermining "the external financial position of the United States" and our "future prosperity."

In Bergsten's Keynesian view of the world, consumption is the driving force. In this one-dimensional approach, fiscal policy is purely a regulator of demand. A domestic budget deficit means too much demand, which spills over into imports, causing a trade deficit. Our prosperity, he believes, is built on debt and will collapse the day we cannot borrow any more.

Fortunately, the facts are entirely different. The budget deficit is not a Keynesian policy deficit designed to spur consumption. Rather, it is the consequence of the unanticipated 1981–1982 recession and sudden collapse in inflation, which wiped out $2.5 trillion of taxable gross national product (GNP) over the 1981–1986 period. The reason the large budget deficits of the 1980s have confounded so many forecasters by not causing the predicted rises in inflation and interest rates is that the deficits are themselves the consequence of the unexpected collapse of inflation. When inflation collapses, it takes interest rates down with it. And if the collapse is not anticipated, it is guaranteed to wreck budget and deficit forecasts.

Bergsten also misinterprets the trade deficit. In his mind, it results from excess domestic consumption spilling over into imports, forcing us to go hat in hand to foreigners for loans to finance our consumption. In other words, as Bergsten sees it, trade flows determine capital flows.

A more sophisticated view supported by the facts is that capital flows determine trade flows. During 1982–1984 there was a tremendous change in U.S. capital flows due to the fact that we ceased to export our capital (see Table 1). U.S. capital outflows fell from $121 billion in 1982 to $22 billion in 1984, a change that had to be offset by a current account deficit. Many writers have implied that this $100 billion change in net capital inflows was due to foreign capital flowing in to finance our deficit. However, during this period there was no significant change in the amount of foreign capital flowing to the United

TABLE 1 U.S. Capital Account, 1980 to 1987 ($, billions)

	1980	1981	1982	1983	1984	1985	1986	1987
1. Capital inflow to U.S.	58	83	94	85	102	130	213	203
2. Less: Capital outflow from U.S.	86	111	121	50	22	31	96	64
3. Equals: Net identified capital inflow	−28	−28	−27	35	80	99	117	139
4. Plus Statistical discrepancy and other (inflows)	26	21	36	11	27	18	24	22
5. Equals: Net capital inflow to U.S.	−2	−7	9	46	107	117	141	161
6. Current account balance	2	7	−9	−46	−107	−116	−141	−161

(+) implies inflow, (−) indicates outflow
Source: U.S. Department of Commerce.

States. Instead, our money stayed at home and financed our own deficit.

Why did we cease to export our capital? The 1981 tax reductions raised the after-tax rate of return earned by real investment in the United States. The American economy began growing faster than other industrialized countries. It paid to invest in the United States. In addition, U.S. bank lending to Third World countries was sharply curtailed. Much of the lending was based on an expected rise in commodity prices, such as oil and copper. When the price rises failed to materialize, the banks realized they had overexposed their capital.

It is interesting that inflows of foreign capital into the United States did not increase until the dollar weakened, which indicates that a weak dollar is more likely to attract foreign investment in the United States than to drive it away. Throughout his paper, Bergsten calls foreign investment in the United States "lending," which could be withdrawn at any point, precipitating a crisis. But in fact, much of this foreign money is invested in real assets, such as plant, equipment, and office buildings that create U.S. jobs and enhance our efficiency. Foreign money is flowing into the United States on its own because it can do better for itself here than in its home countries. It is Germany that has the problem: it cannot attract its own investment capital.

The charge that the United States has become the "world's largest debtor nation" is a good example of how anxious people are to become hysterical. Someone needs to tell the economists who keep fueling this anxiety that it is not possible to be a net debtor while simultaneously enjoying a net creditor's income. Our "net debtor" status is based on the use of undervalued "book values" of U.S. foreign investments (and a $42 per ounce book value of our gold stock). This leads to a paradox: in 1987 we were supposedly $368 billion in the red, but still earned $21 billion more on our overseas investments than we paid to our foreign creditors! It might also help to calm the waters if economists would remember that our foreign debt is denominated in our own currency.

Unlike Keynesian economists, I have never been an advocate of budget deficits, but it is useful to put ours in perspective by comparing it to the rest of the world. During our period of deficit hysteria, the Organization for Economic Cooperation and Development (OECD) and the Bank for International Settlements have been publishing internationally comparable statistics on government budget deficits and the growth of public debt as a percent of GNP. These statistics show that the United States has enjoyed one of the smallest deficits and slowest growth in federal debt as a share of GNP in the world. When the total public sector deficit for each industrialized country is divided by its GNP, the U.S. ratio is below average (see Table 2). In percentage terms, the U.S. deficit is about half that of Canada and Holland and one-fourth that of Italy. Has anyone heard about the Canadian, Dutch, or Italian debt crises? If weaker countries can continue to carry on successfully with proportionately larger deficits, why do our smaller deficits doom us?

Even more astonishing, data from the Bank for International Settlements show that from 1973 to 1986, the period of the largest deficits in U.S. history, German and Japanese federal debt as a share of GNP grew three and four times faster than in the United States (see Table 3). During this period the U.S. ratio of debt to GNP grew 41 percent, the third lowest in the sample of thirteen industrialized countries. The German ratio grew 121 percent, and the Japanese ratio grew 194 percent. Indeed, the Japanese ratio of total accumulated federal debt as a share of GNP is almost twice as high as in the United States. Has anyone heard about the German or Japanese debt crises?

Of course, we should encourage other countries to improve their own investment climates. This would make them more competitive in attracting their own capital and help to correct imbalances in capital and trade flows. And we should continue to keep our domestic deficit on its downward path, both absolutely and as a percent of GNP.

However, we should avoid propagating myths about our dependence on foreign money to finance our budget deficits. The official statistics show that today foreigners hold a much

TABLE 2 Budget Deficits

The OECD publishes data on "internationally comparable general government budget balances." This definition encompasses central, regional, and local government balances, as well as social security financial balances, and is claimed, by OECD, to represent the "most widely accepted basis of measurement . . . for international comparisons." Recent data along with long-term averages and the latest OECD forecasts are included below:

General Govt. Financial Balances	As % nominal GNP/GDP						
	1970–86(av)	1983	1984	1985	1986	1987(e)	1988(f)
United States	-1.7	-3.8	-2.8	-3.5	-2.4	-2.4	-2.3
Canada	-2.6	-6.9	-6.6	-7.0	-5.5	-4.4	-3.3
United Kingdom	-2.8	-3.6	-3.9	-2.9	-2.6	-2.1	-1.9
Germany	-2.0	-2.5	-1.9	-1.1	-1.2	-1.7	-2.3
Holland	-3.3	-6.4	-6.2	-4.8	-5.6	-6.3	-6.3
Italy	-9.4	-10.7	-11.5	-12.3	-11.2	-10.3	-10.0
France	-1.1	-3.2	-2.7	-2.9	-2.9	-2.8	-2.7
Spain	-2.2	-4.8	-5.5	-6.8	-5.7	-4.9	-4.9
Japan	-2.1	-3.7	-2.1	-0.8	-0.9	-1.2	-1.1
Sweden	-0.1	-5.0	-2.6	-3.8	-0.3	+3.9	+2.6
Australia	-0.8	-4.0	-3.2	-2.9	-2.8	-1.6	-0.3

Others not available
f: forecast e: estimated
Source: OECD Economic Outlook, May 1988.

TABLE 3 Federal Debt as Share of GNP

	1973	*1986*	*%Change*
Austria	10.8%	55.9%	417.6%
Spain	13.8	49.0	255.1
Sweden	22.5	68.8	205.8
Japan	30.9	90.9	194.2
Belgium	54.0	123.2	128.1
Germany	18.6	41.1	121.0
Italy	52.7	88.9	68.7
Netherlands	43.2	72.2	67.1
Canada	45.6	68.8	50.9
France	25.4	36.9	45.3
U.S.	39.9	56.2	40.8
Switzerland	30.3	32.5	7.3
U.K.	71.8	57.7	−19.6
Weighted Average	37.5	62.1	65.6

Source: Bank for International Settlements.

smaller percentage of our federal debt than they did a decade ago. For example, in 1987 foreigners held 11.3 percent of gross federal debt as compared to 15.5 percent in 1978. In 1987 foreign holdings accounted for 14.1 percent of the federal debt held by the public as compared to 19.8 percent in 1978. In general the percentage of federal debt held by foreigners rose during the 1970s and declined during the 1980s. The peak year was 1978.

U.S. prosperity is not based on borrowing. Today the U.S. public debt is about the same percent of GNP as when John Kennedy was president. Our prosperity is based on a restoration of incentives and private property rights. The United States is again a good place to invest. During the 1980s the growth of U.S. manufacturing productivity doubled. There was a six-year expansion and the creation of 17 million new jobs without a rise in the rate of inflation. The worsening "Phillips curve" trade-offs between inflation and unemployment that demoralized policy makers in the 1970s were not characteristic of this expansion.

Some economists have blinded themselves to our improved

position by pointing to low net measures of saving and investment in order to bolster their allegations of a precarious prosperity based on borrowing. These net measures are very misleading. The 1981 tax legislation caused a shift in the composition of investment toward assets with shorter lives that increase business cash flow by generating more depreciation. A comparison on a net basis of U.S. saving and investment behavior in the 1980s with prior periods or other countries misreads a change in the assortment of assets as a decline in investment behavior. Comparison on a gross basis tells a different story. Since 1982, gross business fixed investment as a percent of GNP has exceeded the postwar average.

Similarly, those who focus on the decline in the personal saving rate neglect to mention the demographic and other factors that are working to lower the personal saving rate (see Paul Craig Roberts, "Why America's Piggy Banks Aren't Bulging." *Business Week,* June 20, 1988). The remarkable fact is that the rise in business saving during the 1980s offset the fall in the personal saving rate. During the Reagan recovery, the gross private savings rate averaged 16.7 percent, compared to 16.6 percent during the 1947–1981 period. Far from experiencing a collapse in private saving, policy has succeeded in maintaining the private saving rate at its postwar average despite the demographic and other pressures operating to push it down.

After deploring the increase in U.S. external debt, Bergsten calls for the industrialized West to resume lending in a massive way to the Third World. It is extraordinary that Bergsten believes that the United States, a country that produces about 25 percent of the world's GNP, cannot survive a build-up in external debt denominated in its own currency, but that Mexico, Peru, Brazil, Zaire, and the rest of the overindebted Third World can benefit from a large build-up in their external debt denominated in dollars, yen, marks, and other strong currencies. If we have mortgaged our future with debt, as Bergsten claims, why does he recommend an increase in the external debt of much poorer countries?

Bergsten avoids answering this question by asserting that deficits "are far more appropriate for countries at their stage of development." In other words, external debt must not be such a fatal affliction after all.

Commentary:

ARTHUR B. LAFFER

T he Bergsten ten-year plan in my view is fatally flawed. His basic premise that trade deficits are a symptom of misguided policies is just not correct. The fact that his premise is false is more than sufficient to negate the rest of his analysis. The views Bergsten expresses so eloquently are by no means out of the mainstream. When put to the test, however, they fail.

A current account or merchandise trade deficit is not, per se,

ARTHUR B. LAFFER is a member of the Economic Policy Advisory Board to the president of the United States. He was formerly a member of the policy committee and the board of directors of the American Council for Capital Formation and was editor of the Marcel Dekker, Inc. series on economics, finance, and business. He is a contributing editor of the *Conservative Digest* and has been associated with the editorial page of the *Wall Street Journal*. Dr. Laffer has held faculty positions at Pepperdine University, the University of Southern California, and the University of Chicago. From 1972 to 1977 he was a consultant to the secretary of the treasury and the secretary of defense, and he served as an economist in the Office of Management and Budget from 1970 to 1972. Dr. Laffer is the founder and chairman of A.B. Laffer & Associates, an economic research and financial consulting firm.

bad. Far from it. If the loans to foreigners and capital acquisitions by foreigners are not guaranteed by taxpayers, then the existence of a trade deficit is a matter of private concern and should be subjected to public "benign neglect." There is no difference between a Pennsylvania firm's borrowing from a Sensei from Stockton, California, and that same Pennsylvania firm's borrowing from an ethnic Japanese from Hokkaido. In either case, the successful or nonsuccessful performance of that loan is an issue solely between the lender and the borrower. Public policy should not be concerned.

There is also good reason to expect and even welcome trade deficits when an economy experiences a renaissance of performance as has been the case for the United States during the six years from 1982 to 1986. Just as growth companies borrow money, so too growth countries borrow. The accounting counterpart of the current account deficit is the capital account surplus.

To see the non-Bergsten side of the debate, one need only ask whether you would prefer to see capital lined up on your borders trying to get out of your country or lined up on your borders trying to get into your country. Clearly, a country's capital surplus is a sign of economic health, not malaise. The only way investors can generate a dollar cash flow in order to invest in the United States is for the United States to run a current account deficit.

With the inflation and interest rate successes of Paul Volcker, the tax successes of Howard Jarvis, Bill Steiger, and Ronald Reagan, the United States has become the Bermuda of the developed world, a veritable magnet for foreign capital. Capital goes to where the action is.

As a consequence, foreigners have provided the United States with the real resources to increase our output, employment, and productivity. Far from being a problem, the U.S. trade deficit has been a solution. Since the commencement of our trade deficit in the first quarter of 1983, the United States has created over 15 million jobs net. Our foreign deficit has not cost jobs, but instead has provided the resources to facilitate our labor force's surge toward full employment.

This paper is not the appropriate forum for a detailed evaluation of the scientific literature. Suffice it to say that the fact that West Germany and Japan were the two countries with the largest trade deficits in the period 1946 through 1960 is a reasonable, albeit extreme, parallel with the United States of the Reagan era. The trade deficits of Third World countries are not at all comparable to the current U.S. trade deficit. Third World trade deficits are more a consequence of government interventions subverting free market forces rather than private miscalculations. Countries that increase their growth rates, as a natural course of events, attract foreign investors and thereby experience trade deterioration.

The recent sharp deterioration of the British trade accounts following their massive tax rate reductions is similar to what happened in the United States. The argument that somehow indulgent fiscal policy is the root cause of these deficits is surely not the case for Britain—their budget is in surplus. The received doctrine over there, as it is here, is that trade deficits must be stopped. Convoluted error has replaced simple truth. The problem is not the red ink splashed on the trade ledgers, it is with faulty analysis. If believed, the faulty analysis will result in real solutions being imposed on nonproblems.

The United States, from the mid-seventeenth century until the 1870s, ran by the prevailing standards of the time, huge trade deficits. These trade deficits lasted for over two centuries. Ultimately, those U.S. trade deficits provided America the wherewithal to create the preeminent economic force in the world.

The Bergsten analysis despairs over the observation that the United States has become a net debtor nation of incredible and increasing magnitude. International assets are book-value data and most likely are unrelated to market values. Because the United States in 1987 had a surplus of investment income, it would seem more reasonable to assert that U.S. assets abroad are sufficiently undervalued relative to foreign assets in the United States, that the United States is, in reality, not a net debtor nation in market-value terms.

Whether the United States is or is not a net debtor nation is beside the point. The relevant point, which Bergsten does not address directly, is whether the United States is better off or not as a consequence of its debt position. Reliance on the number zero is no defense against the market's assessment of what should be. The essence of international trade as a discipline is that trade in goods and assets improves welfare.

To worry that foreigners are somehow like a herd of deer in a meadow waiting anxiously to bolt at the slightest sign of danger is clearly way off base. Japanese investors over the past three years have suffered large annual yen losses and yet remain active participants in the U.S. capital markets.

Why Japanese or other foreign investors' criteria would differ from their American counterparts' is not self-evident. If economic policies were to change such that the long-term investment horizon of the United States were to worsen, then foreigners might well wish to take some of their capital back out of the United States. This would, as Bergsten correctly argues, precipitate a sequence of unpleasant events.

American investors, however, would also want their capital out of the United States and, if foreigners did not beat domestic investors to the punch, they would precipitate the ominous consequences first. It is unreasonable to assume that somehow foreigners are any different from Americans. In matters of the pocketbook, nationality does not count for much. Therefore, whether foreigners have a large or small involvement in the U.S. economy is really of little importance. Bad economic policies will cause capital flight for both domestic and foreign capital.

No policy that I can think of is more generically disruptive to investors than is a tax increase. Given the current political milieu, tax increases show a total inability of governments to control their spending and, in addition, they illustrate a failure of the body politic to control government. The tax side of the Bergsten proposal to eliminate the budget deficit is, in my view, the *sine qua non* of the debacle he so earnestly wishes to avoid.

3

Choices for the 1990s: Preserving American Security Interests Through the Century's End

HAROLD BROWN

Introduction

The calendar prompts reappraisals of predicted futures as well as of observed past trends. The 1990s lead to a new century and millennium, and will include the fiftieth anniver-

HAROLD BROWN, secretary of defense under President Jimmy Carter, is currently chairman of the Johns Hopkins Foreign Policy Institute at the School of Advanced International Studies. At the beginning of his varied career, Dr. Brown lectured in physics at Columbia University, Stevens Institute of Technology, and the University of California, and he served as a research scientist with the radiation laboratory at Livermore, University of California. Dr. Brown was director of defense research and engineering from 1961 to 1965, when he became secretary of the Air Force, a post he held

sary of the end of World War II. Which of the changes since recorded require fundamental redefinition of U.S. interests? What choices do these force, among what alternatives? What are the most likely lines of evolution of the international security context; what, and how likely, are their alternatives? How much can the United States influence the nature of the evolution of change in the international political-military configuration? Which policy choices are likely to be most critical in exercising that influence?

William Bundy's chapter in this volume, charting with skill and in detail the changes between 1960 and what may be expected in and after 1990 in the state of the world, makes rehearsal of that catalogue unnecessary here. Yet it may be useful to note the broad similarities that exist between today's challenges and those that were being faced or anticipated forty years ago.

In 1948, with almost no U.S. conventional forces in Europe and few elsewhere, the primary *military/technological* challenge the United States confronted was to maintain peace in the face of massive Soviet conventional military forces. The four decades of nuclear deterrence that followed—based first on a monopoly, then superiority, then parity in nuclear weapons—along with U.S. force deployments in Europe, and a variety of (so far principally nuclear) arms control efforts, proved effective in denying direct Soviet military expansion beyond Eastern Europe. Now, however, as only occasionally since 1948, defending against, as distinct from deterring, a nuclear attack has become a major issue of U.S. policy. This new policy focus arose first in the form of President Ronald Reagan's 1983 Strategic Defense Initiative (SDI), and has since gained wider at-

---

until 1969. From 1969 to 1977, Dr. Brown was president of the California Institute of Technology. He has served in several governmental advisory capacitites throughout his career, including being senior science advisor at the Conference on the Discontinuance of Nuclear Tests in 1958 and 1959, and a delegate to the Strategic Arms Limitation Talks, beginning in 1969.

tention because of SDI's complex interaction with proposals for deep reductions in strategic nuclear weapons.

The *ideological* challenge of 1948—namely, to prevent the spread of state-sponsored revolutionary communism—has been met successfully. Arguments exist as to the balance of indigenous factors and Soviet support in the ascent to power and later survival of Communist governments in Cuba and Nicaragua. Yet without the indigenous factors, Soviet support alone—even Soviet invasion, as in Afghanistan—has produced no true Leninist states since 1948, though some Third World nations so proclaim themselves. Indeed, the ideological question we face is to determine whether the United States can and should assist the indigenous—including Communist—elements in China, Eastern Europe, and perhaps even the USSR, that appear to be rolling back, or at the very least sharply redefining, communism themselves. The prime ideological challenge now is to contain the spread of state-sponsored religious fundamentalism and sectarianism, as well as their expression in terrorism.

In 1948 the *economic* challenge was to create new structures that would rebuild destroyed industrial plant, restore trade and monetary balances, and encourage economic growth, especially in the industrialized democracies. The first and last of these objectives have been fulfilled so well that, especially since the early 1970s, trade and monetary balances have again become unstable, often in directions reversed from earlier times. The debt problems of, and (now shaky) control of oil supplies by, the Third World are relatively new factors, as are the vastly increased interdependence and much more influential multilateral economic structures now employed by the wealthy countries. But requirements for new structures to restore the trade and monetary balances are again upon us. A new cycle of ingenuity and adjustment is needed if growth patterns of the 1990s are to approach the historically exceptional levels of 1948–1973, rather than continue at the much lower levels of 1973–1988.

And finally, the *political* challenge of 1948 was to preserve democracy in Western Europe and Japan while extending it to the new nations emerging from the decolonialization of colonial (especially European) empires. In Europe, democracy has been extended to Iberia; in Japan it has been fully successful. In the Third World, however, performance has been spotty. To be sure, independence has been achieved more quickly and widely than had been foreseen. And, with multipolar power increasingly the rule, adherence to U.S. or Soviet blocs has waned more than waxed. But democracy has not made much progress in Africa and has even regressed in South Africa. In the Middle East and South Asia, it exists only in Turkey, Israel, and India. Still, in East Asia and Latin America it is clearly on the rise, if still a young and fragile plant. We now face the problem of how to encourage the growth of democracy in the Third World through various forms of economic and technological aid, through help with debt management, and with programs that link this assistance to the overall advancement of the political and economic structures of the recipients.

To some extent, the foreign policy and many of the security policy challenges of today parallel those of 1948. Indeed, some of the most prominent issues are the same, although changed in seriousness, nature, or circumstances: Soviet domination of Eastern Europe, as well as the Soviet threat, whether military or political, to Western Europe; the Israeli-Arab conflict; and arms control, to cite but a few.

But many matters that now preoccupy us (and some that will do so even more in the future) were hardly imagined as major issues in 1948: Mexico, which by the year 2000 may be as important to U.S. foreign policy as Japan is now; Central America and the Caribbean; ballistic missiles—the Soviet nuclear threat to the United States did not exist in 1948; Islamic fundamentalism; and the Organization of Petroleum Exporting Countries (OPEC), among others. The economic "miracles" of the rebirth and growth of the destroyed economies of Japan and Western Europe belonged to an ill-defined future; the newly industrializing economies (NIEs) were obviously on no lists, though China and India were sometimes seen, then as now, as future giants. And "imperial overstretch," though occasionally predicted, was not a widespread concern in 1948, as it often is in many quarters today.

What concerns us in this chapter is whether, in the light of changes in the past decade—the economic stagnation and political evolution of the USSR, the diffusion of economic power formerly centered in the United States—and of likely future trends, the United States should define its political and military security interests more narrowly than it usually has during the past forty years. Which functional and geographical areas are vital to U.S. interests, which are important and which marginal, and what are the prudent levels of resources to devote to each? If we can preserve strategic nuclear deterrence and avoid accretions to the Soviet bloc, whether externally or internally inspired, should the United States greatly care—from a national security standpoint—about wars, political changes, or other miseries elsewhere? And what policies and programs will be needed to assure that even the two modest policy goals just mentioned will be achieved? Can the second objective in fact be met if the United States assumes a much lower international security profile?

The answers to these questions depend on our assessment of U.S. resources and capabilities in the light of past and anticipated economic, technological, and political trends, and on our judgments of what future developments in the external world—whether helpful or threatening to U.S. interests—are likely to be. In other words, how do we balance resource costs against the totality of security risks, and how do we prioritize among responses to individual security risks? Let us now examine these general issues before turning to more specific functional and geographic areas.

Suppose—to take an extreme case—the United States decided to reduce its military role to the bare minimum to sustain a high degree of confidence that the nation would preserve the physical security of its own territory. Its present strategic forces, modernized as necessary in response to Soviet force changes, would be geared to deter direct attack from that quarter. It might well be possible to build strategic defense adequate to protect the United States (rather than deter attack) from nuclear powers other than the USSR, a category whose membership would proliferate under such circumstances. U.S. conventional forces could be decreased to half their present size without real risk of foreign invasion; the savings could be used for active strategic defense, for foreign aid (which could be increased in such a scenario), and for reducing domestic fiscal imbalance. The total of 6.5 percent of gross national product (GNP) now spent on defense and foreign aid might well be reduced to 4 percent. Barring hegemony extending to the Western Hemisphere by another power, the United States could continue to import to the extent of its needs and export as necessary to pay for these imports.

In the medium run, the Soviets probably would not overrun Western Europe, but rather concentrate on improving their economy. They would, however, gain influence in Western Europe and elsewhere because U.S. redefinition of its security interests to its own borders would not banish force as a major (though not sole) arbiter of international relations— indeed, this American redefinition would probably elevate force as a factor. Western Europe might be pushed toward closer unity; or else, and perhaps more likely, a *sauve qui peut* attitude could fragment it, with Germany, especially, making individual bargains with the USSR. Japan could move toward both rearmament and accommodation with the Soviets under these circumstances, though these moves would conflict in the long run. It could be argued that many Third World conflicts would lose their steam if the USSR emulated a U.S. withdrawal, or vice-versa; was not the Somali-Ethiopian conflict exacerbated by U.S. and Soviet involvement? My own judgment, however, is that such chronic adversaries as Iraq and Iran, Israel and its Arab neighbors, India and Pakistan, Somalia and Ethiopia need no superpower encouragement to sustain their conflicts, that they would, as in the past, find other arms suppliers when necessary, and that such Third World conflicts would actually increase in number and severity if the United States were to retire from the world scene. These conflicts would have serious economic impact on the United States—for example, a

Persian Gulf oil cutoff—but in the long run the more general-
ized effects of an even less ordered international environment
than now prevails would be likely to prove more important to
U.S. security than any short-term crisis.

Of course, a policy of U.S. withdrawal would be likely to
evolve gradually, giving time for other nations—allies, adversaries, nonaligned—and for international organizations to adjust and take on more of the load. And there are many less
extreme versions of a withdrawal policy. The sharp shift
painted in broad strokes here simply serves to sketch one end
of the spectrum of policy choice.

Toward the other end of the spectrum lies a modest modification of past U.S. international security commitments. This
approach would adhere to a strategy of alliances and associa-
tions, but encourage a redistribution of responsibilities *and* of
influence over decisions that would create a balance more in
accord with the change in relative resources that has taken
place in recent decades. In practice, this approach would combine elements of present policy with greater selectivity in political commitment and military engagement. It would involve
more reliance on and cooperation with—which inevitably
means more deference to—allies and associates. The details
would involve creating the appropriate mixture of these elements, applying them judiciously in particular functional and
geographic areas, and determining the precise methods to be
employed in each such area. These details would need to be
worked out with careful regard for the limits on the capacity of
the United States to finance even a more restrained active international role with a resource allocation to international security affairs that is consistent with our present domestic habits. In any event, we can no longer expect to consume at length
more than we produce. This change would also be required,
but perhaps more easily met, under a withdrawal policy. We
must either alter our patterns of consumption, savings, investment, productivity, and trade or else be severely constrained
in our international security policies (as in domestic ones) by
exchange rates, international debt, and balance of payments
deficits. On the political front, greater continuity than hitherto

will be required in the rhetoric and in the details of foreign and security policy—both functional and geographic—a continuity that has been far less apparent in rhetoric and detail than in the broad realities of U.S. policy over the past four decades.

Changes

We turn now to two scenarios for the future. One is an extrapolation of the trends of the past decades; it seems to me the most likely. The other can be seen as an accentuation of some of these trends together with some new elements that, together, by the year 2000 could produce a world quite different from that in the first scenario. To some limited extent, U.S. policy can influence the course of these events.

Extrapolating recent trends suggests a continued, though perhaps decelerating, decline from U.S. economic hegemony and a reversion to a more normal distribution of economic power, in part as a result of the success of the post–World War II U.S. policy of rebuilding allies and former enemies. The redistribution has been intensified by the rise of the newly industrializing powers (primarily in East Asia, but also including India, Brazil, and others), many of which did not exist as independent nations in 1945. This scenario would involve a further increase in U.S. dependence on trade (both imports and exports). Japanese predominance in manufacturing and trade would continue, with at most a gradual development of a more assertive Japanese foreign policy, but probably without a significant Japanese security policy. Further movement could be expected toward European economic unity, but political unity would not progress beyond symbols during the rest of the century.

The U.S.–Soviet military balance would continue to reflect the condition of strategic parity that has existed since the early 1970s, as well as the subsequent growth of Soviet conventional forces, giving the USSR an advantage in the force balance on its periphery, along with some force projection capability. But extended deterrence would also persist in a limited form. That is, a Soviet conventional attack on a vital U.S. interest (Western Europe, for example) would continue to bear so high a risk of escalation to strategic nuclear war as to constitute an important deterrent, even though the United States does not have strategic superiority. In such a military context, political and economic factors take on added weight. The ebb of the ideological appeal of the Soviet model as compared with its attractiveness to many in the 1930s and 1940s, and Soviet Secretary General Mikhail Gorbachev's trumpeting of the systemic and managerial failures of Soviet economy and technology, would clearly reduce the chances of expansion of Soviet power. At the same time, the appearance of greater plasticity and experimentation in the Soviet system would encourage some political elements in Europe, especially in the Federal Republic of Germany (FRG), to explore alternatives to the present close military-political connections with the United States. Gorbachev is attempting to modernize and to improve the efficiency of the Soviet system by mobilizing the intellectuals and technologists as a lever on the bureaucrats and the work force. He recognizes that loosening of the political straitjacket is required to ease Soviet economic and systemic arthritis, but intends to retain essentially all political power ("the vanguard role") in the hands of the Communist party. Perhaps this approach will work. More likely, after four or five years of at most modest growth, the results will flatten out. The choice will then be between more fundamental acceptance of political pluralism and a market-driven price structure, or a reversion to centralized economic planning and political tightening. In my judgment, the latter would be more likely. At that point, or even earlier, Eastern Europe or some of the nationalities in the Soviet Union might explode into open rebellion, creating grave risks both within the Soviet bloc and in its relations with the West.

The diffusion of political and military power beyond the superpowers and other industrialized nations is likely to continue under this scenario. The fragmentation of former colonial empires into scores of new nations that followed World War II will continue to find an echo in irredentism, tribal conflicts, and separatist movements in the Third World. Regional power centers (China, India, Iran, Brazil) will increase their local roles, some seeking regional hegemony (which India has, in effect, already gained) and often threatening and even engaging in military conflict. Overlapping these are the NIEs, whose economic growth will continue to make them both competitors to and debtors of the industrialized democracies. The "nonalignment" of the 1950s and 1960s has been succeeded by a growing predominance of regional issues, groupings, and powers. The regional security organizations sponsored by the United States outside of the Atlantic Pact and Northeast Asia—the Central Treaty Organization (CENTO), the Southeast Asia Treaty Organization (SEATO), and the Organization of American States (OAS)—have atrophied in their security function, while indigenous ones, which vary in cohesion and purpose, have appeared—the Association of Southeast Asian Nations (ASEAN), the Organization of African States, and the Gulf Cooperation Council. This trend will continue and may intensify.

Democratic pluralism will continue to be the exception in the Third World, but this scenario suggests continuation of a favorable trend, especially in Latin America. In many of the NIEs, the growth of the educated middle class and skilled work force necessary for industrialization will create even more pressure for political participation and democratization; U.S. human rights policy probably also has had, on balance, a positive effect; Korea, Brazil, and Taiwan are leading examples of both effects. India has been democratic from the start. Election results in Mexico confirm the pattern. They also remind us that democratization is likely to be accompanied by nationalist and populist manifestations that will trouble the United States in the short run—whether they concern base rights in the Philippines or opposition to debt repayment in Mexico—no matter how much we welcome pluralism as a long-term benefit. Of course, countertrends also exist—as in Singapore and Malaysia. And the Soviet Union is clearly a model of industrialization without democracy. But the Gorbachev program of *perestroika* and *glasnost* suggests that even the current Soviet leadership recognizes the case for and association between advanced economic growth and political pluralism.

West Europeans will seek more say in the voluntary alliance that this scenario assumes will continue, and we can expect intensification of their ambivalence between fear of being abandoned by the United States and concern that the United States will involve them against their will in conflicts with the USSR or elsewhere in the world. Western Europe will move toward, but not achieve in this century, substantial political union, and will become more of a unit in economic and military matters. There, as in the United States, the elites who have traditionally formulated foreign policy will have to pay more attention to domestic political constituencies. Eastern European governments will continue to face internal challenges to their legitimacy. Moreover, the dilemma created for Moscow by the economic drain and political strain required to support dominant Soviet political influence there, and to maintain Communist party control within Eastern Europe while decentralizing within the USSR, will intensify.

The United States, too, will have larger challenges nearby in this scenario, in Mexico, in Central America, and in the Caribbean. The combination of economic stagnation and stress, the difficulty of finding a democratic middle, and the decreasing tolerance of the U.S. body politic for protracted military intervention, along with immigration pressure from such areas, is likely to require more U.S. resources, allocated according to a more coherent and integrated political-economic-security plan, if further conflicts like those in Nicaragua, El Salvador, and Panama are to be avoided. The most severe development would be an economic collapse or a sharp leftward turn, or both, in Mexico; the United States could cope with any resulting security threat, but the required redirection of American attention could have severe effects elsewhere.

Technological changes and resource related developments complete this list of assumed trend continuations. Microelectronics now, and biotechnology in a couple of decades, will change the definition of what constitutes a modern economy.

Highly accurate "smart" weapons, automata and remotely piloted vehicles, space-based support systems, longer range aircraft, and more destructive munitions will continue to change the nature of warfare. Their dissemination to lesser powers will make "gunboat diplomacy" less feasible; Nicaragua is not Grenada, and Iran is not Libya or even Lebanon. NIEs and regional powers will develop advanced military weapons and sell them to other Third World nations (China and Brazil are already doing this with ballistic missiles of ranges exceeding 1,000 kilometers). Military technology will increasingly ride on the back of a civil technological base, making technology transfers for any purpose more central to security questions. Instant worldwide communication will make public relations a weightier and even less controllable element (the feasibility of revolution by cassette was demonstrated by Iran's Ayatullah Ruhollah Khomeini). OPEC, though weak now, will strengthen as energy dependence regains importance sometime in the 1990s, after U.S. oil imports rise to or even beyond the 50 percent level once again. Other "strategic mineral" concerns will not materialize under this scenario, however. The population explosion will continue in some regions: Latin America, Africa, South Asia, most of the Arab world. This will intensify current disparities in per capita GNP ($20,000 per year versus $500 or even $200), and increase North-South tensions.

Thus, broadly sketched, the most likely scenario is one of continuity—a scenario of intensified but still familiar problems, and more hopeful developments that differ from the present scene in degree but not in kind. Now, as at any time, such a scenario represents the most plausible future evolution of events, and therefore the most appropriate basis for security policy planning. But prudent planning must also take into account the fact that discontinuities are also possible—indeed, they occur. The industrialized democratic regions of North America, Europe, and Japan might move sharply apart in both economic and security terms. The post–1992 "integrated Europe" could choose the highest rather than the lowest of the barriers that its individual members erect against imports from

outside Europe. The Western European Union could become
a substitute for, rather than the second pillar of, the North
Atlantic Treaty Organization (NATO). The United States
could itself succumb to protectionism, convinced that a "level
playing field" is not achievable and that foreign "buying of
America" is a grave danger. Japan could—after a wrenching
constitutional crisis—conclude that the U.S. security umbrella
is being folded, and that Japan's leading economic role must
be protected by a self-sufficient military capability suitable to a
world power. The already eroding willingness of America's
European and Japanese allies, and of such other nations as the
Philippines and Korea, to provide overseas bases could decline sharply. Many of these developments would be encouraged should there be an easing of Soviet security pressures in
Europe, the Far East, and the Third World beyond any we
have hitherto considered possible, combined with major reductions of conventional and nuclear Soviet bloc and U.S. alliance forces, whether as a result of Soviet or U.S. initiative.
Indeed, Soviet temptation of the FRG might in an extreme
case lead to a unified (or at least federated) and neutral Germany, changing the face of Europe as nothing has since the
onset of the cold war.

This broadly alternative scenario would represent a sharp
acceleration of present trends. If the countervailing forces that
trends normally evoke, and that usually make for preservation
of relative continuity, should prove insufficient, a very different world would ensue. Of course, U.S. policy itself affects the
likelihood of such a scenario, and could deliberately or unintentionally help to prevent it, encourage it, or—accepting
some version of it as inevitable—try to lengthen and smooth
the transition to it. Such a world—or belief in its likelihood—
would arguably encourage a minimalist U.S. security strategy
of the sort described in the introduction, especially (and perhaps only) if U.S.–Soviet relations should take on the rosy glow
just described. Though not nearly so likely as slower and more
continuous change, this scenario is not to be ruled out.

Technological and environmental changes also could produce a sharply different world. If ground- and space-based

sensors and directed-energy weapons were to make possible a near-perfect defense against strategic attack by large and responsive ballistic and airbreathing forces (which I consider infeasible for decades, and probably forever), the world would become very different. So it would also if U.S.–Soviet relations became so friendly that each decided a few hundred strategic weapons would suffice, that defenses that would intercept all but a few of those would not be destabilizing, and that such a strategic configuration would also deal adequately with potential attacks by third nuclear powers. (I view this as the political equivalent of the technical infeasibility of a near-perfect SDI.)

An environmental catastrophe such as rapid climatic change (a "greenhouse effect" greatly accelerated, say) might, as the equivalent of a Martian invasion, produce international cooperation across ideological and economic boundaries. Since I fear the opposite result—intensification of rivalries—I welcome instead the likelihood that such change will be slow enough to manage by evolutionary means.

Other alarums and excursions are almost certain, however. Revolution or civil strife in Korea, India, the Philippines, or Saudi Arabia, another round of war between Israel and Arab nations—none can be ruled out. Some such events, whether there or elsewhere, will certainly occur. They have, after all, been occurring during the forty years of essential continuity of post–World War II U.S. foreign and security policy. Which will be next, or when, cannot now be foretold. For basic planning purposes, the continuity scenario is the appropriate point of departure. With this brief exposition of possible alternative futures, therefore, we now return to the scenario that extrapolates recent trends to consider specific issues and options.

Issues and Options

The USSR

The Soviet leadership now acknowledges the failure of the Soviet Union to become a modern and prosperous state, its continuing economic difficulties, and its failure to deliver either material goods or the satisfactions of the spirit to its citizens. Despite the fading of its ideological appeal and the easing of any apparent immediate Soviet military threat, the USSR will remain, properly, a central preoccupation of U.S. foreign and security policy. The Soviet Union's massive military power, the extent of its empire, its continued competition with the United States for global influence, but most of all the startlingly new style and substance of the Soviet leadership—and perhaps of future Soviet domestic and foreign actions—will provide new challenges during the years immediately ahead.

Nuclear Force Strategies. With respect to the strategic nuclear balance, the United States has several options, not all of which are mutually exclusive. First, we could seek to restore the degree of U.S. superiority characteristic of the 1950s and early 1960s. This was the apparent goal of many in the Reagan administration. Or we could seek stabilization at the present level or some modest fraction thereof (the Strategic Arms Reduction Talks [START] framework of "50 percent" reductions amounts in fact, given the expected warhead counting rules, to a reduction of about 30 percent in warhead numbers) with improved crisis stability and "arms race" stability—in other words, stabilization of a force structure with characteristics and limitations that would reduce any advantage to striking first and make it more difficult for either side to upset the balance. Or we could seek reduction to a "minimum deterrent" level (say a few hundred to a thousand highly survivable warheads of whose ability to penetrate defenses we were highly confident). Or we could, perhaps in combination with one of the other approaches—especially the last—seek a transition to a "defense dominated" balance where nuclear war could well result in only a few to a few tens of thermonuclear warheads penetrating U.S. and Soviet defenses.

The first of the above options, a return to a clear U.S. superiority, is infeasible, in my view, in the face of a determined superpower, which the USSR remains. Moreover, after Soviet acquisition of a substantial nuclear force in the 1950s, even such U.S. superiority as existed provided quite limited leverage. Conventional force balances, economic assistance, geography, alliances, and the political balance and degree of stability in any contested region have played the decisive role, though the nuclear factor—more a mutual than a unilateral deterrent—has hung and will continue to hang in the background.

The present course of U.S. policy, stabilization at lower levels, has much to recommend it. It could lead to any of the remaining options, it is consistent with a gradual improvement of U.S.–Soviet relations, and it probably will not upset U.S. allies to any appreciable degree. Many details of definition, balance, and verification need working out, but that is a familiar though never fully satisfactory process.

The "minimum deterrent route" is trickier ground. The effects of cheating or breakout, and correspondingly the needs of verification, tend to become greater as the numbers of weapons become smaller. Survivability gains in importance, and could require a completely new generation of strategic weapons—airbreathers, submarine-launched ballistic missiles (SLBMs), intercontinental ballistic missiles (ICBMs)—in terms of basing, vehicles, or both. This could be difficult to fund in the political context of the U.S.–Soviet love-in that would presumably either produce or result from such an agreement. Stabilization at such a force level would still provide a clear deterrent against nuclear attack by the Soviets or by anyone else (providing they had no effective active defenses). And, as a symbol of a turning back from competition in the world's most dangerous race, it could have a substantial and positive political effect. This course would, however, signal a sharper division between nuclear and conventional war, especially if, as would be likely, it were accompanied by a deep reduction in numbers of tactical nuclear weapons, or by elimination of their deployment outside of the United States and the USSR. There would be few strategic weapons available to attack the nuclear strike forces of the other side (which would presumably have been made survivable and therefore difficult or impossible to target anyway—though one would always worry about the vulnerability of one's own command and control structure), let alone to attack conventional military targets. The world would indeed have been made safer for conventional war, and we would hear loud screams from allies unprepared to depend more completely on (and to pay for) conventional arms to deter it. (One remembers Allied anguish at the momentary Reykjavik agreement, perhaps induced by the vapors of Icelandic hot springs, to abolish nuclear weapons completely.) But the minimal deterrent approach should not be lightly dismissed. If accompanied by massive reductions and redeployments (inward) of Soviet conventional forces, it could represent a much safer world—at least in its superpower dimension, although the nastinesses of the great mass of weaker nations could well persist or even intensify.

Finally we have the possibility of a policy aimed at defense dominance. In my judgment, active defenses are both a promise and a snare. The minimal deterrent could well be upset if only one side had them, even though the efficacy of ballistic missile defense and air defense against a responsive threat is worse than doubtful. One million (the number of tons of TNT–equivalent carried by a one-ton thermonuclear weapon) is a difficult factor to overcome, which makes the prospect for defense dominance dim. But a vigorous research and technology development program in ballistic missile defense and air defense might turn up something new, and a combination of unlikely political evolution in U.S.–Soviet relations and reductions to a minimum deterrence level of forces might make defense dominance a feasible option instead of the empty slogan that it is today. Even then, however, there would still be the problem of a stable transition, which many studies have shown to be an extremely hazardous process at best. All things considered, stabilization of force structures at lower levels strikes me as the preferable short-term goal of U.S. policy. It would be consistent with a subsequent consideration of further reductions anywhere down to minimum deterrent level if the evolution of international relations and technical-military considerations warrant.

Conventional Force Strategies. Conventional force balance options are still more complex and less thoroughly explored. An obvious, but I think infeasible, one is building up Allied forces in Europe to parity with their Eastern bloc counterparts. The fact is that neither European nor American publics will pay the price of such a build-up. Seeking more confidence of Allied capacity to repel a Warsaw Pact attack (or at least the capability to contain it for a month, thereby adding a strong conventional deterrent to the nuclear deterrent) is more nearly within political feasibility in my view. But estimates of the outcome of such an attack vary considerably, depending on the starting military circumstances and political conditions and on who makes the estimate. Those estimates range from the Soviets advancing to the English Channel in a week or less (as prophesied by recent SACEUR [Supreme Allied Commander, Europe] estimates) to a Soviet failure to penetrate more than a few tens of kilometers (as suggested in a recent analysis by Joshua Epstein of the Brookings Institution). And most European governments and publics assert (wrongly) that conventional war would be as damaging to them as nuclear war, while either doubting the proposition that increased conventional forces add to the existing deterrence of conventional war or, even if accepting that judgment, being unwilling to divert resources to pay for more conventional forces. Thus, seeking highly asymmetrical reductions and redeployments of Soviet forces with the same goal—a balance such that a Warsaw Pact attack would be very unlikely to succeed, thus reducing both the chance of an attack and the utility of Soviet military capability for political intimidation—is probably a more productive approach.

The two approaches are not inconsistent; modest Allied force improvements—or at least their prospect—are likely to stimulate Soviet acceptance of asymmetrical reductions. One issue that arises in connection with U.S. redeployments, however, is return of U.S. units to the continental United States. Since the added cost of new facilities, let alone of the lift capability to return them in a crisis, would make return more expensive than continued overseas deployment, it is almost certain that they will be demobilized or reduced to reserve status if withdrawn. A suggested alternative is to demobilize units in the United States, but that would lead to elimination of the rotation base; many troops would have to spend most or all of their careers outside of the country, an option of doubtful tolerability. Other alternatives that could be explored include one-year, unaccompanied (by dependents) tours as are now served by U.S. troops stationed in Korea, or moving some active-duty units in the continental United States to reserve status. Both of these measures would probably require reductions of overseas deployments. It should be noted, however, that levels of deployments of U.S. troops in Europe in the 1960s were well below present levels. A combination of mutual reductions and redeployments and unilateral rearrangements of forces is a likely outcome of successful negotiations on the conventional balance, and it may be the only outcome that is practically and politically feasible. Redeployment to the United States of some Air Force units, which are more easily and quickly returned overseas, might be traded off against demobilization of Soviet ground forces.

Relations between the United States and the USSR in East Asia are more complex: there is no long and continuous geographical line across the land in that theater, with nuclear weapons and heavily armed conventional forces in two clearly defined blocs facing each other across it—except for the Sino-Soviet border. There are also many differing players: Japan, the People's Republic of China (PRC), and the two Koreas. Japanese attitudes toward the nature of the Soviet threat are quite different from those in Western Europe. The United States has the option of encouraging an increased Japanese security role vis-à-vis the USSR; we will return to this issue, and the region, later in this chapter.

Elsewhere in the world, U.S. and Soviet interests are potentially most dangerously engaged, in a directly adversarial way, in the Middle East and the Persian Gulf: the United States because of the dependence of the industrialized democracies on Gulf oil and because of U.S. commitment to Israel; the Soviet Union because of its geographical propinquity and the connections of some of the indigenous peoples with the Soviet Union's own Central Asian ethnic groups. For each super-power, the strategic location of the area as a crossroads heightens the concern about the other. U.S. options include attempting to minimize or exclude the Soviet Union as a major participant in settling regional disputes between the Arab world and Israel, Iran and Iraq, and others, or seeking to involve the USSR in precisely that role. Arguing for the first course is the historical Soviet behavior as the patron of regional adversaries of the United States and of its allies or associates, and the Soviet policy of undermining U.S. influence in the region. On the other hand, the continuing Soviet influence on the "spoilers" of peaceful settlement suggests that Soviet acquiescence, even active pressure, will often if not always be required for successful mediation. And recent Soviet foreign policy rhetoric—and even some faint signs of actual behavior—suggests that cooperation may be possible in some cases. Though the strains and even the wars are indigenous, the respective superpower interests are intense, for the reasons given above.

In Eastern Europe, the United States could encourage attempts to break away from Soviet dominance, but this would be an extremely dangerous game. Next to maintenance of the Soviet system in the USSR itself, preserving Marxism-Leninism in Eastern Europe is the icon for whose retention Soviet leaders will risk (indeed, go to) war. Alternatively, we could actively discourage unrest there to avoid the risk of destabilization, though it is hard to devise a formula for execution of such a policy that would not stick in our throats. A third option is to continue current U.S. policy, which seeks to loosen controls at the margin by differentiating our political and economic treatment among Eastern European countries according to their own domestic and foreign policies. This is likely to appeal even more in a situation where the Soviet leadership continues to pursue a policy of change that half the Eastern European national leaderships find uncomfortably liberalizing. In any event, Soviet rule in Eastern Europe is likely to weaken over the next decade, providing both opportunities for the policy of differentiation and risks of a U.S.–Western European policy split, with the West Europeans urging more rapid steps in policy toward Eastern Europe.

In other regions, from Central Africa to Central America, the United States can deal with events as though they are manifestations of an East-West conflict, or treat them as basically indigenous, with a greater or lesser East-West overlay of influence. The more the policy approaches the latter, the more likely the United States is to take a restrained, even hands-off, approach to specific conflicts, and the stronger the argument for the generally minimalist strategy and military force structure outlined earlier as the extreme alternative to that of the past four decades. For either option, however, the degree of involvement will depend sharply on perceived closeness of the issue to U.S. interests, whether through geography or history. The United States will be more interested in conflicts in Central America, in the Caribbean, or in the Middle East than in Central Africa, the Andes, or Burma.

Economic Relations. Economic relations and trade with, and technology transfers to, the USSR are likely to become more prominent issues—the more so if the political-military situation eases. Our options include at least the following three: denial of credits, trade, investment, and technology transfer from the United States, and pressure on others to do the same; encouragement of private U.S. participation in such activities within prudent limits of military security, in exchange for concessions on other matters (regional security issues, arms control, and especially human rights); neutrality on U.S. investment or joint ventures and caution on technology transfer, but acceptance of decisions for closer economic relations with the USSR and Eastern Europe by U.S. allies (especially likely to occur in the case of the FRG). A graded spectrum of specifics lies between these options. The Soviets themselves (unlike the PRC) are likely to prefer dealing with the other industrialized democracies rather than with the United States on these matters, but even symbolic deals with the United States will encourage and legitimize much farther reaching economic/

technical relations with others. This gives the United States some—but still quite limited—leverage in extracting concessions in regional or other military-political areas and in human rights. One limitation is that Gorbachev has clearly emphasized bootstrapping the Soviet economy from within, though encouraging more interaction with Western industry, both to speed Soviet acquisition of technology and of management skills and to provide a quality yardstick for indigenous products.

Fundamentally, U.S. attitudes toward all U.S.–Soviet issues will, appropriately, be conditioned by our view of the USSR and its possible future development, and of the ability of the United States to influence that development. In that sense, moreover, linkage of various aspects of U.S.–Soviet relations—regional issues, arms reduction, human rights—will remain a fact of U.S. political life, however justifiable and necessary it is for U.S. administrations to separate out and pursue, for example, negotiations to reduce the risk of nuclear war. Various policy options have been proposed, and some have been followed.

One option is to put pressure on the Soviet system through a further U.S. military build-up, especially in high-technology areas such as SDI, to force systemic change or collapse. Some in the Reagan administration claimed that this was their policy and that it had worked, crediting it with whatever shifts have occurred under Gorbachev. But, however ill-equipped economically the Soviets are for such a competition, even the most macho U.S. leaders display a remarkable disinclination to inflict pain (in the form, say, of conscription or increased taxation) on the American citizenry. And a hungry, frightened, desperate, "collapsed" Soviet Union with 50,000 nuclear weapons is hardly an adversary that a rational U.S. leader would wish to have helped to create.

A second option often suggested is that the United States help the "good guys" in the Kremlin against the hard-liners by making concessions, seeing their point of view, even extending economic assistance. This presumes a knowledge of detailed individual intentions and internal Soviet politics that is certainly beyond what has hitherto been available. Even now, in the days of *glasnost,* one would wish a better past record of accurate, detailed predictions of Soviet behavior before assigning "friend" and "enemy" labels or equating Soviet with Western political processes. As an example, although it is clear that there is strong resistance to many of the internal changes that Gorbachev is pressing, there appears to be little overt opposition among the top Soviet leadership to the change in foreign policy, or at least in foreign policy rhetoric, that has been promulgated during the last few years. Thus there is little correlation between advocacy of internal reform and of more flexibility in foreign relations, though Gorbachev uses the latter to advance the former. Moreover, even among advocates of both, there are believed to be those who intensely dislike the United States.

In the end, American policy makers are likely to conclude that Soviet political development will be driven almost entirely by internal forces. Soviet political development will in turn be the predominant determinant of Soviet foreign and military policy. U.S. actions can influence the latter to some degree, depending on the issue, but the former only marginally. We must live in uncertainty as to whether economically successful reform of the Soviet system (if it occurs) will produce a more effective and therefore more threatening adversary, or whether the loosening of the economic system, and the accompanying loosening of the political system very probably required to achieve it, will moderate the adversarial nature of the U.S.–Soviet relationship. Such a U.S. attitude leads naturally to a policy of encouraging at the margin political, economic, and human rights reforms in the Soviet Union, by explicitly linking to them U.S. attitudes on economic relations and technology transfer, but limiting linkage of political-military issues with internal Soviet reforms to the minimum level that is implicit in the American political process.

U.S. Allies

Dealing with U.S. allies, who are now our principal economic competitors (the newly industrializing countries or

economies—NICs or NIEs—following behind apace), presents a variety of challenges. The generation that remembers
the United States as World War II savior, generous postwar
rebuilder, and their defender from Soviet political intimidation or military conquest is now passing, and by century's end
will have passed, from leadership. The new generation
remembers Vietnam instead. At the same time, the rhetoric
and style of the new Soviet leadership appeal to many, even in
advance of any concrete actions demonstrating a reduced Soviet military threat. European publics increasingly dislike nuclear deterrence because they reject the destructive consequences of even the relatively modest plans for tactical nuclear
war fighting thereby implied. For their part, European policy
elites recognize that they lack a conventional force strategy
that could fully substitute for the nuclear force strategy and
that they would be willing to fund. Increasingly, both groups
seek to escape the dilemma by (again wrongly) pronouncing
conventional war equally destructive and also by turning to
arms control and the hope of political evolution in the USSR as
dei ex machina.

U.S. economic predominance is gone, though the United
States is still the largest single market and economic entity
(until Europe really abolishes economic borders, national currencies, and individual economic policies—which will take
much longer than the end of 1992), and its industrial and technological leadership is seen by many as passing to Japan. At
the same time, the United States is increasingly ambivalent
about its own place in the world; the minimalist position,
though far from dominant, has respectability and substantial
strength. This is exhibited on such specific issues as protectionism and burden sharing, as well as by various proposals
from all segments of the political spectrum to withdraw from
alliances, or halve the U.S. force structure and defense budget,
or both. Trade issues abound and are real, though abused in
U.S. politics as an excuse for American failures in competitiveness and in management of the economy.

Burden Sharing. Burden sharing is properly viewed in a
broad context including not only military expenditures but

foreign aid and Third World debt, as well as output measures of military capability, conscript forces, and, not least, the sharing of military and political risk. One approach often suggested is for the United States to negotiate an increase in contributions by its allies, for military or other purposes, that equals or exceeds its own reductions in expenditure. Failing that, unilateral U.S. reductions are suggested in the expectation or hope that others would take compensating rather than parallel steps. Political experience suggests the contrary, however, especially in the light of the changes in the views of Allied publics during the last two decades. A second possibility is muddling through. If the external world changes slowly enough, that could work. A third option is to aggregate military and foreign aid responsibilities. This has several advantages. Since U.S. military expenditure levels are unlikely to increase in real terms (as are those of our European allies), the criterion of success could be set as improved military effectiveness, which can be achieved by rationalization of development and production, better integration of national forces, whether under the NATO military structure or bilaterally (France and Germany, Germany and the Netherlands), along with logistic specialization (host country support). Pressure for modest upward adjustments in percentage of GNP spent on defense by those nations for which the figure is now notably low could be more acceptable in such a context. Moreover, increased Japanese contributions would then appropriately be primarily (though not entirely) in the form of united economic and security assistance, largely outside its own region and including Third World areas facing security threats. Holding Japanese military build-up to a modest level and avoiding any direct Japanese regional security role outside its own territory and the adjacent sea and air lanes would avoid both the internal stresses that would flow from a change in Japanese security policy and the fears of revived Japanese militarism that are deeply felt by other nations in East Asia.

Out-of-Area Cooperation. U.S. hopes for out-of-area cooperation by our allies in security matters must, in my judgment, be either very modest or doomed to disappointment. Few allies see their security interests as very similar to ours in Central America, Southern Africa, the Middle East, or even the Persian Gulf. Given these differences in perspective, the parallel actions in the Gulf during 1987–1988 stand as perhaps the best that can be expected. Certainly a NATO action, which requires unanimity, could not be carried out in any of those areas. We should seek agreements to use alliance bases for staging U.S. forces elsewhere, but these will have to be handled bilaterally and probably on an event-by-event basis. It is not unreasonable to ask our allies not to favor anti–U.S. forces in the Western Hemisphere, but they will not always comply. There will be an increasing number and intensity of third-party relationships by our allies in the light of the diffusion (and the word is diffusion, not transfer) of economic and political power from the United States. Western Europe, especially the FRG, will seek closer relationships with Eastern Europe. Japan sees markets in the PRC and investment in the NIEs in and beyond East Asia. The debtor less developed countries (LDCs), whose exports now go principally to the United States, will have to shift more of them toward Japan and Europe if world trade imbalances are to be eased. In such out-of-area relations, economic or military-political, U.S. options overlap the traditional and minimalist strategies. In the latter, we would not do much ourselves but might sometimes act in concert with others. In the former, we have frequently acted by ourselves, though sometimes trying to get others to follow us. As U.S. resources become a smaller fraction of the whole, one may expect that even an active U.S. policy and strategy will increasingly but not exclusively consult with others, attempt joint action, and sometimes urge others to take the lead locally or regionally.

Third World Issues

Third World issues differ so much by region that it is appropriate here to treat instead some of their more general aspects.

Policies and Attitudes. The most fundamental question asks: as criteria for its policies and attitudes, what relative weight should the United States give to a country's internal political structure and behavior (including its record in human rights), to its behavior toward its neighbors, to its attitudes toward the United States, to its position on East-West issues, or to the nature of its economy (market or centrally managed)? The combinations are too many to explore, but some principles are at least worth considering. Direct military action on the basis of another country's internal behavior alone is not justifiable, unless one believes in a U.S. version of the Brezhnev doctrine, which may work in a case or two, but is not sustainable over the long run. Behavior toward neighbors, or—on a very slippery slope—behavior expected to become real in the near future, is more of a justification. Soviet intervention or arms supply can justify corresponding U.S. action, depending on the previous status, the geographical area, and the local situation, but it certainly does not mandate U.S. action. Beyond this still very high order of generality we have learned that rules become less useful as we look more deeply. Economic and political relations are appropriately influenced by human rights and other internal aspects, political and economic, and by the attitudes of the nation concerned toward the United States and toward East-West issues. But specific decisions about direct or indirect U.S. action must vary with the details of the situation.

Third World Development. How important is Third World development, economic and political, to U.S. economic interests? To East-West strategic interests? We could concentrate on the Persian Gulf for its oil, on East Asian NIEs for trade growth, on the Caribbean, Central America, and Mexico for reasons of propinquity, and ignore the rest. Or we could instead seek intensified global cooperation with the other industrialized democracies to help development in the poorest countries, or at least to prevent further deterioration in their desperate situations. In my judgment the choice we make here will have much more to do with our very long-term perceptions of the kind of world we want to live in than with shorter-range concerns for our physical security. I believe that taking the long view of security is the path of wisdom, so that progress in the Third World is important, though it should not be confused with the immediate demands of the national security of the United States.

Prospective Regional Powers. In considering prospective regional powers, again a list of questions to illustrate the sorts of issues, rather than itemization of options with their pros and cons, is appropriate. Is the PRC a potential threat to U.S. interests in the first decades of the twenty-first century? If so, how should we be acting now in order to minimize that prospect? Are India and Brazil going to be big enough security factors so that the United States needs now to conduct its relations with them on a basis that goes well beyond the economic and immediate political issues? How should the United States manage its post-Khomeini relations with Iran, which through its size and resources is likely to remain the largest single factor in the Gulf?

Terrorism. The effect of increased availability of advanced weapons to Third World nations and to terrorist groups, state-sponsored and independent, may well create a new situation with respect to terrorism. Forms of terrorism that employ guns, bombs, and aircraft hijackings probably cannot be eliminated without police state measures; indeed, these forms occur, though rarely, even in the Soviet Union. It is one of those conditions that, though basically unacceptable, can be lived with. But more advanced or more terrible weapons—chemical and biological, which are easily available and even in use in some quarters, and nuclear, which might become available—combine with the fragility and vulnerability of urban-industrial societies to raise more serious questions. What happens if a terrorist act kills 10,000 people? Can we rely on the revulsion against any group committing such an act to deter it? If not, what, if anything, can be done to prevent it? Or are these only fantasies drawn from the adventures of James Bond? Only time will tell. On that note, we turn now to the consideration of more specific military strategies and dispositions among which the United States will have to choose, whether by reasoned policy debate, inertia, or uncoordinated budgetary and political actions.

Military Strategies and Dispositions

Process. As a matter of process, what is the proper point of departure for military planning for the period ahead? Do we begin with decisions on what political-military commitments are required for U.S. security, then derive the necessary force structure to meet those commitments, and then the corresponding multiyear budget needs? Or do we start with a (one-year or five-year) budget ceiling based on what political leaders believe to be politically and economically feasible, then derive a force structure corresponding to political-military commitments manageable under that budget constraint? Or do we start with our present force structure and then modernize and expand it under the influence of institutional service doctrines and interests and the constraint of budgets and arbitrary executive branch and congressional interventions? Do we then try to make that force structure square as best we can with a set of commitments and stated U.S. security objectives determined by a separate but not totally disjointed set of historical and political factors? The answer to all of these options is yes, in various mixtures and at various times. The official rhetoric has occasionally corresponded to the first option, as in parts of the 1960s and the 1980s. But programs and plans must be viewed over five- to ten-year periods, and the first approach has never been sustained even rhetorically over five years. Moreover, during the past fifteen years, military budgets have varied only between 5.3 percent and 6.7 percent of GNP. While this difference is significant in the competition for resources (nearly $70 billion annually at current GNP levels), it is small compared to the wild swings in U.S. views of the world during that period. Thus budgetary pressures are clearly a constraint, and planning for the rest of the century should, in my view, assume as a first approximation about 6 percent of GNP, barring either some extended crisis, or a major agreed mutual reduction in U.S. and Soviet conventional forces, or a unilateral U.S. turn to a minimalist strategy. Furthermore, both a force structure and political-military commitments exist; we cannot start from zero in either case. Correspondingly, change is likely to be gradual in force structure terms, even if it is discontinuous in political terms. Our only rapid (one- or two-year) build-ups were for wars; our only rapid demobilizations were at their ends, and in the case of Korea and Vietnam the stand-down was not all that rapid.

Despite the inertia implied by the above, security and foreign policy interests can be set forth in a fresh look, as if starting over, categorized, for example, as vital, major, and significant, assigned relative priorities, and assessed in terms of a broader context of international security and national goals. Then, plans and programs can be adjusted for implementation over the following five- or ten-year period; indeed, modest (even major, as the 1969–1975 and 1979–1985 experiences show) changes in the overall defense budget can be made. This is as close to a careful, zero-based review as we are likely to come. Unfortunately, bigger changes could well result from unplanned, externally generated dislocations.

The context of the planning process goes beyond matters of international security. There are (usually implicit) trade-offs with domestic political and economic/technological decisions and programs, not only because the latter provide the infrastructure on which military capability rests, but at a more specific level. An example would be the choice between defending access to Persian Gulf oil with forces usable in Southwest Asia and providing alternative energy sources through synthetic fuels. The trade-off does not bear deep analysis, however, because it disappears into a welter of assumptions. (Is the alternate source stand-by, expansible, or producing? Do we replace 1 million barrels per day of U.S. imports from the Gulf, 7 million total U.S. imports, or 15 million from the entire region? And what about the other reasons, if any, for defending the region?) Thus, although broad trade-offs must be examined and should inform overall government policy over the long pull, the short run poses a series of specific choices, which must be addressed largely in their own discrete terms.

Nuclear Strategies, Doctrines, and Forces. A spectrum of goals defines possible U.S. nuclear strategies, doctrines, and forces for the 1990s. At one end of the range is a strategy of counterforce against Soviet nuclear forces, plus strategic defense (antiballistic missile defense, air defense, and civil defense) to allow the nation to survive a thermonuclear war. At or near the other end of the range is a "minimal" but secure second strike deterrent, capable of inflicting unacceptable damage on the urban-industrial society of an adversary in retaliation, but without significant capability of counterforce, or even of a comprehensive attack on opposing conventional military forces.

It is almost certain that the numbers, and to some degree the nature, of strategic systems will be constrained during the 1990s by strategic arms reduction treaties, the first of which is likely to be achieved fairly early in the Bush administration. Within those limitations a wide variety of mixtures of land-based and sea-based ballistic missiles, bombers, and air- and submarine-launched missiles will be possible. The generally agreed necessity for the strategic forces to be able to survive any technological or deployment breakthrough that the Soviets might be able to effect during the rest of the century will argue for a force that includes both bombers and submarine-launched ballistic missiles. There will be more argument about whether penetrating bombers as well as those carrying cruise missiles are needed, and about whether the land-based ICBM component needs to be highly survivable in its own right, or indeed whether it is needed at all. Past history suggests that the United States will retain both some penetrating bombers and an ICBM force that, if not highly survivable by itself, would be at least very difficult for the Soviets to destroy simultaneously with the bomber force. Arms reduction agreements can improve the survivability of strategic forces and the stability of strategic force balances, but they are no substitute for unilateral force structure and basing decisions.

Could a strategic nuclear war be limited to the exchange of a small number of warheads on each side aimed primarily at military objectives outside of cities and at areas of demonstration—of intent or of will? Could there be a series of discrete rounds of a strategic exchange using highly accurate warheads? These issues will continue to be debated, without definitive conclusion but with some effect on the nature of strategic force structure programs—for example, a program to provide a military-political command structure capable of extended survival. The possibility of moving to a force balance that is dominated by the defense, which was very skeptically viewed in an earlier section, will also remain a central issue. It is organically connected to the issue of arms reduction, because unless strategic nuclear weapons are reduced from the range of ten or fifteen thousand to a few hundred on each side, such a transition is infeasible.

The use of strategic defenses for more limited objectives than provision of a general shield of the population against a massive nuclear attack will be an important decision for the 1990s, whether for the purpose of defense against an unauthorized or accidental launch by the other superpower, defense against attack for whatever purpose by other nuclear powers, or active protection of strategic retaliatory forces. A transition to defense dominance by cooperative means seems very difficult and by unilateral means probably impossible.

Conventional Military Strategies and Dispositions. The reflections in military strategy of the "traditional" and "minimalist" alternatives for future U.S. security interests are the coalition strategy and the maritime strategy. The coalition strategy implies sufficient U.S. ground force and land-based tactical air force deployments in alliance areas to cement the alliance relationships, even though the allies must inevitably supply the bulk of the conventional forces. On the central front in Europe, for example, the allies supply 90 percent of the ground forces and 75 percent of the peacetime tactical air power. A maritime strategy relies primarily on deployments of naval forces throughout the global ocean, and where necessary on the periphery of other continents, and on air power based on the soil of the United States and its territories and dependencies. Correspondingly, it implies a more unilateral U.S. determination of when and how it intervenes militarily. It depends considerably less on the provision of base rights from other nations, although overflight and transit capabilities for aircraft and access to refueling and other naval stores are sufficiently necessary so that the maritime strategy does not allow for complete autonomy. Independence of foreign bases is a matter of degree, as both the Soviet and U.S. navies have found.

Technology has made the ranges of naval and air forces substantially greater than they were in earlier decades. Examples include very long-endurance aircraft, nuclear powered ships (which nevertheless must have their munitions and aviation fuel replenished during combat operations), and large transportable structures anchored on seamounts. But what is technologically feasible is by no means always affordable; the usual case is quite the reverse. The choice of military strategy is thus likely to depend on a political decision by the United States as to where its geographical security boundaries lie and how much of a political commitment it wants to make in each of those geographical areas. Force deployments and basing agreements will follow from that set of decisions. They can perhaps be modified by technological capabilities and thereby made less immediately subject to the vagaries of popular attitudes in the host countries, but the U.S. defense budget would not necessarily be lower as a result.

A parallel set of issues for nonnuclear military strategy and force structure is the specific geographic orientation of U.S. forces and the corresponding structure and organization of those forces. In Europe, where a clear line exists between opposing alliances, highly mobile and heavily armored units play a leading role, though in urban and wooded areas a considerable place remains for more lightly armed defensive units, probably reserves, using lighter ground vehicles for mobility rather than tanks or helicopters. In the Pacific theater, where distances are much greater, and in the Middle East/Persian Gulf theaters, where the distances from the United States are much greater, early arrival may be more important than either the fire power or the mobility of the forces that first arrive. It should be recalled, however, that the dissemination of advanced arms both in East Asia and in the Middle East/Persian Gulf area has been substantial. Thus U.S. forces, even if not facing the Soviets directly, could in many cases require substantial fire power and mobility. Moreover, those two features entail substantial tonnage—mobility in many of these areas is not well provided by human feet, and both helicopters and tanks weigh quite a lot. The trade-off between mobility from the United States and mobility as well as fire power and protection at the other end will be a difficult one.

The organization and equipment of a portion of the U.S. military force for low-intensity conflict will be an important issue, but it should be remembered that recent wars have been low intensity only by comparison with World Wars I and II, or with what we anticipate would be involved in a NATO–Warsaw Pact war. The rate of destruction of tanks and aircraft, as well as human casualties, has been high in the Korean, Arab/Israeli, and Iran/Iraq wars.

In deciding what fraction of the forces and equipment should be stationed, pre-positioned, and delivered by airlift and by sealift, U.S. strategists will need to consider matters of political reassurance, U.S. vulnerability to local political issues, flexibility of deployments, and future arms control agreements that may limit some but not others of these. Almost inevitably, however, a larger fraction of U.S. force capability is likely to be based on U.S. soil than is now the case. This change will probably result from arms agreements with the Soviets, from the decreased availability of overseas bases in a climate of greater political turmoil and the assertion by host countries of more autonomous foreign policies, and from new developments in technology.

In these matters concerned with conventional forces, it is likely to be vital to the orderly formulation and execution of U.S. policy that joint determinations be made with allies of the approaches to commitments, deployments, and procedures that involve them. Moreover, careful consultation with allies, including modification as necessary of U.S. stands, should be carried out before the United States takes a position in East-West negotiations.

Regional Balances. What of regional balances in other geographical areas? Europe and Northeast Asia have been areas of deep U.S. commitment ever since World War II. As a consequence, structures of military, political, and economic relations between the United States and various allies have evolved in those regions. We may decide to change those structures under the pressure of events during the rest of this century, or they may be changed whether or not we wish them to if those pressures become strong enough. But in these regions we begin from a relatively clearly established base, whereas in other regions the balance of the military, political, and economic elements is much less clearly set. Those trade-offs, and the proper balance of commitments among regions, will be major questions for the United States during the rest of this century.

To take three quite different examples, consider Afghanistan after the Soviet withdrawal, Central America, and Sub-Saharan Africa. Afghanistan will by reason of geography and demography continue to be seen by the Soviets as an area of vital interest. For the United States, Afghanistan is more a matter of principle, though the power structure in Afghanistan will continue to affect both Pakistan and Iran, which are of considerably greater geostrategic interest to the United States. Economic and political connections between Afghanistan and the United States are likely to remain slight, but the question of what military supplies should be provided, and to whom, will continue.

Geography makes Central America very important to the United States, while Soviet interests there include both ideological advancement (which at least in the short run is being deemphasized under Gorbachev) and the opportunity to divert U.S. attention and resources from regions of more direct U.S.–Soviet competition. The United States could choose to confine its military support in the region to neighbors of Nicaragua and Cuba that may be militarily threatened either directly or through insurgency supported from those centers, but concentrate more of its effort on building up the economies of the non-Communist nations of the area and strengthening them politically. If Central America and the Caribbean were more like Southeast Asia in culture and history, Cuba and Nicaragua could then find themselves in the same awkward condition as Vietnam now does.

Sub-Saharan Africa is remote from the central geostrategic interests of both the United States and the Soviet Union. It has extreme economic and human problems, and in South Africa the world's most unjust situation of racial oppression. Military intervention or assistance would appear to play little or no role in U.S. policy in the area, although it is clear that there has been some of the latter in Angola. Our political and even our economic leverage is also modest. This would seem a likely case for a minimalist policy, but the South African situation has caused some who advocate a minimalist policy elsewhere to reject it in this region. Southern Africa is likely to continue and indeed intensify as a domestic U.S. political issue in the 1990s, but the rest of Sub-Saharan Africa is unlikely to follow suit.

Conclusion

Expenditures for the support of the U.S. military establishment (including the retirement pay of armed forces personnel only; the corresponding cost for retired defense department civil servants is counted as a social expenditure) and foreign and military assistance amount to about 6.5 percent of the gross national product. Resources for those purposes compete with consumption and with investment, both in physical productive capacity and in human resources (for example, education). Decisions about international responsibilities and the availability of funds to meet them are affected by tax policy; by public attitudes on savings, investment, and consumption; by the state of research and development and of education; and by the competition among income transfers, defense and foreign assistance expenditures, the (very small) direct government involvement in investment, and the somewhat larger government contributions to the physical infrastructure. The 6.5 percent figure for defense and foreign assistance should be set against a 4 percent personal savings rate, a 22 percent overall investment rate in the entire economy, and an 18 percent figure for income transfers, including those made by state and local governments. This means that the defense allocation is unlikely to be the deciding factor in the prosperity of the economy.

Other industrialized democracies devote smaller fractions of their GNP to defense and foreign aid. For some the figure is 4 or 5 percent, for others only 2 or 3 percent. But these differences are dwarfed by the differences among those same countries with respect to the other figures just mentioned—rates of personal savings and income transfers, for example. Even if the political climate in the United States makes it more feasible by executive and legislative branch actions to change the 6.5 percent up or down by 1 percent than to change the savings rate or investment rate by the same amount, a 1 percent change in defense and foreign affairs will not compensate for the much larger absolute differences in the other factors. Thus military and foreign assistance expenditures are unlikely to be the driving factor in American economic performance. Competition between military and civil sectors for research and development, technology, and trained personnel may be a more serious problem, but the extent (and even the direction) of the effect is not clear. Indeed, mobilization of resources toward a goal, even a military goal so unrealistic as the astrodome version of the Strategic Defense Initiative, alarmed Japanese civilian planners as well as the Soviet military. Their respective concerns were that the civilian technological as well as the conventional military spin-off could tilt the balance in favor of the United States. They were wrong, but they were worried nonetheless.

To me, all this implies that the recent widespread concern about U.S. "imperial overstretch" is itself something of an overstretch. Previous imperiums exhausted themselves much more by protracted war than by peacetime military expenditures; their wartime military expenditures were a much higher percentage of GNP than 6 or 7 percent, and the human losses were great as well. The United States was damaged in morale and in human terms by the Korean War and especially by the Vietnam War, and damaged economically by the decision during the Vietnam War not to pay for that war out of current taxation. But World War I and World War II both left the United States stronger economically at their conclusions than at the time of U.S. entry. Thus the problem is not one of economic exhaustion by our present level of military and foreign aid commitments. It is rather a question of *balance* among U.S. capabilities—between our commitments and the degree of risk that we are willing to accept, interacting with the external environment ("requirements" or "threats" in the military jargon) and with the contributions of allies in military forces, in domestic economic policies and foreign aid, and in sharing of political and military risks. A key question for American security policy, and for American diplomacy, in the next decade is how these burdens, risks, and responsibilities are to be shared among the United States, its allies, and its associates in a period of continuing change in the external environment.

Both the developing world and the NIEs will have a much greater effect on the United States than during the past forty years. Japan is already the world's second economic power, and nearly—or perhaps better than—tied for first as a manufacturing and technological one. There is substantial ferment in China, in the Soviet Union, and in Eastern Europe; we may be dealing with Communist societies that will look very different ten years from now. Resource issues will return, population issues will continue, and environmental issues will probably accelerate. Dealing with these matters goes well beyond issues of defense expenditures and military capabilities; the sharing of responsibility with allies must also include foreign aid and political cooperation.

But orchestrating these matters at a time when the United States is far less predominant than it was forty years ago will be more difficult—it will take more skill and more domestic cohesion. The smaller the share of the joint burden the United

States carries, the less weight the United States will have in the joint decisions, in a process that may exhibit stairstep discontinuities as time goes by. The United States will have to balance how modest a share of influence we will settle for against how large a share of our resources and skills we are willing to devote to international matters. The trade-off will be eased insofar as improved domestic productivity, coherence, and economic growth create a greater store of resources and skills to be allocated.

The challenges may seem daunting—and indeed they are. An American secretary of state in the 1950s seldom really had to ask whether U.S. economic or military resources were sufficient to support U.S. objectives; in retrospect it was more a matter of whether to use them or not. But it often did not seem that way at the time. Worries about Soviet invasion of Europe were greater in the late 1940s and 1950s than they are now. Concerns about a prospective Soviet preemptive attack on U.S. strategic retaliatory capability, with what was considered to be a significant chance of success, were strongly reflected in expert writings and even some official studies of the late 1950s. The successive challenges in the 1960s and 1970s, including the Vietnam War and a perceived secular decline of the United States in the face of Soviet military and European and Japanese economic power, also gave rise to understandable pessimism. Some of these challenges were indeed poorly met and have left permanent damage, while others were faced successfully.

As we think about the next two decades, it is important to remember that no other nation comes close to the aggregate power of the United States when economic weight, military capability, technological innovation, productivity, and international experience are all included, though in one or another we can be equalled or even surpassed. Where we must learn to do better is in continuity of policy and adoption of a longer view. A fifty-year perspective is too much to expect from political leaders who know they will not be around nearly that long to reap its benefits. Besides, it is hardly feasible in a world that changes so quickly. But a ten- or twenty-year perspective is not infeasible, and the security issues that have been sketched in this chapter can be faced with a ten- or twenty-year perspective. And, through concentrated, coherent application of America's resources, talents, and skills, I believe that they can be successfully met.

4

Inherited Geopolitics and Emergent Global Realities

SEYOM BROWN

T he cold war alignments and antagonisms that dominated world politics in the aftermath of World War II were at the outset substantially congruent not only with the postwar economic and military facts of life but also with established

SEYOM BROWN is professor and chair of the politics department at Brandeis University and an associate at Harvard University's Center for International Affairs. In a career spanning thirty years, Dr. Brown has written, taught, and conducted research on foreign policy issues at such institutions as Columbia University, the Carnegie Endowment for International Peace, Johns Hopkins University, the Brookings Institution, RAND Corporation, the U.S. Defense and State Departments, the University of Southern California, the University of California at Los Angeles, and the University of Chicago. Dr. Brown is the author or coauthor of numerous books and articles concerned with many aspects of world politics, U.S. foreign policy, and international organization. Although an original essay, some material in this chapter has been adapted from *New Forces, Old Forces, and the Future of World Politics.* Copyright 1988 by Seyom Brown. Used by permission of Scott, Foresman and Company.

Anglo-American geopolitical concepts inherited from the first half of the twentieth century. Ideology, material conditions, and grand strategy were for a time mutually reinforcing. Later, even as the Reagan administration began to grapple with Mikhail Gorbachev's call for a post–cold war relationship, the inherited geopolitical doctrines continued to provide the basic frame of reference for national security planners and for politicians and foreign affairs experts who were urging a renaissance of a "bipartisan" foreign policy. The presidential election campaign of 1988 perpetuated the traditional wisdom, as the nominees of both parties, while giving rhetorical recognition to the new signals from Moscow and elsewhere, vied for public confidence in their ability to stay the basic course of post–World War II foreign policy with minimal risk of rocking the boat.

By the latter 1980s, however, the inherited geopolitical doctrines were no longer congruent with many of the emergent material and political conditions. The formulation of a coherent and realistic foreign policy for the 1990s will require a more substantial departure from cold war orthodoxies than most champions of a new consensus are recommending. But alternative grand strategies—of the kind suggested in this and some other chapters in this volume—are highly controversial, and must await fresh assessment by a leadership in Washington that is not seeking the immediate approval of the electorate.

The Geopolitical Legacy

The core geopolitical ideas of the officials who gave conceptual coherence to U.S. foreign policy during the period since World War II—George Kennan, Dean Acheson, and Paul Nitze in the Truman administration; John Foster Dulles and President Eisenhower himself during the 1950s; General Maxwell Taylor and Walt Rostow during the Kennedy/Johnson years; Henry Kissinger and President Nixon; Zbigniew Brzezinski for Carter; and Alexander Haig at the outset of the Reagan administration—are traceable to a common source: the thinking of the early twentieth-century British and American geopolitical theorists who saw a persisting vital interest of the insular powers (Britain, the United States, and Japan) in preventing one continental power from dominating the Eurasian land mass. The cold war geopoliticians seized upon the "heartland/rimland" concepts of their predecessors to propound a new imperative: America must supplant Britain's former role of maintaining access and influence all around the littorals of the Eurasian land mass. The underlying premise was that if the resources and sea access of the rimland areas, particularly the vast stretch from the Mediterranean through Southeast Asia, were controlled by the power that also controlled the heartland (now the Soviet Union), that power would dominate the world.

By the late 1940s, and with remarkable consistency over most of the next four decades, despite the emergence of complicating realities, the prevailing geopolitical wisdom in Washington was based on the presumed validity of the following propositions.

1. The Soviet Union would expand its sphere of control into western and southern Europe, the Middle East, and Asia if the countries of these areas did not have the protection of the United States. World War II had made this situation unavoidable. By virtually destroying the industrialized societies of Britain, France, and Japan, the war removed the traditional forward bulwarks against an expansionary heartland power. This left the responsibility for organizing and leading a countervailing coalition up to the United States, the only insular power with a sufficiently intact industrial base and military capability to stand up to the new Eurasian imperialist.

2. Even if the leaders in the Kremlin abandoned or postponed their goal of transforming the world into a system of soviets, the Russians would continue to fear "encirclement" by the insular powers—now manifested in stepped-up efforts by the United States to sign up allies and establish military bases on the rimland—and therefore would not abandon their attempts, often coercive, to assure political alignment and military cooperation from neighboring countries all around the USSR.

3. Thus in addition to the possibility of a war in central Europe over the disposition of a still-divided Germany, war in the vast southern rimland area (the "arc of crisis"), perhaps initially involving allies of the rival superpowers, was an ever-present possibility.

4. With the deployment of society-destroying intercontinental nuclear arsenals by both superpowers, effective deterrence of Soviet or Soviet-sponsored aggression in particular theaters or effective military counteraction should deterrence fail—let alone a rollback of the existing Soviet sphere—required U.S. strategies and capabilities that were not dependent on the credibility of our promise to initiate a direct homeland-to-homeland exchange of blows with the Soviets.

5. Consequently the United States would need to assure itself a not disadvantageous global balance of "general purpose" military power and access to a wide variety of zones of potential combat. The inevitable corollary was an intensified rivalry with the Soviets for allies and client states worldwide in order to provide economic resources, military personnel, and bases for military operations.

6. There was, accordingly, no escaping the need to maintain a globe-spanning, U.S. controlled coalition. Indeed, an adequate balance of power vis-à-vis the Soviet Union was seen as so dependent upon reliable support from the coalition that the cohesion and perpetuation of the coalition itself came to be regarded as an indispensable vital interest of the United States, not just one of a number of important means to secure the country's survival and well-being.

The national security incentives for the United States and the Soviet Union to build and sustain worldwide coalitions were reinforced by official ideologies on both sides. Each coalition was defined by its leaders and many of its members as a community of peoples sharing basic beliefs rather than just an alliance to marshal power for the defense of territory and other strategic and economic assets. Although standard code words such as "free world" and "socialist commonwealth" were never adequate descriptions of the values adhered to by members of each camp, they did—particularly during the early decades of the cold war—reflect a very real difference in general approach to domestic and world order that established two rival centers of gravity around which many nations tended to coalesce. The collective military force of each coalition was presumed to be available to protect a "way of life" and certain "rules of the international game," as well as pieces of real estate that were critical to the balance of power.

Emergent Realities

The expectations of the early cold war strategists were that in the decades following World War II the world would become increasingly polarized into two camps, so that for most countries nonalignment would become untenable. As it turned out, those expectations did not materialize.

By the middle 1950s, important centrifugal tendencies already had surfaced in both superpower-led coalitions. The Kremlin rolled its tanks across the Hungarian border in the fall of 1956 to shoot down dissidents on the streets of Budapest not only to prevent the Hungarians from too large a departure from orthodox Soviet models of socialist development; no less a crucial factor in the Kremlin's brutal reaction was the Hungarian reformers' contemplation of taking their country out of the Warsaw Pact. Meanwhile, the North Atlantic Treaty Organization (NATO) was being sorely stressed by the British/French/Israeli connivance—behind the back of the United States—to wrest the Suez Canal away from the Egyptians militarily and thereby topple the Nasser regime. The evidence provided by the Suez crisis of profoundly divergent interests and strategies within the U.S.–led coalition was French President Charles DeGaulle's strongest argument in convincing his countrymen that France should pull out of the NATO military command and develop an independent nuclear force. Similarly, by 1958 Beijing had concluded, especially in light of Moscow's too-little, too-late help in the Formosa Straits crisis, that the Soviets were unreliable allies and that China would need to deploy a nuclear arsenal of its own to resist American nuclear blackmail in future crises.

The Evolving Geostrategic Environment

The early defections by Paris and Beijing were telltale signs, though not widely recognized until the 1980s, of the dirty little secret about "extended nuclear deterrence": the fact that the superpowers' protective umbrellas were full of holes, and that it would be surprising if, *in extremis,* they did *not* collapse. The strategically orthodox continued to argue that the balance of terror between the superpowers, far from nullifying the military reasons for each of their global alliance systems, enhanced their importance; for without very firm and unambiguous commitments by coalition members to come to the defense of each other, the common enemy would discount the risks of aggression. But this only stated the problem without resolving it. It was precisely the disproportion between the terrible physical and economic costs of major war against the opposing superpower and the less tangible political costs of backing out of an alliance commitment at the moment of truth that had reduced the credibility of alliances.

The crisis of alliance credibility was exacerbated further by growing doubts about the military *value* to the superpowers of various members of their coalitions. As first bombers and then missiles became truly intercontinental, neither superpower had as much need of distant allies to extend its lethal reach into the territory of the other. (Remember Khrushchev's perceived need to deploy intermediate-range ballistic missiles [IRBMs] to Cuba, as opposed to the ability of Kennedy—already armed with an effective intercontinental ballistic missile [ICBM] force—to agree to remove U.S. Jupiters from Turkey as part of the resolution of the 1962 missile crisis.) Thus by 1987 it was clear to most strategists that the United States relinquished little of military value in the intermediate nuclear force (INF) treaty abolishing all land-based nuclear missiles with ranges between 300 and 3,000 miles. Moreover, with the deployment in outer space of advanced reconnaissance systems, neither superpower had as much need as previously for bases near the other's frontiers in order to assure adequate warning of menacing deployments, alerts, or impending attack. Prior to the Marxist takeover in Ethiopia, the U.S. communications base at Kagnew was ritualistically cited in Pentagon planning documents as one of our vital security interests; yet no American administration since has had the slightest inclination to go to war to regain it. Nor did the loss of the forward intelligence-gathering facilities in Iran in the Khomeini revolution crucially diminish U.S. strategic warning capabilities as much as the standard assessments had predicted.

The maturing capacities of the Soviets and Americans to stand each other off at the intercontinental level, however, did not initially lead to a downgrading of their respective alliance systems. Rather, the new geopolitical wisdom held that mutual strategic deterrence of the superpowers tended to encourage limited contests for local position with conventional or paramilitary forces. The realization that such limited wars between the superpowers (or their proxies) were still a distinct possibility stimulated military planners to apply the fruits of the technological revolution to conventional operations as well as to strategic ones. But, paradoxically, the development of technologically advanced "tactical" capabilities led in turn to the downgrading of the importance of various locational and topographic factors in determining what foreign objectives are worth fighting for and how to fight for them—with implications not always positive for alliance relationships.

The new communications and transportation technologies are reducing the significance of distance from the zone of battle as a factor-cost in military campaigns. Military operations in remote theaters can be commenced and sustained with greater ease (technically speaking) than previously. The same technological developments are reducing the military significance of some traditional overseas access routes, as improvements in air freight capabilities and economies in ocean shipping lower the costs of substitute routes. By the 1980s, only six straits were geopolitically crucial to the global oceanic powers, whereas in the 1950s the number was about twenty. Developments in airlift, sealift, and instant communications are also reducing the military requirements for pre-positioning troops and weapons in the locale of potential conflict.

Simultaneously, the value of allied military bases for communication links and command and control is declining for local and conventional war as well as for strategic war. For tactical campaigns, too, observation posts, airfields, ports, and command headquarters on the territory of allies can give way to increasingly sophisticated airborne, naval, and space systems that are less dependent upon stationary sites located on friendly territory.

By the late 1980s, most American military planners were advocating strategies and force postures minimally dependent on access to foreign bases. For example, one of the principal recommendations of the January 1988 *Discriminate Deterrence* report of The Commission on Integrated Long-Term Strategy, chaired by Fred Ikle and Albert Wohlstetter, was that "the United States must develop alternatives to overseas bases." Especially in the Third World, where "we have found it increasingly difficult, and politically costly" to maintain them, said the commission (whose members included Henry Kissinger, Zbigniew Brzezinski, and Andrew Goodpaster), "we should not ordinarily be dependent on bases in defending our interests." The commission was pleased, however, to report compensatory technological developments:

Low-cost satellites in space can in some measure replace the communication and intelligence-gathering functions of overseas bases. We can build very long-endurance aircraft for surveillance, manned or unmanned. We also have some impressive naval options. Located in international waters, or in an ally's territorial waters but still out of view, our operations can be far more secure than those on land bases.

All in all, the new mobility and communications technologies exert ambiguous impact on superpower incentives to maintain military allies around the globe, and to intervene on their behalf. As foreshadowed in the Nixon Doctrine of 1969, they make it less crucial for the superpowers to become engaged with their own troops on foreign soil, and easier for them to disengage from previous commitments. But many of

these same technologies also make it physically easier to establish a presence in remote areas (thus the periodic augmenta-
tion of U.S. naval assets in the Persian Gulf and of Soviet naval
assets in the Caribbean). While fewer external interests merit
being considered militarily vital, both the United States and
the Soviet Union can cast their interest nets more widely.

In determining how much to invest in the protection of foreign countries, the superpowers can now give more weight to
nonmilitary criteria—ideological or cultural affinity, economic
advantage, or simply how one's reputation for fidelity and
toughness might be affected by a failure to protect even a marginal interest when challenged. Ironically, therefore, while
there is less clear-cut, survival-based *need* for each superpower
to actively counter the other's expansionary tendencies, there
may well be large numbers of unnecessary conflicts based on
mutual concerns about prestige and fraught with opportunities for bluffing, games of chicken, and dangerous miscalculation.

Eventually, it is very probable that the technologically induced erosion of extended mutual security commitments will
also erode the superpowers' core alliance structures—especially where these involve visible foreign deployments (weapons facilities and troops) and large budgetary outlays that are
in competition with other pressing national needs. Barring the
flare-up of crises that threaten to precipitate a third world war,
statesmen and military strategists throughout each of the cold
war coalitions are bound to perceive the advantages of more
flexible military arrangements that allow them considerable
leeway to opt in or out of alliance actions on an ad hoc basis,
and to seek such flexibility by avoiding the peacetime deployment of weapons, troops, and other military facilities on each
other's soil.

The Weakening of Cold War Ideologies

Just as collective defense imperatives and ideology worked
together to sustain the unity of the U.S.–led and Soviet-led
coalitions during the early cold war period, so the maturing of

the contradictions of collective defense in the context of the superpower balance of terror has stimulated, and is in turn stimulated by, the contemporary disintegration of the global ideological divide. Together these mutually reinforcing developments constitute an enlarging cluster of centrifugal forces urgently tugging at the surviving bipolar structure of the cold war system.

Well before Gorbachev began to question whether it was necessary to project "class conflict" onto the international scene, Soviet party ideologists felt compelled to lay aside the standard Marxist prophecy of a succession of violent struggles against the holdout capitalist powers that would bring about the worldwide victory of socialism. As the Soviets put it in a 1963 doctrinal dispute with the Chinese Communists: "The nuclear bomb does not distinguish between the imperialists and the working people." In another world war hundreds of millions of workers would lose their lives along with their chains. A primary task of the leading Marxist states, therefore, became to stabilize relations among the great powers to the degree necessary to prevent global war, while the historical revolutionary process worked itself out in the varied domestic societies of the world. Moreover, Soviet security motives for peaceful coexistence coincided with strong economic motives for expanding commerce with the capitalists. But an inadvertent and problematic side effect for the Kremlin of the resulting East-West detente has been the undermining of discipline within the Soviet coalition.

Once long-term coexistence with the capitalist West became the prognosis of Soviet ideologists, many Warsaw Pact governments saw no reason to refrain from developing their own relationships outside of the so-called socialist commonwealth. Adapting to the growing national assertiveness of its partners, the Kremlin endorsed the concept of "many roads to socialism," accepting an unprecedented degree of pluralism in its camp—both with respect to designs for the domestic political economy and unilaterally pursued negotiations with Western and Third World countries. In some cases (most dramatically the "Prague Spring" of 1968, and the rise of Solidarity in Poland in the early 1980s), the pluralism went beyond the threshold of Moscow's tolerance, and provoked a conservative backlash. But by the latter 1980s, there were few national leaders remaining in positions of influence in the countries of the Soviet-led coalition who were simply local satraps of the Kremlin, merely implementing policies wholly conceived in Moscow. More and more the leaders of national Communist parties had become just the opposite: agents for their domestic constituents, seeking to extract the best deals they could from the Soviets and the other members of the coalition, and attempting to enhance their bargaining power by cultivating relationships outside the coalition.

In the West changing perceptions of the Marxist-Leninists, from seeing them as a monolithic band of Kremlin-directed world revolutionaries to viewing them as a feuding group of self-interested states and nationalistic movements, also undercut the ideological foundations of the extensive U.S. system of alliances. We now focus concern upon Communists less because of their common and inimical design for organizing domestic society than on the basis of their individual and collective intentions and capabilities for major international aggression against important Western interests. In the United States itself, many influential participants in the policy process no longer accept the cold war premise that the success of communism anywhere in the world is a major threat to the American way of life. This souring of the foreign policy establishment on ideological anticommunism began with the full Americanization of the war in Vietnam, and was an important factor in the unwillingness of the American body politic to sustain the growing blood and treasure costs of fighting communism in Indochina.

By the 1970s, an American president whose political career had been built on anticommunism was ready to embrace the distinctly nonideological policies of detente with the USSR and rapprochement with China. Most high U.S. government officials of that era purged anti-Communist rhetoric from their statements. Taking a leaf out of Henry Kissinger's classical *realpolitik* concepts, President Richard Nixon himself allowed that "it would be a safer world and a better world if we have a strong healthy United States, Europe, Soviet Union, China, Japan; each balancing the other, not playing one against the other, an even balance."

Although ideological anticommunism returned to center stage with the election of Ronald Reagan, there were already too many powerful interests in both the Soviet-led and the U.S.–led coalitions, and in the Third World, with a practical stake in East-West detente to countenance a full international repolarization along ideological lines.

The North-South Axis of Tension

The early cold war view of the Third World as a key arena in the cold war—comprising countries that, because of their poverty and powerlessness, were bound to gravitate toward or be coerced into either the Soviet or American sphere of influence—also turned out to be a gross oversimplification. The basic trend over the ensuing decades, rather, was away from political alignment with either cold war coalition. Increasingly, the approximately 100 newly independent countries, joined by most of the countries in Latin America (most of which achieved independence from their European overlords during the nineteenth century), tried to act as a coalition of their own. They wanted to make it clear to the superpowers and other industrialized countries that they were more exercised by "North-South" issues—principally the disparities of wealth and power between the more affluent and the poorer countries—rather than the geopolitical and ideological rivalry between the Marxist and capitalist camps.

In pressing their demands for help in developing their economies, most of the Third World governments were particularly wary of seeming to accept a new semicolonial (or neocolonial) dependency on one of the superpowers. The need to perpetuate nationalist fervor in order to sustain viable government was particularly great in the multiethnic, multiracial countries carved out of the old European empires. A visible amount of xenophobia toward the new imperialists in

Washington and Moscow was a necessary ingredient of domestic political leadership, especially as popular aspirations
for economic development remained unsatisfied and frustrations mounted.

For their part, the superpowers gradually came to realize the
pitfalls of locking themselves into "mutual security" alliance
obligations to help client regimes sustain themselves against
their internal and external enemies. Regimes that survive primarily as wards of one of the superpowers, however successful
they may look in terms of gains in gross national product
(GNP), often turn out to be political and security liabilities.
Both Washington and Moscow have found it necessary to distance themselves from particular Third World clients who,
using weapons and other resources obtained from their superpower allies and claiming to be fighting on behalf of shared
ideological causes, have moved unilaterally against local opponents in rash, sometimes brutal power plays that are adverse to
the interests of their benefactors. U.S. problems with client
regimes in Argentina, Turkey, Pakistan, South Vietnam, Taiwan, the Philippines, South Korea, Indonesia, Israel, Jordan,
and Saudi Arabia are cases in point. The Soviets have had to
rein in, or disassociate themselves from, moves they considered reckless on the part of China (when it was a Soviet ally),
North Korea, Vietnam, Libya, Iraq, Syria, Ethiopia, Algeria,
and Cuba.

Along with this geopolitical distancing between the superpowers and many of their southern economic and military clients, there was a growing realization all around that the causes
of the persisting poverty and underdevelopment in many
countries were much less tractable than had been supposed by
either Marxist or non-Marxist development economists. Com-
pounding these difficulties, the industrially advanced countries, facing special economic difficulties of their own during
the 1970s and 1980s, became even less inclined to allocate
resources to Third World needs (particularly to major debt
relief) just as the true magnitude of the development problem
began to be appreciated.

Much earlier, the Third World countries sensed their weakness in bilateral bargaining vis-à-vis their affluent patrons, and tried to compensate by concerting their demands—primarily through the Nonalignment Movement in the 1950s and then the so-called Group of 77 in the United Nations Conference on Trade and Development (UNCTAD) in the 1960s. In the 1970s, buoyed by the ability of Third World oil producing countries to compel the industrialized West reluctantly to accept new terms of trade, the members of the Group of 77 coalition used a series of United Nations special sessions on development to press their case for an international economic redistribution regime, which they called the New International Economic Order. Despite their many differences, the developing countries were able to coalesce around a charter of economic rights and duties, calling for international price supports for their primary product exports, special preference access to industrial country markets, commitments from the affluent countries to contribute a specified percentage of GNP to official development assistance for the poor countries, special debt and balance of payments relief, and movement toward one-country/one-vote procedures in most international forums and institutions.

The affluent industrial countries proved unable to concert a common response to these demands; indeed, the European Community appeared pleased to differentiate itself from the official U.S. view that most of the global redistributive measures on the Third World's agenda were unacceptable "socialist" distortions of the international market. In the Lome Conventions and other special treaties the West Europeans negotiated special commodity pricing agreements with many of their former colonies (some of which had socialist, even Marxist, regimes) and extended them special tariff and other market entry preferences. The Japanese and Canadians each followed suit with various of the newly industrializing countries in the Pacific Rim, and even tried to cultivate their own special relationships with some Latin American countries. Belatedly, and reluctantly, the United States joined in the game of cultivating particular Third World economic partners, continuing—more than the Europeans, Japanese, or

Canadians—however, to inject cold war ideological criteria (as in the case of the Caribbean Basin Initiative) into its proselytizing efforts. Thus not only did the rise of the Third World coalition cut directly across the coherence of the East-West divide, but the adaptations to the North-South (rich versus poor) axis of international tension further fragmented the erstwhile bipolar order.

The Technological Revolution and the World Order Crisis

The growing incongruence between the cold war–based political system and many of the newly emergent or reemergent lines of cooperation and conflict is only the surface expression of underlying, perhaps irreversible, material and cultural developments that are transforming world society in the second half of the twentieth century. Most basic has been the dramatic expansion in human power to change and exploit nature, particularly the exponential increase in the mobility of people, materials, and information. Who can communicate with whom, who can easily exchange goods and services with whom, who can injure and destroy whom will at any point in history substantially define the shape of human communities—both patterns of interdependence and of autonomy. It was inevitable, therefore, that the post–World War II revolutions in the technologies of communication and transportation, industrial processes, and warfare would play havoc not only with the established coalitions but with the nation-state system itself.

From the standpoint of the physics of moving persons, things, and ideas, the whole earth may already be described as a community. The lag in constructing political and legal relationships that are congruent with already existing patterns of intense human interaction is attributable to "cultural"—not material—causes. But cultural factors are themselves reacting to the new forces in volatile, unprecedented, and unpredictable ways.

Indeed, a new political/cultural polarization has been developing. It divides those who are part of the new mobility (or at least willing to take their chances with it) from those who feel threatened by it. It is precisely because it has become so physically easy and inexpensive for people, things, information, money, diseases, and harmful substances to cross national borders that there is a thickening apparatus of inspections and controls at most points of entry to and from most countries. Relatively unpoliced national borders, such as among the countries of the European Community or between Canada and the United States, are rare. But the costs of maintaining the barriers, particularly the opportunity costs of contact and commerce forgone, bear differently on different sectors of society. Where tourism has become a large earner of foreign exchange, which is the case in many developing countries, visa and customs regulations that may discourage foreign visitors are matters of intense debate in national parliaments and bureaucracies, often pitting cultural traditionalists and xenophobes against entrepreneurial middle classes and cosmopolitan elites.

The new ideological fault line, showing up in virtually every country, affluent or poor, is the product of the fact that contemporary international commerce is in many respects antithetical to the basic norms of the nation-state system—national sovereignty and noninterference in a country's domestic affairs. More than the legal-constitutional forms of national sovereignty are at stake. The ability of a country to ensure that public safety, orderly commerce, social justice, and cultural integrity within its territory are sustained is undermined when national policies for regulating the national market can be ignored or overwhelmed by buyers, sellers, and investors who are unaccountable to the legal institutions of the country. Most countries today attempt to regulate and moderate their cycles of inflation and recession through alterations in interest rates and currency value—usually administered by a national central bank—in order to affect domestic demand, as well as the country's ability to sell goods and services abroad and to attract foreign investments. But tremendous amounts of money held by private institutions can now change hands so fast that the whole thrust of a country's domestic economic policy can be overwhelmed by nongovernmental financial transactions, let alone the similar effects that can be created by the actions of other, contrary-minded central banks.

Even more direct challenges to the capacity of the nation-state system to discipline the technological revolution, so that it serves rather than undermines the health and welfare of the earth's peoples, have emerged in the environmental field. Typically, the negative environmental side effects of many of the twentieth century's industrial innovations spread beyond the confines of the jurisdictions housing the sources of the disturbances. Much of the acid rain damaging aquatic resources, crops, and buildings in Canada originates south of the forty-ninth parallel; Scandinavian countries suffer a similar inadvertent assault from British industries. Industrial effluents entering the Rhine in France and Germany have dangerously polluted the waters that flow into coastal cities and ports along the North Sea. The Mediterranean became an infected toilet bowl in the 1970s because of its overuse as a receptacle for the industrial and human waste of the littoral states. Lethal radioactivity from the explosion of the Chernobyl nuclear reactor spewed across international boundaries in 1983. Working out respective national responsibilities for corrective action, as well as the liabilities for compensation of victims, is a delicate and controversial diplomatic task—particularly with the growing realization that adequate responses to the new threats in many cases may require permanent transborder monitoring and licensing agencies, perhaps with supranational adjudicatory and enforcement powers.

The most ominous environmental threats—those that degrade the essential biospheric conditions for sustaining human life on earth—are dramatically exposing the mismatch between the spans of effective control possessed by the sovereign nation-states and the globally ubiquitous sources of the dangers. By 1988 three-fourths of the countries of the world had not yet signed the Montreal Convention requiring abatement of activities that produce chlorofluorocarbons and other substances that deplete the ozone layer—the planet's natural stratospheric filter against cancer-producing radiation from the sun. There was an even more sluggish response to the consensus developing among atmospheric scientists that a continuation of the business-as-usual build-up of the atmospheric envelope of particulate matter (mainly carbon dioxide from the burning of fossil fuels) was producing a "greenhouse effect" that would drastically alter the world's climate and sea levels over the coming decades. Only draconian measures to alter existing patterns of energy consumption could slow down the alarming rate of global warming, but as of this writing, most national governments still had an "after you, Alphonse" posture toward the very costly and (for a time) growth-sacrificing policies required.

As anticipated by Barbara Ward and Rene Dubos in their pioneering 1972 treatise on the looming environmental threats, *Only One Earth:*

The global interdependence of man's airs [and waters] and climates is such that local decisions are simply inadequate. Even the sum of all local separate decisions, wisely made, may not be a sufficient safeguard. . . . Man's global interdependence begins to require, in these fields, a new capacity for global decision-making and global care.

Drifting Toward a Polyarchic World

If humankind continues to drift along the dominant currents identified in this and some other chapters in this volume, we are headed toward a largely unanticipated post–cold war configuration of world politics, in which the globe-spanning coalitions organized by the United States and the Soviet Union have lost a good deal of their coherence, and international relationships feature many overlapping and crosscutting alignments and antagonisms. Although there would not be an effective global steering group or agency to supplant the demise of the polarized world disciplined by rival hegemons, the newly forming situation would not necessarily be one of international *anarchy,* in the sense of an absence of rule, hierarchy, or law to constrain sovereign nation-states. Indeed, the currently emerging configuration exhibits some regional enclaves of international order; various still mutually loyal allies and a number of relatively stable balances of military power; increasingly dense and probably durable transnational commercial relationships; and a proliferation of functionally specific international regimes and institutions for regulating the growing economic, technological, and ecological interdependence of peoples (ranging from the International Monetary Fund to fisheries commissions to the International Civil Aviation Association).

The traditional concept of anarchy simply does not comprehend the complex situation of conflict and cooperation, hegemonic and subordinate relationships, interdependencies, and integrating and disintegrating communities that has developed in the last half of the twentieth century. I find the term *polyarchy* to be more descriptive of the intricate global pattern of many communities, spheres of influence, hegemonic imperiums, interdependencies, nationalisms, and transstate religious, ethnic, and ideological affinities—some of which overlap, some of which are concentric, some of which are substantially incongruent—that is the hallmark of the emerging post–cold war system.

Whether the emerging polyarchy will evolve in predominantly benign or dangerous ways cannot be forecast with confidence. But if the contemporary drift toward polyarchy is allowed to continue without channeling by alert and creative statecraft, the likelihood of the human species' being able to survive the next century in a relatively tolerable condition is at least strongly in doubt. It is theoretically possible that some of the benign tendencies of world polyarchy that are sketched below will take shape in the decades ahead. But simple prudence, it appears to me, requires that we operate on the assumption that these benign potentialities may be overwhelmed by equally plausible dangerous potentialities.

Benign Tendencies

The evolution of a largely benign variant of polyarchy is theoretically consistent with some of the trends identified in this chapter. Given the proliferation of groups with crosscutting memberships and interdependencies, the most influential political entities ought to be those that are major participants in the widest variety of coalitions and joint or multilateral ventures. Since they would have the largest supply of usable political currency—in effect, promissory notes for support on one issue in return for support on another—these entities should have more access to more of the levers of power than any others. Conversely, their threats to withdraw support would serve as powerful negative sanctions.

As in previous systems, power in the form of promises to apply or withhold military force would still be of decisive importance to countries in conflict over vital security interests. But in such a benign variant of polyarchy, threats to use military force would have little or even negative utility in bargaining over many of the nonsecurity issues around which coalitions would be forming and reforming. This is because the threat to apply military power would be seen to carry a high risk of devaluing the other bargaining chips in one's possession—alienating the confronting parties to the extent that they dismantled their cooperative projects and withdrew from coalitions to which the other side belongs. Similar disincentives also ought to work against extreme policies of economic coercion, such as the embargo attempted by the Arab oil producers against Israel's supporters in 1973, or efforts by the United States to strangle the economies of Cuba and other Marxist regimes in the Western hemisphere.

In the polyarchic system, with its elaborate overlapping of interests and coalitions, the most effective international bargainers ought to be those whose opponents on one issue are still their supporters on other issues. Therefore, if coercive strategies do seem to be required in a conflict over some particular issue, the prudent polyarchic statesman would nonetheless be restrained in the application of coercive pressures, for he would want to limit the diminution of his ability, on other issues, to positively influence those he is currently confronting harshly. He will be strongly constrained to threaten or inflict levels of pain well below those that would lead to total nation-to-nation or coalition-to-coalition hostility.

To wield effective bargaining power benignly in such a world, one would need to be well connected with many of the most influential groups and to be quite affluent in assets that are of value to these groups. But to state this condition is also to state why, at any given moment, there are likely to be many nations and groups that are unwilling to limit their political behavior to the nonviolent rules favored by the groups benefitting most from the peaceful variant of polyarchy.

The Dangerous Tendencies

It is equally plausible that the high order of unpredictability of political relationships in an unregulated global polyarchy would push world politics in the direction of a brutal might-makes-right system, where any group hoping to survive, let alone protect the range of its interests, would seek to acquire independent capabilities for self-defense—including nuclear weapons or other means of mass destruction or terror—to deter adversaries from intolerable provocations. This could well be the consequence of the severe erosion of the credibility of superpower alliance commitments, occasioned by the crisis of extended nuclear deterrence and the waning of cold war ideologies.

The question of how to avert this predicament is inseparable from the basic prognosis of an emerging polyarchy; for to the extent that the prognosis is correct in attributing the polyarchic trends to social and material forces that are largely irreversible, many of the standard "solutions" to the nuclear proliferation problem are bound to be ineffective. As argued below, more radical measures may need to be considered.

The emerging polyarchic world is also likely to be more conducive to major acts of nonstate terrorism than were either the cold war system or the traditional "anarchic" nation-state system. In the traditional nation-state system the population of the world is divided into definable jurisdictions under the control of sovereign national governments, each responsible for the transnational behavior of the people within its jurisdiction. In the evolving polyarchy, however, with its rapid and elusive mobility of materials and people, the existence of alienated subnational and transnational groups able to obtain sophisticated weapons and lethal substances on the open or black market portends widespread chaos and insecurity.

Government-to-government negotiations and threats in the traditional state system have a reasonable chance of prodding officials into apprehending and controlling the sources of international violence and criminality. But as the prevalence of transborder terrorism, hijackings, and drug running during the 1970s and 1980s attests, the reduced ability of national governments to be fully sovereign within their own jurisdictions in the polyarchic world could be particularly tempting to groups who are not squeamish about using indiscriminate violence to achieve their ends and who are too internationally dispersed to be targets of deterrent or retaliatory strategies.

Choices for U.S. Foreign Policy

As the emergent realities make the inherited geopolitical world view increasingly anachronistic, those responsible for the conduct of U.S. foreign relations will need to choose between significantly different courses of action. One course—passive adaptation—would be to react to the new threats and opportunities only as they become immediately unavoidable, responding pragmatically on the basis of assessments of near-term costs and benefits to particular national interests, situation-by-situation, without an overarching strategy to set basic direction and establish priorities. Another response, characteristic of the Reagan administration during its first few years in office, would be to recommit U.S. power to the restoration of a disciplined and ideologically unified "free world" coalition. The assumption here would be that under a revived strategic consensus on the priority of resisting the common enemy, cooperation—multilateral, if need be—to deal with the new challenges in the law and order, economic, environmental, and health and welfare fields will also be feasible. A third response is one of creative adaptation, attempting to anticipate the emerging new forces, and to ride with those whose energies can be turned to the task of constructing a just and peaceful world society consistent with basic American values.

Passive Adaptation

A "go with the flow" approach to threats and opportunities arising out of the polyarchic trends that are pulling apart the security alliances and challenging the viability of the nation-state system has the virtue of being compatible with the dominant atheoretical style of American policy making. The lawyers, economists, masters of business administration, and public policy school graduates who staff the high echelons of the foreign affairs and national security bureaucracies today are for the most part pragmatic marginalists—trained to think case-by-case, and to assess costs, risks, and benefits on the basis of what the market will bear in the immediate future. Moreover, because the increasing pluralization of American post–cold war international interests is reflected in a factionalization not only of the bipartisan foreign policy consensus but also of the consensus within the Republican and Democratic parties, there is very little prospect of mobilizing the necessary congressional support for a new foreign policy "grand design" at this time.

Unfortunately, if for these reasons the country continues to drift on the increasingly turbulent international tides, it may find itself in the worst of possible world situations. On the one hand, it may experience the severe gap between international commitments and capabilities that scholars like Paul Kennedy (author of *The Rise and Fall of the Great Powers*) foresee if we fail to take major corrective action, but it may also have a hangover world view and a set of conditioned foreign policy responses from the period of cold war bipolarity that are now both ineffective and excessively dangerous. For if the interests of America's erstwhile allies and international clients, as they perceive them, diverge from as often as they converge with U.S. interests, then U.S. efforts to invoke the old loyalties and impose an East versus West definition on crises where the sources of alignments and antagonisms are more complicated will tempt us inappropriately into romantic postures of confrontation with "the enemy." The perpetuation of such a foreign policy is likely to induce the Soviets also to overcommit themselves to foreign adventures if only to help their friends call the American bluff. But if we then refuse to retreat with the whole world watching, we increase the risks of being drawn into mindless and terrible games of chicken with the Soviets in which each side feels it will suffer too much humiliation from backing down.

Alternatively, a passively adaptive U.S. policy under a more dovish leadership might allow highly destabilizing asymmetry to develop in the evolving polyarchic world. It is most plausible, after all, for the breakup of international security alliances and the challenges to the predominance of the nation-state to be more rapid and extensive in the U.S.–led coalition than in the Soviet-led coalition. This could provide dangerous temptations for an imperialistically inclined Soviet leadership, and its allies in other countries, to stage aggressive *fait accompli* power plays (even involving the use of major military force) under the assumption that the United States and its friends are too disorganized to engage in timely counteraction.

A passive U.S. policy also is unlikely to avert another dangerous imbalance in the evolving polyarchy: the prospect of a worsening gap between the affluent and mobile segments of society and the poor and relatively handicapped segments, with the latter becoming increasingly frustrated and alienated. This scenario envisions the likelihood that in the United States, Western Europe, and Japan, where the transnational economy is developing most rapidly, and in portions of the Third World that become dependent on the finances and technologies of the affluent industrial world, power would gravitate to elements of society that are largely unaccountable to the less-developed, less-mobile elements. The upper transnational tier would probably comprise corporations and professionals in the high-technology fields, and bargaining among these corporate elites would largely determine the social order. As is already the case to a more limited degree, the transnational power structures would lack legitimate authority coextensive with their actual influence and scope of operation. Widespread discontent among the disadvantaged groups would increase the likelihood of active conflict, perhaps including physical combat and terrorism against and among the power elites, so that contracts and other intergroup commitments would lose stability. Polyarchy could thereby evolve into full-blown anarchy, where raw power is the principal social arbiter.

Restoration of the Cold War Consensus

If the principal observations in this chapter about the sources of change in the contemporary world are correct, then an American foreign policy directed toward reconsolidation of the free world coalition would be a nonstarter. Even the effort to reinstitute such a policy would undermine U.S. influence abroad and would ill serve the security and welfare of the American people. It would be contrary to the emergent realities to once again attempt to enlist friendly countries all around the world in a "strategic consensus" premised on the belief that the main threat to their independence and way of life comes from the Marxist-Leninists and that military power should again provide the principal means for containing this threat.

This kind of policy was tried in the early 1980s in reaction to the embarrassments suffered as a result of the passive adaptation policies of the 1975–1980 period. But both the need for such a policy and the opportunities for genuine success that it offered existed more in the minds of the inexperienced Reagan administration than in the world of practical international relations. The repolarization of world politics that it assumed and implied was totally inconsistent with the continuance of an efficacious U.S. strategy of continuing to play upon the Sino-Soviet split. It was also grossly at variance with the complex, crosscutting relationships characteristic of the Middle East. It risked alienating the United States from many of the more influential countries in Latin America, Africa, South Asia, and Southeast Asia. And it put the United States at cross-purposes with the international economic policies of its principal NATO allies and Japan, which were increasingly oriented toward developing new opportunities for commerce with the Soviet Union, the East Europeans, and the Third World. A dogged persistence in efforts to revive the now-anachronistic cold war consensus would have denied the United States the opportunity to take positive advantage of the switch in Soviet grand strategy instituted by Mikhail Gorbachev, allocating resources away from military aggrandizement and international power plays and toward domestic economic and political restructuring of the USSR, which Gorbachev correctly perceived would require a restoration of Soviet-American detente, further expansion of East-West commerce, and major arms limitation agreements.

Moreover, to iterate a central argument of this chapter, repolarization of world politics into two camps under the aegis of the United States and the Soviet Union would be inconsistent with the increasing inability of the superpowers to provide credible security protection to members of their own camps. Such a bipolar world would also be inconsistent with the unwillingness of most countries to let their ideological inclinations (which, in any event, have produced hybrid regimes with both capitalist and socialist features in most instances) interfere with currently advantageous commercial relationships, or with balance of power concerns vis-à-vis local adversaries.

Creative Adaptation

A U.S. foreign policy that would positively exploit the centrifugal forces that are eroding the superpower-led coalitions, and at the same time help the human species ward off the threats to its own existence, is also possible, in my judgment. Many of its ingredients are evident in adaptive measures already undertaken by the United States and other countries in particular fields, and in proposals by special international commissions of concerned and experienced world leaders. The larger challenge, to echo an observation made in 1968 by Henry Kissinger at another historic juncture for adapting U.S.

policy to emergent realities, is "philosophical" more than it is technical in nature.

The obsolescence of some of the principal arrangements for stabilizing the post–World War II international system need portend neither anarchy nor Armageddon, *provided* the forces causing the obsolescence are adequately understood. For then it will be realized that many of these forces can be channeled to the task of building a more civilized and just world order, and perhaps one even more conducive to the furtherance of basic American values than were the institutions of the cold war.

First, the centrifugal forces pulling apart the superpower-led coalitions can be harnessed to a deliberate strategy of de-polarization. The United States would become a credible champion of a world no longer bifurcated into rival ideological camps balancing one another's power through militarily bristling coalitions. We would encourage the genuine nonalignment of the Third World countries, instead of begrudgingly tolerating it, and even look forward to the dismantling of NATO and the Warsaw Pact.

More concretely, we would negotiate a series of military disengagement/neutralization arrangements with the Soviet Union, proceeding from tertiary to secondary to primary areas of traditional geopolitical importance. The premise of these arrangements would be that it was no longer the objective of either side to deny the other influence in these areas, but only to retain its freedom of access and opportunity to compete for influence. As a minimum, neither side would maintain military bases in the selected areas; optimally, both would also refrain from the military build-up of local and surrounding client states and movements.

This mutual military disengagement policy would be complemented by superpower tolerance for ideologically divergent domestic regimes, particularly among the nonaligned, but even in countries still nominally within each of their camps. There would be no insistence by the U.S. government, for example, that countries wishing to qualify for economic assistance renounce Marxist principles of political-economic organization and not be headed by Marxists or by governing coalitions that included Marxists; nor would the United States actively sponsor anti-Marxist groups with the objective of subverting or overthrowing the Marxist regimes. The Soviets, for their part, would allow members of their camp and client states more leeway to experiment with market economies and pluralistic political systems. The result might be some wins and some losses for democratic capitalism, but if Americans genuinely believe in the attractiveness of free societies as much as we claim, then we should be willing to take our chances in the competition if it occurs on a reasonably level playing field.

Both superpowers, in short, would respect the determination of indigenous peoples to resist outside domination and would rely principally on the strength of this basic cultural force to contain the other's imperial temptations. In a depolarized world where most countries maintained cooperative relationships with both the United States and the Soviet Union while remaining politically independent of each so that nonalignment was the norm, neither superpower would need to be compulsive about protecting its ideological brothers and sisters wherever they might be threatened. The United States and the Soviet Union each would be provided with acceptable justification for refusing to become militarily involved in conflicts whose outcome, one way or another, would not really threaten its security interests.

Of course, such a depolarization strategy would run the risk of stimulating other countries to acquire their own means of self-defense, including weapons of mass destruction—nuclear or otherwise. Although additional nuclear proliferation would not be primarily the fault of the depolarization of world politics (mutual superpower deterrence having already eroded the confidence of nonsuperpowers in the efficacy of extended deterrence), the likelihood of the depolarization strategy even marginally exacerbating the problem would make it imperative that collateral policies be pursued to denuclearize both global and local military balances and to delegitimize the actual use or threatened use of nuclear weapons. While achieving these policy objectives would be very difficult, their potential would still be far more promising than past efforts to avoid proliferation through mutual security alliances. Indeed, solving the nuclear proliferation problem through attempts to firm up alliance security guarantees is quixotic tilting at windmills. It worsens the very predicament it is supposed to deal with, since it gives new emphasis to superpower reliance on nuclear weapons while further exposing the nakedness of those who lack their own.

A nonproliferation regime with any real prospect for avoiding the otherwise inevitable spread of nuclear weapons in a polyarchic world would need to deemphasize the political and military value of such weapons for those already possessing them. This has been signalled repeatedly in the periodic review conferences among the signatories to the Nonproliferation Treaty, where the nonnuclear members have been angrily demanding that the superpowers take more seriously their pledge in Article VI of the treaty to pursue negotiations leading to their own nuclear disarmament. The message is unmistakable. The majority is unwilling to put up with its second-class status much longer, including subjecting themselves to international inspection to ensure that they are not violating the treaty, unless the superpowers themselves reduce their own reliance on nuclear weapons.

A new statecraft has also become imperative to deal adequately with new predicaments resulting from humankind's technological inventiveness: the porousness of national borders to the global circulation of people, things, money, and information—even in the face of national legislation to prevent unwanted ingress and egress; and the fact that the remarkable biospheric envelope that has sustained living organisms on this apparently unique planet is being placed in jeopardy by a variety of everyday human activities.

The new statecraft would build upon the dominant material and social forces that are simultaneously intensifying and diversifying the interactions and interdependence of peoples around the globe. It would be directed to constructing regimes of political and legal accountability congruent with the variegated and complex patterns of interdependence that will be featured in the emergent polyarchy. The normative

core of accountability in these regimes would be the principle
that those whose actions substantially affect the way other people live are accountable to those whom they affect, and normally should act only with the consent of those affected.
Procedurally, this would mean that the substantially affected
populations (or their representatives, as approved by them)
would be participants in the decision processes that authorize
those actions. Or, put negatively, internationally significant actions—whether by national governments, subnational governments, nongovernmental groups, transnational organizations,
or regional or international institutions—are illegitimate to
the extent that those opposing such actions have not been
given a fair opportunity to influence the relevant decisions.

Stated in the abstract, this principle, of course, begs many
important questions. How are the accountability-assuring, decision-making processes to be organized, and how will nonstate actors be represented in them? And, particularly for the
nonstate actors, which groups of people deserve to have representatives seated at the principal tables of decision? And on
what basis are the various groups to choose their representatives? (Should democratic principles of selection be insisted
upon, or should each population group be permitted its own
system of selection?) Which populations are indeed likely to
be "substantially affected" and therefore legitimate consent
groups in more permanently organized decision-making institutions in particular fields?

Most of the answers to these complex questions cannot be
derived directly from the core accountability principle. As in
the case of the analogous questions in complex domestic political systems, the answers will have to be worked out through
political bargaining among the groups that set up and participate in such regimes. But the fundamental philosophical shift
away from the constitutive principle of the inherited system—
national sovereignty—and toward mutual accountability as a
new central constitutive principle will in itself affect the bargaining. Liberated from the obsession with national sovereignty, political leaders would have more leeway to respond to
the new needs of human society—many of which cannot be

adequately tended to without a broader and more open conception of community than has prevailed for centuries in the modern state system.

The emergence of a denser network of institutions transcending national jurisdictions, with authority to resolve disputes and allocate resources in various fields that are critical to human security and well-being, would put a premium on the political leadership skills that enable effective functioning in the significant international forums. Leaders with a cosmopolitan orientation, who could speak and debate knowledgeably about the "world interest," would be sought by constituencies eager to defend their particular interests in the emerging global arenas of politics and governance, just as in a previous era of change leadership gravitated to those whose horizons extended beyond their own towns and villages and who could make cogent connections between the parochial interests of their immediate constituents and the more inclusive interests of the national polities then emerging.

Fortunately, the imperatives of such a policy of creative adaptation to the polyarchic trends of the contemporary world need not be inconsistent with an efficacious containment of Soviet aggressive expansion, should that threat rematerialize in the future, nor with the deepest values of American society, nor with a world order conducive to the continuation of the American democratic experiment.

It must be emphasized that the basic policy urged here does not contemplate the United States' unilaterally abandoning any of the standard foreign policy instruments or foreign commitments that we have relied upon in the post–World War II period to protect the security and well-being of the American people and to maintain a tolerable world order. There is no suggestion for nonreciprocal reductions in the U.S. military arsenal or for one-sided disengagement from international objectives over which the United States and the Soviet Union are in rivalrous contention. Rather, the argument is that the instruments the United States has been relying upon for prosecuting the cold war—and, indeed, the predominance of cold war geopolitics in the overall definition of U.S. world interests—have become woefully insufficient tools for a diplomacy responsive to the polyarchic trends now evident.

Nor should the arguments here in favor of enhanced international and transnational accountability be confused with inclinations that surface from time to time in the American body politic to slough off our accumulated global responsibilities by passing the buck to international organizations that are constitutionally ill-equipped to act vigorously. On the contrary, my brief is for even closer direct attentiveness by the United States to the needs of other peoples and to how our acts of commission (or omission), say, on matters affecting the global economy or the natural environment, can very significantly help or harm them. By championing the norm of international accountability for an increasingly interdependent world, Americans would also be acting in their own enlightened self-interest. It is no longer only the United States and its allies that can stabilize or destabilize the international monetary system. It is no longer only the advanced maritime powers that can interfere with vital lines of communication and transportation. And poor as well as rich industrialized societies can disrupt the planet's crucial environmental systems.

As world society becomes both more pluralistic *and* interdependent, neither the cold war nor the traditional nation-state system can simply be left behind. But those whose world view and statecraft are circumscribed by the inherited geopolitics will be.

5

National Security Strategy
for the 1990s

GRAHAM ALLISON

Introduction

At the last turning of the centuries, Theodore Roosevelt
proclaimed: "As the nineteenth century belonged to
Europe, the twentieth century will belong to the United
States." What about the twenty-first? Is the curtain now falling
on the American century? That proposition has dramatic appeal—and even a certain plausibility, as evidenced by the response to historian Paul Kennedy's *Rise and Fall of the Great
Powers*. Whatever its merits, this argument will undoubtedly
find a popular audience, quite possibly providing a plot for a
television series before the century closes.

GRAHAM ALLISON has served as dean of Harvard's John F.
Kennedy School of Government since 1977. He has also been a professor there since 1968. Dr. Allison is author of *Essence of Decision;
Remaking Foreign Policy; Hawks, Doves and Owls; Fateful Visions;* and *Windows of Opportunity.* He was a founding member of the Trilateral Commission, a director of the Council on Foreign Relations, and a director of several private corporations. From 1985–1987 he served as
special advisor to the secretary of defense.

The rise and fall of nations is heady stuff. In the realm of such "big think," criteria for distinguishing sense from nonsense are few. One can, for example, read all 677 pages of Kennedy's provocative analysis without learning that the U.S. share of world output today (roughly 23 percent) is identical to its share in the mid–1960s and—not accidentally I suspect—the same as it was before World War II.

Inviting as the topic is, this essay will not debate America's rise or fall. Rather, my assigned topic is to "state a realistic vision of the world that American foreign policy should be seeking to realize in the year 2000—and a strategy for achieving it." The editor asked that the essay not be primarily analytic or explanatory, but rather a piece of "advocacy" aimed at provoking debate. Finally, the editor suggested that I proceed as myself: a "centrist" who is unapologetically enthusiastic about the main lines of postwar American foreign policy. I recognize reasonable analysts both to my left and to my right who judge postwar American policy more failure than success. But I will leave to their essays and commentaries the task of balancing my advocacy of the proposition that, in the main, American postwar national security policy has been both well conceived and remarkably successful.

In the 1990s the United States will confront an environment profoundly different from that of the 1950s. This new world has emerged in no small part as a result of the success of the strategy America chose earlier. Advancing American objectives in the 1990s will not require—in my view—an abandonment of this postwar strategy. Nonetheless, we must take significant steps beyond the concepts and policies that have brought us to this point. Thus as a basis for addressing the question of a strategy for the 1990s, this chapter begins by examining strategy and performance in the first four decades of the postwar period.

The Postwar Period: National Security Strategy and Performance

By what yardstick should U.S. performance since the surrender of Germany and Japan in 1945 be measured? The critical question is: relative to what? Britain after World War I? The United States in the interwar period? Britain after the Crimea or after the Napoleonic Wars? Bismarck's Germany? Or, stretching even further, the hegemony of Rome or of Athens?

Suppose a Martian historian were to review earthly history since 1945. He or she would find the basic features of international affairs in the last half-century relatively clear. Indeed, some major characteristics of the decades to come should not be too opaque.

To Martian eyes, the main feature of postwar international politics would not be the expansion of the Soviet Union, the resurrection of Japan and Europe, or the multiplication of independent nations. Instead, it would be the *global expansion of American influence*—military, political, economic, and cultural. That influence was exerted in the form of ideals, ideas, and products; alliances, treaties, and international institutions; military forces second to none built at a cost exceeding $5 trillion; reconstruction efforts financed by foreign aid spending of more than $300 billion; the production of half the world's total manufactured products in the immediate aftermath of the war, and roughly a quarter thereafter. The extent and character of American influence fulfilled, indeed exceeded, Henry Luce's 1941 vision of "the American century."

As a careful scholar, our Martian would note that this extended American influence differed in significant ways from empires of the past. First, the phenomenon was more subtle than a classic "empire." The United States sought neither to exercise direct political control over key allies nor to return to traditional balance-of-power politics. Rather, it set out to build an alliance of values and interests. Second, the American commonwealth was remarkable for its fundamental generosity, its promotion of freedom, encouragement of democratic government, support of economic development, and commitment to international order. Never before had so much capital and energy flowed from the victors to the vanquished in the aftermath of war. Third, America's extended influence emerged as much by default as by design. The country responded to perceived threats in a manner that seemed so clearly defensive to most Americans that few even noticed the extent to which their nation shaped and maintained the political and economic order around the globe. Fewer still predicated their foreign policy views or aspirations upon any conscious desire to achieve or maintain global predominance.

Who in 1945 would have dared to hope that the new era of peace would last more than twice as long as the period between World War I and World War II? Who could have imagined that in twenty-five years, Germany, Japan, and Italy would have become leading democratic industrial powers? Few in the late 1940s or early 1950s expected that the ideals of freedom, individual human rights, and market oriented economies would triumph so soon and so decisively over the ideology of communism.

Issues of strategy in foreign policy are not much discussed in the United States. Americans are by nature more pragmatic than strategic. When the subject arises, it is most often to explain why a political system as open, and a government as fragmented, as ours cannot have a strategy. Alternatively, the subject is raised to a level of metaphysical abstraction far removed from recognizable policy choices.

In contrast, this chapter will adopt a common sense definition of strategy as a plan that identifies where one wants to go and how to get from here to there. While military usage distinguishes strategy from tactics, the concept of strategy has been adopted recently and enlarged by the American business community to incorporate the broad formula that defines an organization's business, its basic goals, and its policies for achieving those goals. Thus defined, macrostrategy combines the ends (goals) toward which a firm strives and the means (microstrategies, policies, and programs) by which it seeks to get there. The essential notion of strategy is captured in the relationship of means to ends—the combination of purpose, instruments, and policies that guides the enterprise.

Used in this way, strategy, like policy, is an "accordion" word. In addition to the broad goals of the firm, strategy incorporates the key operating policies through which a firm seeks to achieve its goals in each functional area: finance, research and development, manufacturing, and distribution. Effective corporate strategy must balance the goals of the organization with both its internal operating capabilities and its external opportunities and threats. A sustainable corporate strategy must match the particular strengths of the corporation with current and anticipated demand and competitive factors in its markets.

In assessing American national security strategy, I will use this enlarged conception, which includes connections between ends and means at several levels of specificity. A broad plan of action for achieving one's "ultimate" objectives generates requirements that, at the next level, become objectives for which one needs a strategy. To understand the nature of our strategy, therefore, it is necessary to examine the coherence of successive layers of linked means to ends.

As Nietzsche reminded us, the most common form of human stupidity is forgetting what one is trying to do. The assessment of strategy thus starts with objectives: what were we trying to do? A second issue is contextual: what features of the international environment constituted significant threats and opportunities? Then we come to microstrategies and plans: what was the plan of action for advancing these objectives in this environment—starting with the broadest strategic choices, but including successively more specific microstrategies for achieving important subordinate objectives? Finally, performance: given its objectives, how did the United States perform?

Objectives: What were the major objectives of postwar American foreign policy?

America's basic postwar national security objectives crystallized in the period of the Marshall Plan. They are stated clearly in the top secret (now declassified) National Security Council (NSC) document of 1950 that became the charter for postwar policy: NSC-68. The key "one-liner," reiterated annually in public documents thereafter, was: *"to preserve the U.S. as a free nation with our fundamental institutions and values intact."*

NSC-68 recognized that this goal includes security, political, and economic interests:

Militarily, the objective was to protect the American state, values, and institutions, and the freedom of American citizens against attack or intimidation—so far as possible without war.

Politically, the objective was to preserve the United States' central political values of freedom, individual rights, and democratic institutions.

Economically, the objective was prosperity: to sustain real improvements in the American standard of living and quality of life.

Beyond U.S. borders, the basic objective was to advance similar security, political, and economic interests of U.S. allies, friends, and other nations (in that order), so far as possible in the pursuit of primary objectives for the United States.

In a sharp departure from prior American foreign policy, postwar statesmen recognized—or defined—as "vital" the United States' interest in shaping an international order in which American freedoms and democratic institutions could survive and prosper. This view—defining interests beyond U.S. borders as vital—constitutes a choice of one strategic path, rather than others, as the preferred way to advance narrower American interests. It is thus appropriate to recognize that as an initial strategic choice and assess it, as well as successive choices, in terms of narrow, selfish, "bottom-line" American interests.

ENVIRONMENT: What features of the postwar environment constituted major threats and opportunities to American interests?

The primary threat to American national security has been posed by the Soviet Union. In 1946 when Ambassador George Kennan sent his "long telegram" from Moscow proposing a policy of containment, he feared that Soviet communism would become an ideological firestorm, engulfing key countries in Europe and Asia much as Islam had spread in the seventh century. Demoralized by a devastating war, exhausted economically, and faced with powerful indigenous Communist parties, these nations seemed especially vulnerable to Communist ideology. As the Soviet Union consolidated an outer empire of occupied countries in Eastern Europe, and threatened a combination of internal subversion and external intimidation in Greece, France, and Italy, a vigorous U.S. response seemed necessary to forestall a Soviet dominated Europe.

This Soviet threat was especially dangerous because the war had left both the United States' defeated enemies (Germany, Italy, and Japan) and its European allies in a severely weakened condition. Were the Soviet Union to add the military-industrial capacity of Europe or Japan to its own base, the resulting concentration of power in the hands of a single nation would violate a geopolitical axiom that had guided British policy for four centuries. Even without a well-developed geopolitical strategy, American pragmatists could see that such a consolidation of strength could pose an unacceptable threat to the United States.

Another critical contextual factor was the perceived need for new international institutions and conventions to preserve the peace, revive and stabilize the war-torn economy, and provide a framework for a wholly new order of international cooperation. American statesmen recalled vividly the failure of international institutions of the interwar years to prevent a depression that spilled over into politics and provided fertile ground for the growth of fascism in Germany and Italy. The League of Nations and European alliances had proved important at the time of the remilitarization of the Rhineland, or later at Munich, when resistance to Hitler's aggressive ambitions could have made a difference. Thus it was clear to most American policy makers that new international architecture was essential for any hope of a durable peace.

Moreover, nuclear weapons were transforming the character of war and military threats. As early as 1946, the strategist Bernard Brodie had concluded: "Thus far the chief purpose of our military establishment has been to win wars. From now on its chief purpose must be to avert them. It can have almost no other useful purpose." Previously, it was necessary to defeat an enemy's army before subjugating its population. Nuclear weapons and long-range delivery vehicles made it possible to destroy a society without engaging its conventional military forces—while also rendering large parts of its territory (and perhaps the planet) uninhabitable.

A final noteworthy feature of the postwar environment was the rapidly awakening nationalism of colonized people, coupled with deep-set imperial fatigue. Even before World War II, nationalistic aspirations in India were undermining British domination. Other colonized societies from Indonesia to Algeria to Kenya showed similar stirrings, while the benefits of empire for European powers exhausted by the war had declined significantly.

MICROSTRATEGIES: What was the plan of action for advancing U.S. objectives in this environment?

Most essays on this subject argue that the United States is incapable of pursuing a consistent course of action: the culture is too parochial and innocent; the government is too divided; and administrations change too frequently. Certainly, Americans spend more time debating issues that divide them than in celebrating what unites them. Yet beneath this superficial turbulence there has been a noteworthy steadiness of purpose and progress.

At the broadest level the United States had a number of options for advancing its interests in the postwar environment, including: (1) going it alone, as in the period after World War I; (2) seeking to dominate Germany and Japan on a long-term basis, perhaps as the Soviet Union did in Eastern Europe, or alternatively adopting some version of Henry Morgenthau's plan to turn Germany into a demilitarized dairy land; (3) creating a form of world government to which the United States and other nations would cede substantial sovereignty (for example, over nuclear weapons or other military forces); and (4) attempting to establish an extended American empire, either globally or in selected regions, perhaps enforced by preventive war to preclude acquisition of nuclear weapons by its rivals.

The strategy actually chosen was quite different from any of these. Nowhere was strategy fully articulated; indeed, few Americans understood it clearly, or even recognized that the United States had a grand strategy. Nonetheless, the strategy revealed in repeated operational choices and actions can be characterized in terms of its political, military, and economic thrusts. It can be analyzed in its application to specific nations and regions. In sum, the American postwar strategy was:

Militarily: to deter attack upon the United States and its vital interests by maintaining standing military forces and demonstrating a credible determination to use them in ways that would make the costs of aggression against American vital interests substantially greater than any benefit an aggressor could hope to achieve.

Politically: to promote democratic institutions and values, not just by example (as a "city on a hill") but by actively building democratic institutions around the world.

Economically: to create an international economic system that encouraged growth in commerce, investment, expansion of economic development, and stable monetary relations, thereby promoting expansion of the world economy and the U.S. economy, and providing incentives for market oriented economic progress in other nations.

These three strands were interwoven in a strategy to "contain" the overriding threat to U.S. interests: the Soviet Union. While George Kennan worried most about political containment of Soviet ideological initiatives, NSC-68 envisioned a combination of military, political, and economic means to frustrate Soviet advances in all three areas. Politically, the United States supported non-Communist leaders in Western Europe and opposed Communist subversion and intimidation. Economically, the Marshall Plan aided reconstruction of the nations of Western Europe, while American initiative in Japan played a similar role there, so that these nations would be able to resist Communist initiatives and have a growing stake in a free world alternative. Militarily, the North Atlantic Treaty Organization (NATO) and the U.S.–Japan mutual security treaty signaled vividly the United States' vital interest in the security of these regions; the presence of substantial American forces, the rebuilding of indigenous military forces, and the explicit American plans for forward defense drew the line of deterrence at the borders of our allies.

The least precedented strand in this strategy of containment called for the most substantial and sustained effort in world history to reconstruct the vanquished in the aftermath of war. That effort went beyond reviving the economies of Europe and Japan to a deliberate commitment to assist each country in becoming a viable democratic political system. While less discussed, and less fully articulated, it is clear that this U.S. policy went beyond the geopolitical ambition of preventing Soviet domination of these areas. It went beyond a reconstruction and recovery aimed only at restoring a world balance-of-power politics. It was based on a broader vision of what would be required to create a genuine community of nations, as well as a deeper and more optimistic faith in the responsibility-building characteristics of democratic institutions and procedures.

The Bretton Woods institutions constituted an attempt to prevent occurrences such as the Great Depression, which created the conditions in which Hitler came to power. The International Monetary Fund, the General Agreement on Tariffs and Trade, and the World Bank together created the institutional structure of an international economic system that promoted growth in the world economy and market oriented national economies. Although governance of these institutions was made to reflect the relative economic strength of member nations, no effort was made to assure absolute American predominance, even though such a demand might have been made. The first priority was security, which was seen to require mutual and collaborative effort by individually strong allied nations.

Toward the Third World, it is more difficult to identify a coherent U.S. strategy. U.S. policy projected American values.

Despite risks to its relations with our allies, that policy encouraged decolonialization and provided aid to encourage local economic development. It also established a network of alliances designed to inhibit the spread of communism, and offered security guarantees and an economic environment that encouraged development in countries of special security interest—for example, in Korea, Taiwan, the Philippines, Iran, and Turkey.

In dealing with nuclear weapons, America's broadest strategic choice emerged more by default than by design. The United States did not try to preserve an American monopoly of nuclear weapons, which would have necessitated preventive attacks on other nations seeking to acquire this capability. Nor did it cede control of nuclear weapons to an international authority, along the lines explored by the Baruch plan, or to stigmatize nuclear weapons as was done with chemical weapons. Instead, the United States integrated nuclear weapons into its defense posture as a key element of military containment through deterrence. Extended deterrence of Soviet attacks upon America's European allies relied explicitly on the threat of nuclear response. As the NATO alliance proved unwilling to meet its conventional force objectives beginning with the Lisbon goals of 1952, nuclear weapons became, in effect, a much cheaper substitute for conventional forces. But the chosen strategy implicitly accepted the eventual emergence of a condition of *mutual* assured destruction capacity. Thus by the late 1960s the Soviet Union had developed nuclear forces that, like their U.S. counterparts, could survive a first strike and retaliate to destroy the United States as a functioning society.

PERFORMANCE: How well did the United States meet its objectives?

In focusing on current problems, Americans tend to lose sight of enduring accomplishments. While chauvinism runs deep in the national psyche, so too does the tendency to blame the United States for whatever ills exist or are imagined. Moreover, assessments of policy are seldom undertaken in a purely analytical spirit. Usually they are intended to criticize opponents or inspire renewed efforts. It is thus difficult to disentangle the evaluation from the exhortation. For example, in 1962 Henry Kissinger's *Necessity for Choice* found the policies of the previous fifteen years a substantial failure. So too did Stanley Hoffmann's 1978 assessment, in *Primacy or World Order,* of Kissinger's strategy of detente in the late 1960s and early 1970s.

Without wishing to encourage complacency, I nonetheless judge the postwar record a substantial success. The peace of the past forty years compares favorably with the achievement of statesmen who declared World War I the "war to end all wars." At that fundamental level, the American alliance system has secured for the United States and its partners the most vital of all national interests in international relations: each state's continued existence and independence.

The international economic order fostered by the United States in the late 1940s has permitted the fastest and most sustained expansion of the world economy in history. Since 1950 the world product has quintupled to some $20 trillion. Americans' standard of living has tripled. While the U.S. share of world product declined from its anomalous high (nearly 50 percent) at the end of the war to 23 percent by the mid–1960s, the Soviet Union's share, which expanded slightly from 1945 to 1960, has shrunk slightly since then and now stands at about 11 percent. Together, the United States and its allies in Western Europe and Japan have a combined gross national product (GNP) more than five times that of the Soviet Union and its satellites.

Indicators of domestic political development and individual freedom are more difficult to formulate. Clearly, however, the past forty years compare very favorably in this regard with the preceding four decades, or with any comparable period of the modern era. The defeated nations of Germany, Italy, and Japan are now vigorous, democratic, market oriented societies. Democratic political systems, individual human rights, and the incentives of a market oriented economy are the dominant symbols and values of the era, West and East, North and South.

Containment of the Soviet Union has, over time, had the

effects George Kennan forecast: the emergence of divisions within the international Communist movement, the erosion of communism and the resurgence of nationalism, and the exhaustion of communism as an ideology that ultimately consumes itself. Moreover, to an extent Kennan never foresaw, the Stalinist attempt to plan and control every aspect of national life has proved incompatible with the degree of operating flexibility and independence of thought essential to effective participation in an advanced technological economy.

Thus assessed in terms of the objectives, fears, and hopes of the late 1940s, American postwar policy must be judged a striking success. Nonetheless, strategies chosen to address one set of problems have given rise to new problems in at least three areas of serious concern.

First, the U.S. nuclear strategy allowed the Soviet Union to acquire the military capability to destroy the United States as a functioning society. In part, this was an inescapable consequence of the technological fact that offense dominated defense in this era. A policy of preemptive attacks or permanent domination to prevent the Soviet Union and other nations from acquiring nuclear weapons would likely have proved even less acceptable, as would the creation of an international institution to manage the nuclear weapons. Such options would probably have required continuous American military action to secure and sustain Soviet compliance. But the fact remains: the basic national security strategy that has preserved the United States as a free nation has also left it vulnerable to destruction. Moreover, as other nations become able to deliver substantial numbers of nuclear weapons by ballistic missile or aircraft against American targets, the ability of the U.S. strategy to preserve our fundamental institutions and values is arguably at greater risk than at any previous point in our history.

Second, while applauding the massive growth of the world economy over the past four decades, we must nonetheless worry about the viability of a global village in which more than a billion people (one-fourth of the total population) try to survive on less than $200 each year. The unevenness of economic development, particularly in Africa and some regions of Asia and South America, threatens our values, and ultimately our security.

Third, the capacity of the U.S. economic base to provide sustained real increases in the average standard of living of American citizens is less certain today. The danger emerges partly from external threats, but even more importantly from failures within. Perhaps most important, the very success of U.S. attempts to foster the growth of freestanding, productive, fiercely competitive Western trading partners has led to a situation where the success of the national economic strategy adopted by the United States is far more dependent upon the cooperation—even, as at present, the forbearance—of other nations.

In the British game of cricket, after a particularly successful "at bat," a team can voluntarily "declare" its turn at bat over and play defense against the opponent's batsmen, and thus hope to win the game. Were it possible for the United States to stand down on the record of the postwar period, one could be tempted to do so. It is not likely that our batsmen will be as successful in their next inning. But international relations provide no such option. The game continues without respite, bringing an unending succession of new opponents with new pitchers and batsmen never encountered before.

A Strategy for the 1990s: Beyond the Cold War?

The 1990s could see the end of the bipolar system of international relations—that is, the end of a bipolar system primarily defined by the cold war. The distinguishing feature of that protracted struggle was not the great power competition that Tocqueville foresaw between the United States and the Soviet Union, but an ideological competition between "freedom and slavery," in the words of NSC-68. If the cold war ends in the 1990s, it will be in victory for the ideas of individual freedom and human rights, market oriented economies based on incentives for individuals, and democracy. Such a victory is far from won. While the Soviet Union is adopting many of the words and symbols of the West, Soviet practice remains quite different. The Soviet movement toward Western values is fundamentally a pragmatic and distinctly uncomfortable adaptation forced by the failure of Stalinist economic and social structures. Gorbachev and his associates see the current period as a *pereduishka,* a breathing space in which the Soviet Union does what is necessary to maintain its position in the world.

Nonetheless, events now unfolding may represent the opportunity NSC-68 sought—*if* the West can muster the imagination to engage the Soviet Union aggressively in restructuring Soviet relations, within and without, in ways that advance our interests and values. We must ask ourselves, what agenda would we wish for a Soviet leadership under current circumstances? What agenda could a Soviet leadership viably pursue to reach our preferred settlement of the cold war? The similarity between that agenda and Gorbachev's today is, I believe, not coincidental.

The challenge to the West in the 1990s is first of all *conceptual:* to stretch our minds beyond familiar, comfortable application of concepts and policies to grapple with new opportunities and new threats. The opportunity is reminiscent in some ways of 1944, when the Allies began to recognize that victory was probable. It became necessary to consider terms of surrender and the postwar settlement: what did the United States want beyond the defeat of Germany and Japan? What should the victors try to create thereafter? This period is also, paradoxically, one of heightened risk. What if Gorbachev succeeds in carrying through on his threat to "deny the West an enemy"? More precisely, what if he effectively denies the West the *perception* of the prospect of being hanged separately unless its members hang together? Absent this vivid threat, the attempt to sustain the structures of NATO and the U.S.–Japan treaty in the 1990s will prove more challenging than in any prior decade. Thus if Gorbachev sustains present external policy, the 1990s could see shifts in the tectonics of international politics: not only along the primary axis, but along the secondary and tertiary axes as well.

How far does Gorbachev mean to go? How long will he remain in office, or his "revolution" continue? How likely is an explosion in Eastern Europe, or a Western economic depression, a great surge of protectionism, or even a revolution in Mexico? Without answers to such questions, statesmen must nonetheless act. Choosing under uncertainty risks great mistakes, but waiting for events to clarify the facts misses great opportunities. As Winston Churchill observed, if France or Britain had resisted Hitler in 1936 when Germany remilitarized the Rhineland, or even in 1938 during Germany's confrontation with Czechoslovakia, the German generals would almost certainly have turned Hitler out of office. World War II, as we knew it, would have been avoided. No doubt, a Western leader who took such actions would have been criticized for acting too quickly or too forcefully. Hitler would now likely be regarded as a misunderstood nationalist. By the time the facts are clear for all to see, it is frequently too late to act effectively or at acceptable costs.

OBJECTIVES: What should be the major objectives of American foreign policy in the 1990s?

America's basic national security objectives in the 1990s remain unchanged: preserving the United States as a free nation with its fundamental institutions and values intact. This goal requires security from attack or intimidation, sustenance of our political values, and continued real increases in standards of living—first for ourselves, and thereafter for allies, friends, and others. Strategic choices about how to achieve these national objectives define subordinate objectives for successive layers of strategy.

ENVIRONMENT: What features of the environment of the 1990s must be addressed by strategy?

The truly significant features of the international environment of the 1990s are not given as simple facts but have to be creatively identified. Changes in the underlying structure of international politics are producing continental and regional shifts. The first task is therefore conceptual: to understand what is happening and why. Intellectually, we must begin to stretch:

Beyond containment of an ideologically fervent, emerging super-power on the rise, to policies for coping with an ideologically exhausted military superpower on the decline. In short, containment worked. The combination of time, NATO's determination not to yield to the Soviet Union any exploitable military advantage, the performance of Western market oriented economies, and active opposition to Soviet external adventures has made Moscow increasingly realistic in its assessment of the fact, and even the causes, of failure. Now we must begin establishing the terms on which the Soviet Union can become a "normal" country and enter into the industrial democracies' economic and political order.

Beyond traditional Western alliances against aggression by an unambiguous hostile adversary, to a clearer, positive articulation of the values and interests, and indeed the international order, that the Western industrial democracies are *for.* Possibilities for the allies in the 1990s differ profoundly from the 1950s, not just in the changed Soviet threat. Europe and Japan have recovered as successful industrial democracies. Japan and Germany now outperform the United States in per capita GNP. A new array of divergent interests will become more salient. There are no bigger question marks about the 1990s than the international roles to be chosen by Europe and Japan.

Beyond bipolarity. In the year 2000, the Soviet Union will almost certainly remain the single largest military threat to the United States. Nonetheless, it has fallen behind Japan to third place among national economies of the world. If the European Economic Community were taken as a single unit, the Soviet Union would be fourth. If China can sustain the economic growth rates achieved in the past decade, by the year 2000 its GNP will approach the Soviet Union's. Other significant regional powers include India and Brazil. Thinking beyond the clarity of bipolarity to the variability of a world of multipolarity will tax even the most imaginative American strategists.

Beyond nuclear deterrence based on a credible threat to deliberately initiate a nuclear war. Loose talk at Reykjavik about "getting rid of all nuclear weapons" frightened many Europeans and Americans. Strategists like Henry Kissinger criticized President Reagan for stigmatizing nuclear weapons. But the deeper truth is that before Ronald Reagan, nuclear weapons were stigmatized by the facts. A policy that promises to destroy the people it would defend is difficult to sustain in a democracy. As Kissinger has observed, "I cannot believe that a democratic public will indefinitely sustain a policy that bases security on the capacity for total civilian devastation." When the United States could attack the Soviet Union with nuclear weapons without suffering a retaliatory response, that threat had real plausibility. As the Soviet Union acquired a survivable second-strike capability against the United States, the U.S. threat was transformed into a threat to commit mutual suicide. Such conditions led President Reagan to his bumpersticker that captures the heart of the matter: "A nuclear war cannot be won and must therefore never be fought."

But what then of NATO's current strategy of "flexible response," which relies upon NATO's initiation of the use of nuclear weapons to deter a Soviet conventional attack? The credibility of that posture has been strained by recurring questions since the late 1950s about whether the United States would deliberately trade Boston for Bonn; by assertions of former Secretary of Defense Robert McNamara and others that the United States never intended to fulfill its NATO commitment to use nuclear weapons to meet a conventional attack; and by statements like former German Chancellor Helmut Schmidt's assertion that "after the first explosion of a single nuclear weapon on German soil, the German Army will surrender."

At a minimum, such statements demonstrate that the leaders of the alliance largely have lost the capacity to talk coherently to their publics about nuclear weapons, or indeed to themselves. Without some cogent account of a role for nuclear weapons that stops short of destroying those defended, NATO is highly vulnerable to Gorbachev's campaign to denuclearize Europe.

Beyond East-West Competition in the Third World. Instead of considering the less developed countries primarily as a front line along which to resist Communist expansion, the advanced industrial nations need to refine and differentiate their strategies for addressing these countries.

Beyond sovereignty understood as "complete independence," to a more refined conception of autonomy within a setting of tightening interdependence. An ongoing technological revolution relentlessly undermines national boundaries. Globalization of economic activity means that even actors as powerful as the United States can no longer unilaterally maintain the value of their currencies or domestic interest rates. Pollution, radioactivity, and acid rain fall on capitalists and socialists alike. Nuclear arsenals have denied all nations, including the superpowers, the capacity to independently assure their citizens' safety or their nations' survival. Coping with contradictions between technologically driven facts of life on the one hand, and historically determined jurisdictional sovereignties on the other, will be the institutional challenge of the decades ahead.

Beyond complacency about the American economic base. In 1950 American economic dominance was widely taken for granted. No one then imagined an era in which Japanese products would be more competitive in world markets than American ones—and even less that Japanese goods would be preferred by American consumers. Most postwar planners accepted America's economic base as a self-renewing resource that could be spent freely to advance security and political interests. Today, observers of various political stripes are leaping from greater economic parity and continued American defense spending to foggier concepts of "imperial overstretch" and misleading explanations of a misidentified "American decline."

In fact, the U.S. share of world GNP has *not* declined since the mid–1960s. It remains around 23 percent—as it was in 1938. The point the "declinists" take as the natural baseline, 1950, was in fact the exception in this series—when America produced almost half of the world GNP, reflecting the exceptional circumstance of the aftermath of war. Thus the real issue is not American decline from this point, or even relative decline, since the best current projections have the United States maintaining its current position in the year 2010. Rather, the issue is the weakening of the American economic base that has resulted from a combination of declining productivity and excessive borrowing for consumption.

In sum, the intellectual challenge is to begin thinking beyond the cold war: beyond concepts and policies created for the frozen environment of ideological competition, a single military threat, American nuclear superiority, American economic and political preeminence. With the loss of American nuclear preeminence and military superiority, concepts such as nuclear deterrence, extended deterrence, escalation control, and strategic stability no longer comfortably fit the phenomena they were invented to describe. So too with many of our notions in the realms of economics, politics, and culture. Concepts that have done so much effective work over the past decades need not be discarded. Rather, the task for the period ahead is to extend and refine these ideas in order to replenish our conceptual arsenal. As we reaffirm the central purposes of postwar American policy, we must stretch our concepts—and our minds.

MICROSTRATEGIES: What broad plan of action should the United States adopt to advance its objectives in this environment?

Two principal conclusions follow from my diagnosis of the environment of the 1990s. First, the changes now under way are likely to be revolutionary—in the sense that they will strain to the point of obsolescence familiar concepts for characterizing our problems. Second, the United States must actively collaborate with other allied nations both to understand the environment and to choose a strategy for addressing it. Neither the diagnosis nor the prescription can be "made in America." The challenge is not to impose our solutions but to evoke the creative energies of others. A workable strategy for the next phase must emerge from a genuinely consultative process. Here I shall outline four key strategic issues Americans should be debating among themselves and discussing with their major allies. In addressing each issue, I shall first state what I believe to be the appropriate strategic objective, and then sketch an agenda of possible actions.

1. Restoring the American Economic Base. The U.S. objective should be to secure America's position as the world's largest and most productive economy for the next half-century, ensuring sustained real increases in our standard of living and providing the base for preserving our security and our values. To this end, we must eliminate the twin American deficits—the budget deficit and the trade deficit—in an orderly fashion that avoids a deep American recession, a global depression, or a hard landing for the dollar that undermines the financial system.

The long-term health of the U.S. economic base depends primarily on what we do at home. George Bush should summon the American people to a national effort. During President Reagan's first term, his commitment to "rebuild American military strength" succeeded in increasing defense spending by more than 50 percent in real terms. Restoring the American economic base, unfortunately, will require decades of much harder choices and actions.

Eliminating the federal deficit is a relatively straightforward task, once it is faced seriously. The current Bipartisan Economic Commission offers an appropriate device for political absolution from all the sins required—if the Bush administration will accept it. Alternative means of deficit reduction abound. Every penny on the gas tax generates $1 billion of federal revenue. Thus, a $1 increase in the gas tax would raise

$100 billion (minus some cutback in consumption), encourage conservation of a scarce resource, help reduce the trade deficit, and still leave American gas prices below those in Europe and Japan. In the near future, unfortunately, powerful political considerations are likely to rule out such an increase. A more likely outcome is a mixture of higher taxes on gasoline, luxuries, alcohol, and tobacco, combined with limits on the growth of domestic and defense spending, which could eliminate the federal deficit in an orderly, flexible manner over the next four to five years.

Increasing the rate of savings, which has fallen to its lowest level in American history, will be more difficult. The policy options include increased incentives, such as individual retirement accounts (IRAs); a federally guaranteed indexed savings bond; restriction of consumer credit; greater attention to the public and private policies that could encourage savings, such as providing annual wage and salary increases in a single lump sum rather than as part of the monthly check; and making credit card borrowing less attractive. More ambitious programs would tax consumption or impose a value-added tax.

The toughest nut on the list of needs is increasing productivity. After almost three decades of annual increases that averaged about 3 percent, American productivity growth began to fall in the early 1970s, and growth has averaged only 1.1 percent per year since 1979. A national campaign to increase productivity will have to improve the quality of education significantly (e.g., by applying technology, or engaging businesses and universities in a competition to improve local schools), as well as encourage capital investment, more targeted research and development, entrepreneurship, and initiatives to shrink the gap between technological invention and marketable product.

Beneath the symptoms these steps address, some analysts see deeper cultural causes, recalling economist Joseph Schumpeter's analysis of the "contradictions of capitalism" more than fifty years ago. The ethic of consumption that fuels capitalism also undermines the character necessary to sustain saving and increase productivity. There is undoubtedly some truth to this observation. But finding effective ways to revive the ethic of production remains as illusive as it is essential.

Rebuilding the American economic base will also require work abroad: in eliminating barriers to American exports and strengthening international institutions to manage ever-tightening independence. Breaking down protectionist barriers in countries like Korea, Singapore, and Japan will require more than discussions about the virtues of free trade. Washington's trading partners must revise expectations and practices learned over decades in which Americans were willing to provide relatively open markets without insisting on reciprocity, reflecting the subordination of economic concerns to security interests. Americans' singular approach to business-government relations will be a handicap in this effort. But the U.S. government must work aggressively to obtain a level playing field for American producers.

The rapid emergence of a global economy—in capital, technology, goods, and increasingly even labor—raises deep questions about how to assure the orderly functioning of such markets. After October 19, 1987, the Brady Commission discovered that the New York and Chicago securities markets are not entirely separate, and thus cannot be effectively regulated on an entirely independent basis. The same could be said of other markets—such as London or Tokyo. The Group of Seven's recent success should not encourage complacency. Rather, taking advantage of what the Seven have learned about monetary and fiscal coordination, efforts should be made to regularize this process and bring it within the framework of international institutions and international law.

2. *Aggressive Engagement of the Soviet Union in Setting the Terms on Which to Settle the Cold War and Integrate the Soviet Union into the Political and Economic Order Established by the Industrial Democracies.* The United States' first strategic objective must be to maintain and adapt the structures that have prevented war and won the peace for the past four decades. These begin with NATO and the U.S.–Japan treaty. Far from

being "solved," the challenge of avoiding nuclear war remains to be addressed every day. In fact, the coming years are likely to be particularly dangerous. The least implausible scenario for a nuclear war starts with miscalculation, accident, and inadvertence that give rise to a conventional war, which in turn escalates to a nuclear war. As Soviet power declines, ambitions in Eastern Europe, China, and elsewhere, long held in check, will rise. Historically, periods of transition in the relative positions of great powers are fraught with risks of uprisings, put downs, and other events that spill over—as did Austria-Hungary's attempt to settle its score with Serbia in 1914.

Talk of "settling the cold war" unsettles many for whom this is one of few fixed points. But we should remember what we were trying to accomplish. NSC-68 was quite explicit. With respect to the Soviet Union, the United States' objective was (1) to "frustrate the Kremlin's design" (which the document identified as the "domination of the Eurasian land mass") and (2) to "foster a fundamental change in the nature of the Soviet system." Toward that end, NSC-68 recommended the combination of military, political, and economic strategies described above. But containment was never conceived as an end in itself.

Rather, NSC-68 identified its objective precisely, and its answer deserves to be quoted at some length:

1. It is only by developing the moral and material strength of the Free World that the Soviet regime will become convinced of the falsity of its assumptions and the precondition for workable agreements can be created. By practically demonstrating the integrity and vitality of our system, the Free World widens the area of possible agreement and thus can hope gradually to bring about a *Soviet acknowledgement of realities* which in sum will eventually constitute a frustration of the Soviet design.

2. Short of this, however, it might be possible to create a situation which will induce the Soviet Union to accommodate itself, with or without conscious abandonment of its design, to *coexistence on tolerable terms* with the non-Soviet world. Such a development would be a triumph for the idea of freedom and democracy. It must be an immediate objective of U.S. policy.

3. [Moreover] there is no reason, even in the event of war, for us to alter our overall objectives. They do not include unconditional surrender, the subjugation of the Russian people, or a Russia shorn of its economic potential . . . Rather, *these objectives contemplate Soviet acceptance of the specific and limited conditions requisite to an international environment in which free institutions can flourish,* and in which the Russian people will have a chance to work out their own destiny. [Emphases added.]

In sum, NSC-68 asserted: "We should limit our requirement of the Soviet Union to its participation with other nations on the basis of equality and respect for the rights of others."

If Soviet deeds matched Gorbachev's words, the Soviet Union would be nearly there today. Unfortunately, that is not the case. To "take Gorbachev at his word," as German Foreign Minister Hans Dietrich Genscher and others have proposed, is to confuse words with actions. But Western critics who dismiss Gorbachev's words and actions as mere propaganda are equally misguided.

The task for the 1990s is to formulate an aggressive diplomatic agenda aimed at *testing Gorbachev at his word.* The basic recipe for a program of testing begins by clearly identifying U.S. interests and objectives. Second, we should examine Gorbachev's "new thinking" for concepts and statements that indicate a willingness to move in directions that further our interests. Third, we should devise proposals for Soviet actions that advance Western interests—propositions that Gorbachev cannot refuse if he means what he says. Such tests can be devised across the entire agenda of U.S.–Soviet relations.

Something profound is happening in the Soviet Union today. We are witness to the early stages of a "quiet revolution," the conclusions of which neither Gorbachev nor we can foresee. As NSC-68 envisaged, Gorbachev's efforts to adapt Soviet actions spring from a "frustration of the Soviet design" fostered by failures of the Soviet system and successes of Western containment. In his indictment of the failings of the Soviet economy and society, Gorbachev is as harsh and penetrating as any Western observer. He states the bottom line bluntly: unless the trend of the last decade is reversed, the Soviet

Union will not enter the twenty-first century as a great power.

The core of his response has two elements: common sense and pragmatism. Nothing is more revolutionary in the Soviet system than common sense. Previously, ideology so distorted common sense and required so many epicycles of rationalization that most Soviet citizens had a better idea of what was not true (namely, the things that were said officially) than what might actually be so. Gorbachev is clearly committed to moving Soviet rhetoric toward "calling things by their real names," as he puts it.

Gorbachev's pragmatism is also heretical, for it implies a willingness to experiment with alternative ways of achieving a goal. Prior Soviet planning presumed a central monopoly of wisdom in the analysis of problems and design of a plan, and a monopoly of power in assigning players the roles they should perform in carrying out the script. In contrast, pragmatism requires that individuals be engaged and active enough to think for themselves and to adapt as they go.

At its core, Gorbachev's new thinking is a radical rejection of the Stalinism that has ruled the Soviet Union for more than half a century. Like Luther's denunciation of papal authority, Gorbachev's acknowledgement that the Communist party of the Soviet Union has no "monopoly of truth" has earthshaking implications. *Glasnost* is predicated on the incandescent idea that truth emerges from discussion and debate among many people, each of whom lays claim to a piece of reality. *Perestroika* revises the notion of an economy centrally planned by all-knowing authorities, in favor of greater local autonomy, individual incentives, and, over time, market forces. As—and if— the Gorbachev revolution continues, we should expect to see additional repressive features of the Stalinist society subjected to scrutiny, and buried.

These fundamental changes have significant implications for Soviet national security policies: primarily a subordination of foreign policy to domestic priorities, starting with reduced investments in the defense sector. The Soviet Union cannot solve its internal problems without a substantial relaxation of competition with the United States. Moreover, substantial restructuring of the Soviet economy will require resources now consumed by the Soviet military.

Gorbachev's evident ambition is to assure and even enhance the Soviet Union's position as a great power. But, fortunately, U.S. interests do not require that the Soviet Union cease to be a great power. Gorbachev is trying to cope with competing challenges: to secure his position in the struggle for power at home; to shift resources from defense to more productive investment; and to constrain Western arms through arms control. At the same time, he is obviously sorting out what he really thinks about a confusing, changing international environment. It would be a mistake to assume that Gorbachev has mapped out the future in a clearly specified long-term plan. Rather, he and his associates see the world as in flux as they journey into uncharted territory.

The West has an opportunity to reach beyond containment and engage the Soviet Union in ways that encourage Gorbachev's reformist instincts to restructure Soviet external relations and internal institutions. (That, after all, is what we set out to do.) Externally, Gorbachev says:

The fundamental principle of the new political outlook is very simple: nuclear war cannot be a means of achieving political, economic, ideological or any other goals. . . . Security can no longer be assured by military means. . . . Attempts to achieve military security are preposterous. . . . The only way to security is through political decisions and disarmament. (*Perestroika: New Thinking for Our Country and the World,* 1987)

If Gorbachev really believes this, what should the Soviet Union be prepared to do? Clearly it should be willing to restrain the continued growth and modernization of the Soviet military establishment, which now consumes 15 to 20 percent of the Soviet GNP. Over time, such a government should be prepared to reduce Soviet military forces sharply and restructure them. So far, there is little evidence that Gorbachev's fine phrases have been translated operationally in the military realm. Defense spending has increased, both nuclear and conventional forces have been modernized, and new equipment has been delivered to front-line forces. On the other hand, Gorbachev has accepted NATO's proposal to eliminate inter-mediate-range nuclear forces, including highly intrusive verification procedures on Soviet territory. That success invites further Western testing. Note the formula for NATO's success in this case: a reasonable although radical proposal combined with persistence and hard bargaining. NATO should be testing Gorbachev's words about nuclear weapons with proposals to restructure the Soviet nuclear arsenal in ways that reduce the threat of surprise attack (i.e., by eliminating the first-strike weapons Americans fear most: the Soviet heavy, land-based SS-18 missiles).

Nowhere does the USSR pose a greater military threat to American vital interests than in Europe. Hence the appeal of Gorbachev's concept of Europe as a "common security house" in which tenants can legitimately provide for their own security—but not by stockpiling explosives that could destroy the building. At the June 1988 Moscow summit, Gorbachev reiterated his acceptance of the Western concept of an Atlantic-to-the-Urals arms reduction zone. His proposals included an exchange of data on conventional forces in this zone, verified by on-sight inspection; the identification and elimination of asymmetries in the forces of the two sides; and the restructuring of conventional forces in Europe to give them a solely "defensive" orientation. His stated criteria in such restructuring is "to eliminate the capacity for surprise attack of offensive operations."

It is a pointed indictment of U.S. leadership in NATO that such promising suggestions have been spelled out by Gorbachev alone, essentially talking to himself. Little wonder that allied publics saw Gorbachev as more interested in peace than President Reagan. NATO should test Gorbachev's seriousness by immediately taking up his offer to exchange and verify data about both sides' military forces. Our response should set the terms of reference for an exchange that could include a detailed order of battle broken down to the level of regiment or battalion, including location, designation, personnel levels, and equipment by type and model. While data on NATO forces are publicly available, Soviet data have been top secret since 1917, despite fifteen years of Mutual Balanced Force Reduction Talks. If Gorbachev responds positively, NATO should quickly follow with a detailed proposal to reduce the Warsaw Pact's capacity for surprise attack and large-scale offensive operations. The largest asymmetries—and the key to surprise attack capability—are the tens of thousands of Soviet tanks and artillery in Eastern Europe and the western Soviet Union.

The West should also encourage "confidence-building measures" to increase transparency and constrain military activities. The intermediate nuclear force (INF) treaty proves Gorbachev's willingness to be less secretive about Soviet territory and military forces. NATO should propose creating mutually recognized trip wires that the Soviet Union would have to trigger in preparing for war. These measures should include positioning permanent international inspectors at militarily important arms depots, airfields, fuel dumps, railheads, and perhaps even command and control centers; specific constraints on forward deployment of tanks, artillery, bridging, and mine-clearing equipment; and a year-in-advance schedule for force mobilization and maneuvers.

The West should also follow up on Gorbachev's demonstrated willingness to pull back from regional conflicts. Soviet withdrawal from Afghanistan without victory blatantly refutes the predominant Western geopolitical explanation of Moscow's intentions there: Afghanistan was a war that a committed Soviet Union was determined to win and could not afford to lose, a calculated step in Russia's centuries-old quest for warm water ports, with domination of the world's strategic oil reserves as the unspoken prize. Yet Gorbachev has accepted defeat in Afghanistan with only the fig leaf of calling it stalemate, without even demanding a "decent interval." Similarly, he has encouraged Vietnamese withdrawal from Kampuchea and urged Cuban troops out of Angola.

The lesson is that the West should actively engage Gorbachev in adjusting in ways that advance our interests. Nowhere is this approach more promising than in Central America, where Gorbachev has explicitly supported "the Contadora process and the Guatemalan accords" for moving toward a political settlement. Nevertheless, Moscow continues to ship arms to the Sandinistas (more than a billion dollars' worth of Soviet bloc aid in 1987) and to guerrillas in El Salvador and Guatemala. The United States should join the Central American presidents in proposing immediate cessation of all military aid (Soviet, Soviet bloc, Cuban, and American) to the Sandinistas and the contras, and devising effective guarantees that the Nicaraguan government will cease all material support for insurgent movements.

Internally, Gorbachev's *glasnost* and *perestroika* steadily reduce the "slavery" that was a major target of NSC-68. Progress on releasing political and psychiatric prisoners and allowing emigration for refuseniks has come slower than we would like, but faster than ever before. Economic restructuring moves toward markets and incentives, with the openly expressed hope of joining the world economy rather than being left behind. The West should explain that if the Soviet Union hopes to become a "normal" participant in international trade and to produce goods that are globally competitive, it must reorganize its internal pricing system so that it can meet the terms for inclusion in the General Agreement on Tariffs and Trade, as China has been working to do. The benefits to the West of economic decentralization (delegating economic decision making to the heads of industries, firms, farms, and collectives) should not be underestimated. Decentralization of economic power inevitably weakens the central monopoly of political authority. A totalitarian political system is not compatible in the long run with a decentralized market economic system, because people who have economic power have power per se.

The West should continue to push Moscow on both economic and human rights issues. Both publicly and privately, we should explain why a society that is less repressive at home is more trustworthy abroad. Reforms that provide greater freedom for Soviet citizens and restrain ideologically motivated expansionism will erode the moral features of the Soviet regime that most offend Western values and interests.

Such a strategy of testing Gorbachev is not without risks. As the USSR passes such tests, some Western observers will proclaim prematurely that "peace has broken out." We could be tricked. The web of interdependence we spin could entangle the West more deeply than the Soviet Union. Nonetheless, consider the dangers presented by the alternatives. The surest way to undermine the alliance is to pretend that nothing is really changing in the Soviet Union. Lectures by Americans to Europeans on the perils of gullibility only reinforce their determination to prove us wrong. Should Gorbachev fail, his successor might pursue similar internal reforms, although more slowly and with a less active foreign policy. Equally plausible, however, and considerably more dangerous would be a new leader who tried to exploit Soviet military advantages of the moment in the hope of preventing decades of relative decline.

A strategy of testing Gorbachev at his word will absorb a decade of Western imagination and initiative. It is fair to ask: to what end? Our primary purpose in pressing for bold actions that follow logically from Gorbachev's bold words should be to establish a sustainable structure for *peaceful competition*. The effort can build on lessons learned in restraining conflict between the superpowers for the past four decades. The risk of mutual destruction has motivated a search for ways each nation can defend its values and interests without war. In effect we have mutually discovered unwritten rules of prudence: avoiding any use of nuclear weapons, avoiding any use of military force directly against the other or its vital interests, avoiding direct confrontations between U.S. and Soviet forces. Over time, many of these rules have been embodied in written agreements and codes of conduct, with associated procedures and institutions. A relationship of peaceful competition should extend and enhance these constraints. In time, we should move toward greater collaboration, for example, in combating terrorism, nuclear proliferation, and the spread of advanced weapons such as ballistic missiles. In some areas, however, competition between the values and views of the United States and the Soviet Union can be productive—spurring each nation to greater vigor and creativity. Which political system can better meet the needs of its own population, better realize cultural and spiritual aspirations, or attract the hearts and minds of citizens around the world? Answers to such questions should be left to peaceful competition.

3. Strengthening U.S. Alliances with Europe and Japan. Our strategic objectives should be, first, to preserve alliances with Europe and Japan in a period of increasing strain; second, to continue progress toward a full and equal partnership among these allies; and third, to make explicit and effective the concept of this "commonwealth of industrial democracies" as the foundation of a more stable, benign international order.

This ambitious agenda begins with the recognition of three deeper truths. The first is that for Americans, Europeans, and Japanese, in the words of the beer commercial, "It doesn't get any better than this." This alliance itself has provided a longer peace, more sustained economic growth, and greater freedom than any of the parties enjoyed under any earlier arrangements.

Second, the alliance always had positive goals beyond defending *against* the Soviet threat. Containment was a means to an end. NSC-68 outlined a strategy for building alliances of values and interests. What values? The United States, Europe, and Japan share fundamental commitments to:

freedom of individual citizens in political, economic, and cultural life;

democratically chosen governments in which two or more parties contend in regular, free elections;

economies in which prices and wages are basically determined by forces of supply and demand;

an international economic order that encourages efficiency and equity through specialization and trade; and

an international political order that permits nations to determine their own evolution free from outside interference.

Each nation's prospect for success in maintaining these values is enhanced by the fact that each is not alone. Each nation's confidence in these values is reinforced by the successes of the others. Espoused by leaders throughout the world, these values were more often breached than honored in most other nations in the world in the 1980s and, unfortunately, will be so in the year 2000 as well.

To appreciate the interests served by these alliances, consider possible alternatives. A neutral Japan, for example, would pose serious problems for the American defense structure in the Pacific. An openly antagonistic Japan would be still more disturbing. Global markets would shrink, imposing substantial costs on North America and Europe. Conflicts could easily arise over trade, raw materials, or even the Pacific trust territories. A remilitarized Japan, with a superpower arsenal, could threaten neighbors and come into confrontation with the United States. When this "what if" exercise is conducted from the perspective of Japan or Europe—contemplating the United States as neutral or hostile—the attraction of the current alliances becomes even clearer.

Third, the alliance of industrial democracies contains the seeds of a concept of international order. There was more than hubris and moralism in American efforts to reconstruct Europe and Japan as democracies. Farsighted leaders saw connections among freedom, democracy, and stability. The preference for market oriented economies was not just parochial. Postwar statesmen understood the symbiosis between capitalism and freedom. It was no accident that the Bretton Woods system allowed nations to meet essential needs for resources and markets without political domination: Japan's inability to do so in the 1930s was clearly seen as a contributing factor to World War II. In the U.N. Charter, the U.N. Declaration of Human Rights, and more recently the Helsinki Accords, the insistence upon human rights and freedoms for all individuals represents more than a preference. Those values are essential ingredients in a commonwealth of industrial democracies that promises peace as well as freedom.

How can the alliance be preserved and strengthened? The agenda for action includes four related initiatives. The first is to prepare for the strains that will arise as Gorbachev reduces the perception of a Soviet threat, as public support for nuclear deterrence diminishes (especially in West Germany), as Eastern Europe offers opportunities for historic change, and as we lose the generation who remembers the world before the alliance. Leading the alliance in the era of the cold war has been somewhat akin to managing an iceberg in a long freeze. In a thaw, contradictions and conflicts previously frozen over appear as fissures. An aggressive Soviet Union led by sclerotic, unresponsive ideologues posed a formidable but focused threat. Whenever NATO was tempted to forget, the Soviet Union reminded us: in East Germany, Hungary, Czechoslovakia, Afghanistan, and Poland. But now we face a young, energetic Soviet leader intent on saying "da" to many Western demands and cunningly crafting proposals of his own. To use an analogy from baseball, if the West's hitters are no more effective than in the last two decades, this new Soviet pitcher could well shut them out. A 1988 public opinion poll offered West Germans a hypothetical choice between Reagan and Gorbachev for president of Germany. Germans chose Gorbachev.

Gorbachev's thaw is presenting opportunities to help the East in ways that will increase freedom for Europeans in the East, and reduce risks for Europeans in the West, at least in the short run. Seizing this opportunity without undermining the Western alliance will require greater intelligence in design and higher competence in execution than the West has mustered in the past decade.

The INF story demonstrates that such capabilities are not unattainable—just rare. The Reagan administration's "zero-option" was smart: ambitious, publicly attractive, and evidently fair. It put the Soviet Union on the diplomatic defensive and helped create a climate in which deft management and courageous Western leadership overcame significant public opposition and an all-out Soviet diplomatic campaign. Having won the battle of deployment, however, the West stood pat with the original zero proposal. That was foolish, particularly after Gorbachev came to power. When Gorbachev accepted NATO's proposal, we had no alternative but to agree. The result: elimination of the longer-range missiles capable of reaching targets in Eastern Europe and the western Soviet

Union, leaving in place the shorter-range missiles and artillery, all of which would explode on German soil. Our success therefore unintentionally triggered a debate in Germany about the denuclearization of the Federal Republic over the period ahead.

NATO's current agenda includes modernization of the short-range Lance missiles in West Germany and formulation of a position on conventional arms control negotiations with Moscow. If the managers of the Western alliance show no keener sense for politics within Germany in deciding about Lance modernization, and no more agility in advancing persuasive conventional arms control than they demonstrated on average in the INF history, NATO's future will be in jeopardy.

A second agenda item is to continue the evolution of the alliance toward "responsibility sharing" in a more equal partnership. Europe and Japan have long since recovered. Everyone rhetorically agrees that they should assume more of the alliance burden, and have a larger voice in shaping the burden to be shared. But the difficulties of organizing collective actions to achieve common objectives are imposing. How can we mobilize the leadership required to sustain such collective action? What criteria and procedures should be used to allocate burden and influence in addressing common concerns? How can the "free rider" problem be solved?

A promising starting point is the Japanese concept of "comprehensive security," which recognizes the military, economic, and political dimensions of security. In a partnership that serves the comprehensive security interests of the United States, Europe, and Japan, burdens and voice should be allocated by a principle of "rough equivalence." If we followed the model of international commercial practice, contributions to collective efforts should be roughly proportionate to the capacities and interests of the parties and the benefits each derives, and influence over partnership decisions should be roughly proportionate to contributions. Leadership, always in short supply, should be provided by any party with the necessary imagination, capacity, and will.

As a longer-term objective, the United States should aspire

to *tithe for comprehensive security:* to increase our contributions over time to roughly 10 percent of GNP for the combined goals of defense, maintenance of an international economic system (including aid), and promotion of common political values. We should invite our partners to make an equivalent effort, starting with 5 percent as an initial objective to be achieved over the decade ahead. Moreover, partners need not all contribute an identical mix of defense, economic, and political effort; they should be able to choose the areas in which they will take leadership roles.

As our partners pay more, they will legitimately demand a larger role in defining the burden to be shared. Americans accustomed to U.S. leadership of the alliance will find this a painful adjustment. Our commitment to maintain our current efforts should not be dependent on our partners' willingness to match our effort in the short run. Considering the other areas in which we spend equivalent amounts, we should count this a wise investment in advancing our interests and values.

A third item on the agenda involves dealing with specific issues in Europe and Japan in ways that promote comprehensive security. NATO should maintain the current military alliance, including American troops and a credible nuclear deterrent, as a basis for aggressive engagement of the Soviet Union in restructuring: (1) the Soviet threat to Europe, (2) Soviet domination of Eastern Europe, and (3) relations between the West and the East in Europe. To the extent that Gorbachev is prepared to constrain Soviet capacity for surprise attack and offensive operations, security will be enhanced. The challenge for European and American leaders is to fashion a common approach to Eastern Europe that allows our values to drift eastward, increases freedom and autonomy for Eastern Europeans, and involves them in European-wide institutions that promote the security interests of all parties. Otherwise, there may be repetitions of the Hungarian and Czechoslovakian uprisings, or a Balkanization that could undermine the peace in both West and East. The current possibilities lead statesmen as serious as Henry Kissinger to contemplate "the first comprehensive discussion about the political future of Europe since the outbreak of World War I," and the concept of a "European house that would extend from the Polish-Soviet frontier to the Atlantic."

A more immediate objective for the next several decades might be closer to "Finlandization" of Eastern Europe: an evolutionary process that would permit the peoples of Eastern Europe considerable autonomy in government, economy, culture, and personal freedom, and encourage the evolution of a larger framework that would meet security concerns of the Soviet Union and other neighbors. Essential to any evolution of this sort is a more highly integrated Western Europe. The United States should encourage continued progress along the path, including establishment of the single, integrated European market in 1992 and greater European cooperation in providing for its own defense.

Relations between the United States and Japan could well get worse before they get better. Japan accepts the benefits of the partnership, but remains reluctant to accept any major responsibility. Rather, it does the minimum necessary to respond to U.S. pressure on a case-by-case basis. Japan's contribution to the common defense effort amounts to 1.5 percent of GNP. Despite the fact that it is the principal beneficiary of the open trading system, Japan currently runs a trade surplus of more than $50 billion with the United States and continues to resist opening its own markets on equivalent terms or taking other initiatives that would strengthen the international financial system.

American long-term interests are not served by scapegoating Japan, however. Japanese military forces, which rival those of Germany and Britain, make important contributions to the overall U.S. security posture. Japan's current self-defensive objective—to protect itself and its sea lanes out to 1,000 nautical miles—provides a framework for increasing the Japanese defense effort in a manner consistent with the overall objectives of the alliance. Japan's military posture also provides a powerful example in the longer-term international order: it is a superpower without proportionate military might. Were

Japan to become a military power, it would undoubtedly discover independent ambitions, with harmful results for its own security interests and those of its Asian neighbors and the United States.

Japan must identify and assume a major role within the framework of the alliance. Fortunately, a consensus seems to be forming around Japan's taking the lead in economic development. Its own national experience offers a striking model. In 1988 Japanese overseas development assistance became number one in the world, exceeding that of the United States. Japanese Finance Minister Kiichi Miyazawa and others have been talking about a Japanese initiative to address the issue of Third World debt, perhaps restructuring and relieving as much as half of the $600 billion of dubious debt outstanding. The United States should encourage such Japanese initiatives, not only on international development but also on trade. Within the framework of "comprehensive security," such initiatives should count toward Japan's share of the burden.

A fourth item on the agenda is the most elusive, but perhaps the most important: to realize the concept of international order implicit in the commonwealth of industrial democracies. This should begin by unpacking and making more explicit the impulses that created the postwar alliance. We should specify how the foundation that has been laid can provide a stable, benign international order for all countries.

Our objective has always been more than peace achieved through cold war or balance-of-power politics alone. Though less well developed, a conception of peace built up from a commonwealth of industrial democracies goes back at least two centuries. In his *Perpetual Peace,* Immanuel Kant outlined the conditions of international and domestic politics that would, in his view, lead to the "ever widening pacification" of international life. Kant's analysis is both subtle and complex, but, simply stated, his conditions for peace are three. The first and most important relates to domestic political regimes: peaceful nations must be "republics," in which citizens have rights and governments depend on the consent of the governed. As Kant argued:

If the consent of the citizens is required to decide that war should be declared, nothing is more natural than that they would be cautious in commencing such a poor game, decreeing for themselves all of the calamities of war. Among the latter would be: having to fight, having to pay the costs of the war from their own resources, having painfully to repair the devastation war leaves behind, and to fill up the measure of evil, load themselves with a heavy national debt that would embitter peace itself.

Kant's second condition focuses on economics: these republics should have market economies aimed at improving citizens' well-being. Then, given an international division of labor through free trade, economic interdependence will evolve. Benefiting from these arrangements, citizens will be more reluctant to break the ties of trade.

Third, because democratic states respect other democratic states, international law among such nations would have an ever-widening scope, encouraging the reasoned resolution of conflicting interests, and ultimately leading to peace. Because war was becoming increasingly destructive, Kant maintained that peace would become more attractive and even necessary.

Kant did not think such a peace would come about quickly. Rather, he foresaw a lengthy process in which democratic republics would form an implicit "pacific union" among themselves. Peace would be the norm in relations among such states. As new democratic republics appeared, this pacific union would expand; by gradual extension, peace would become global and finally perpetual. In fact, in the almost 200 years since Kant wrote, there has been virtually no war between democratic republics.

4. Coping with Nuclear Weapons. The strategic objective of the United States should be to design policies that would minimize the likelihood of the use of even a single nuclear weapon against the United States, our allies, or anyone else—or by us. This will require success in preventing war between the Soviet Union and the United States or our allies, and in avoiding any accidental or unauthorized use of nuclear weapons. An essential strand in this strategy for war prevention must remain a credible nuclear deterrent. In the shorter run, this means both continued modernization of existing forces and continued pursuit of arms control agreements to reduce the Soviet threat (by reducing both numbers of weapons and the risk of their use). Over the longer run, it means attempting to reduce the role of nuclear weapons in international affairs and to reduce numbers of nuclear weapons in the superpowers' arsenals to levels below a capability for a species-threatening nuclear war.

If nuclear weapons had never been invented, nonnuclear world wars would be more probable, such as World War II, which claimed 50 million victims. In such a world, governments would more vigorously pursue alternative technologies of mass destruction, including chemical and biological weapons. Thus, some strategic thinkers argue, a world with nuclear weapons is preferable, even if a nuclear war could conceivably destroy all human life. If permitted to choose, my colleague Thomas Schelling has said that he would take a world with some very small probability of a species-threatening nuclear war but very few nonnuclear global conflicts, rather than a world without nuclear weapons in which World War IIs occurred every fifty years.

Such a choice is purely hypothetical, since nuclear weapons cannot be disinvented. Barring societal amnesia, we will continue to know how to make nuclear weapons. Even if the United States and the Soviet Union eliminated every one of the nearly 50,000 nuclear weapons in their combined stockpiles, each would be able to reconstitute its capability to destroy the other's society within weeks or months. Every future state of this earth can be characterized in terms of a *mobilization timetable* to superpower nuclear arsenals.

Whether we have many nuclear weapons or few, the essential issue remains the probability that they eventually will be used. That probability reflects the risk of use by accident; the incentives to launch a nuclear first strike, either out of the blue or in a crisis; and the likelihood of circumstances, for example a conventional war in Europe, that could lead to a deliberate choice to use nuclear weapons to prevent the loss of a vital interest.

The effectiveness of any deterrent posture depends on two elements: the weapon's capability to make the cost of aggression substantially greater than its benefit, and the credibility of commitment to use that capability. Physical capacity to cause catastrophic harm is relatively easy to maintain, given current technologies. But neither superpower now is capable of eliminating its adversary's capability to destroy its own society in retaliation. As noted earlier, to the extent that fulfillment of a threat could mean societal suicide, credibility declines.

It is natural to seek an escape from the unpalatable condition of mutual assured destruction (MAD). The logical options include: (1) making it impossible for the opponent to destroy one's own society, either through an offensive capability to disarm the adversary, or a defensive capability to render nuclear weapons impotent and obsolete; (2) creating a "fire break" that would prevent an escalation from any limited conflict to general nuclear war; and (3) maintaining a posture (real interests, treaty commitments, and deployed forces) that makes the odds of nuclear use, whether deliberate or accidental, higher than a potential adversary would accept. No technology available today or on the horizon offers any prospect of denying the Soviet Union the capacity to destroy the United States. A sustainable fire break would raise the probability of nuclear weapons' being used below the threshold and might not be observed by the losing side in a war in any case. The third option is, in effect, NATO's current choice.

NATO's strategy of "flexible response" combines conventional and nuclear weapons, including British national nuclear forces, a commitment to forward defense in the event of war, and a refusal to inform the adversary when and under what circumstances nuclear weapons might be used. All of these elements are meant to undermine the confidence of a Warsaw Pact commander or Soviet leader about to assess accurately the prospects of success in attacking NATO. Warsaw Pact commanders face the chance that the West would use U.S. battlefield, short-range, strategic, or British or French nuclear weapons in a way that could escalate to the destruction of Soviet society. In abstract calculations, nuclear planners and

Western leaders may question the credibility of NATO's posture. But the Soviet leadership has come to understand that a Warsaw Pact attack on NATO would likely become a general war, conventional and nuclear, with consequences no one can foresee but with high risk of an ultimately self-defeating ending.

In the decades ahead, the West should seek to reduce reliance on nuclear weapons, modernizing its arsenals as necessary to assure that they are safe and effective—but simultaneously seeking a strategy to reduce numbers of nuclear weapons below the level at which a nuclear war could threaten the species. Note that this is *not* a posture beyond nuclear deterrence. Nuclear weapons will remain part of the inescapable background; their use will always be a possibility if vital interests are attacked. To move in this direction, we should recognize and defend credible nuclear deterrence as part of NATO's strategy, which has produced four decades of peace; recognize nuclear weapons as part of war prevention strategy (to prevent a nuclear war, we must prevent a major conventional war that might escalate into nuclear war); modernize and reduce numbers of nuclear weapons in Europe and in the strategic nuclear arsenal through unilateral action or negotiations; reduce early reliance on nuclear weapons as we build a more credible conventional deterrent (negotiating Soviet forces down to a conventional balance, or building NATO forces up through the application of technology to conventional forces); explore defenses as part of the mix, without any expectation that we can create an impermeable shield in the foreseeable future; and appreciate that the "long pole in the tent" is the political relationship between the United States and the Soviet Union. Any comprehensive vision of a world beyond MAD must involve a more cooperative U.S.–Soviet relationship. In concert, the superpowers could indeed limit the capacity for destroying each other's society or the species. Moreover, such cooperation is a necessary condition for reducing nuclear threats posed by other nations.

In order to achieve the refinement in U.S. nuclear strategy that we must accomplish over time, we should stand back from this ambitious agenda, and the current debates about the vulnerability of the U.S. land-based intercontinental ballistic missiles (ICBMs) and the modernization of short-range, land-based missiles in Western Europe. This will permit us to reflect on deeper questions beneath our nuclear posture.

Conclusion

In conclusion, the next decade will bring us to the start of a new century, in fact a new millennium. To achieve America's basic national security objectives in a period of revolutionary change, it will be necessary to replenish our conceptual arsenal. Stretching minds beyond familiar concepts that have served well is painful and frightening. Moreover, conceptual adaptation is only the beginning. Recognizing the Soviet threat, imagining the reconstruction of Europe and Japan, and conceiving of alliances of interests and values were necessary first steps. But there remained the yet harder work of mobilizing support for great exertion, establishing organizations like NATO, the U.S.–Japan Mutual Defense Treaty, and the Bretton Woods structures, making these institutions work.

Will statesmen of the 1990s be equally successful in addressing the four challenges discussed above: restoring the American economic base, engaging the Soviet Union in settling the cold war, strengthening U.S. alliances with Europe and Japan, and coping with nuclear weapons? What about other major challenges to national security in the year 2000 which have not been discussed here for lack of space? After four decades of sustained effort, if faced with a less clear and present danger, many will conclude that we are overstretched and attempt to draw back. Others will seek to cling to old verities in the hope that we can just hang on.

This chapter's conclusion is quite different. Statesmen of the 1990s may succeed or fail to protect the security, prosperity, and freedom of the U.S. and our allies into the twenty-first century. The outcome will not be determined by objective limits on resources or capabilities. Threats to national interests will indeed be severe and more complex than in the late 1940s. Obstacles to effective strategy will loom larger. Leadership will require less unilateralism and more subtlety in evoking thought and action by others. But our response to these challenges remains our responsibility—to fulfill or to fail.

6

The 21st Century: American Foreign Policy Challenges

LAWRENCE S. EAGLEBURGER

M ost of the world's peoples—or at least those over fifty years of age—know, as few Americans can, that the twentieth century has not been a vintage era in human history.

LAWRENCE S. EAGLEBURGER left the State Department in 1984 after serving twenty-seven years as a foreign service officer. In the 1960s he served on the staff of the National Security Council, was special assistant to the under secretary of state, and was political advisor and chief of the political section of the U.S. Mission to NATO in Brussels. In 1971 he was appointed deputy assistant secretary of defense, and in 1973 he became acting assistant secretary of defense for international security affairs and then deputy assistant to the president for national security affairs. In 1977 President Carter appointed Mr. Eagleburger as ambassador to Yugoslavia. In 1981 President Reagan appointed him assistant secretary of state for European affairs, and in 1982, under secretary of state for political affairs. Mr. Eagleburger has served on the boards of major national and international corporations and as president of Kissinger Associates, Inc., a firm founded by Dr. Henry Kissinger to offer strategic consulting services to international companies. He is currently Assistant Secretary of State, Designate.

Indeed, the American historian Barbara Tuchman has argued with substantial justice that we must go back to the fourteenth century to find a period as unstable and bloody as our own times. Two world wars, the deaths of tens of millions in those wars, a disastrous depression, the rise and fall of national socialism, the end of colonialism, with its attendant instability and economic chaos, and the rise of Communist totalitarianism, all are evidence of the abysmal failure of most of those who led in the West—particularly in Europe—from the close of the nineteenth century through the first four decades of the twentieth century. The common task of the West since the end of World War II has been, above all else, to see that the errors that marked that time are not repeated by succeeding generations.

By any reasonable standard we have not done badly so far. Europe, at least, has enjoyed a longer period of peace than at any time in the past hundred years, thanks largely to the NATO alliance and the commitment of the United States to the defense of its allies. And we have, together, built a host of institutions—particularly in the economic arena—that have established a commonly accepted set of rules which have mitigated the worst aspects of unilateralism and unfettered nationalism. Bretton Woods, the International Monetary Fund (IMF), the World Bank, the General Agreement on Tariffs and Trade (GATT), the Organization for Economic Cooperation and Development (OECD), and the European Community (EC), have all played a major role in leading the industrial democracies toward a far more rational international economic order than history has known before.

The Western democracies, then, have much about which to congratulate themselves. And Americans have a right to be particularly proud of the part they played—a role unique not only in American history, but in world history as well.

But times change, and with those changes comes the need to adjust old patterns of thought, and the international institutions which served them, to the new realities. Yet history is replete with examples of the failure to adjust in time, and the instability and chaos that followed from the failures.

The United States and the democratic West (including Japan) now face such a time of transition. How well we adjust to the demands of this time of change may well decide whether the first half of the twenty-first century will resemble its twentieth century counterpart or be a time of broadly based prosperity, stability, and peace. Perhaps as at no time since the close of World War II, the conditions are ripe for the democratic West to build that better world if it but has the wit and wisdom to seize the opportunity. Equally, however, a failure to act wisely carries with it the danger of a return to the kind of world that so afflicted our parents' and grandparents' generations.

The beginning of wisdom for Americans, and for America's friends and allies, is to recognize that we are leaving the atypical period of a bipolar world in which two superpowers reigned supreme, and are returning to a more traditional and complicated time of multipolarity, with a growing number of countries increasingly able to affect the course of events despite the wishes of the superpowers. Japan and the European Community, although still dependent on the United States for their security, wield great economic power, and will be increasingly important in the years to come (the EC "single market" by the close of 1992 inevitably will, over time, vastly increase Western European economic power and influence). The Association of Southeast Asian Nations (ASEAN), Korea, and Taiwan are now significant players on the international trade scene, while the People's Republic of China (PRC) may slowly be moving toward a more market oriented economy that could lead it to a more influential international role early in the next century.

While, with the possible exception of the PRC, none of these nations today occupies a position even approaching the military relevance of either the Soviet Union or the United States, history would seem to teach us that at least some of them— particularly a more united Western Europe and Japan—will eventually translate some of their growing economic power into increased military strength.

The issue for the West, then, is how well the United States

accomplishes the transition from overwhelming predominance to a position more akin to a "first among equals" status,
and how well America's partners—Japan and Western
Europe—adapt to their new found importance. The change
will not be easy for any of the players, as such shifts in power
relationships have never been easy. The United States, inevitably, will react against the fact that it no longer can so often
have its way. Europe and Japan, also inevitably, will find their
new independence a heady experience and be inclined to flex
their muscles for the joy of it. Yet the reality is that the *collective*
strength of the West will be greater in this new multipolar
world than in the era of American predominance. The test will
be whether, under these new circumstances, we regress to the
bad old days of unilateralism, with each nation intent on
achieving its narrow objectives, or, having learned the lessons
of 1900–1945, we are able to take synergistic advantage of our
combined strength to deal with the truly difficult challenges of
the new century.

Nor should we be under the misapprehension that this time
of transition is a Western phenomenon alone. The USSR is
passing through a similar period, but with problems that significantly outweigh our own. The Soviet economy stagnates,
industrial goods are of questionable quality, consumer goods
are in short supply, and the ability to take part in the high-
technology race becomes increasingly more difficult. These
facts underlie the Gorbachev *perestroika* and *glasnost* initiatives,
for without major reforms (assuming they are possible), the
USSR will in time find itself occupying a place at the top of the
list of developing countries, ever less capable of competing
effectively with the developed West. Additionally, the Soviets
have nowhere to look for the kind of support that Western
Europe and Japan potentially represent for the United States.
Their allies are, in most cases, suffering from the same disabili-
ties as the Soviets themselves, facing the same wrenching ago-
nies of reform, and governed by regimes that are now, as they
have always been, unpopular with the vast majority of their
peoples.

I remarked earlier that the new century poses difficult challenges for the West. It would have been more accurate to say that the transitional period through which we are now passing is itself the author of substantial problems *and* makes a creative Western response to a host of other challenges more difficult. For example, the rise of Western Europe and Japan, accompanied by America's growing recognition of its own limits, increases the difficulties in maintaining Western cohesion on defense matters and on the development of an international trade regime that furthers growth and avoids protectionist pressures. At the same time, there exists a host of new problems—or in some cases, old problems which have taken on a new sense of urgency—which we must begin to deal with now despite the fact that in the best of all possible worlds it would be better if their solution could await the outcome of the West's transition to a new and more balanced sharing of responsibilities. The disastrous state into which much of the developing world is sinking, in large part because of its heavy debt burden, must be arrested soon or instability on a broad scale will be the consequence. Collective efforts to begin to address the increasingly obvious threats to the environment cannot await a more propitious organization of the Western community except at great cost in resources and probably lives.

It is time, therefore, for the industrial democracies of the West to begin a collective examination of the problems they will confront as they move into the twenty-first century. It is, as well, a time to begin to plan how to deal collectively with those problems, for most are not amenable to unilateral solution, but can be managed—and a creative outcome assured—if the combined wealth and talents of the Western community are brought to bear. And while the United States is no longer capable of solving these problems alone, it is probably only the United States that, because it is a global power and therefore thinks (if not always well) in global terms, has the breadth of vision to lead the West to understand the nature of the challenge and the magnitude of the opportunity that is before us.

What follows is a brief description of some of the most important of those challenges and opportunities.

Europe, West and East

The past decade and more has seen a slow deterioration in the transatlantic relationship between the United States and the Western Europe of NATO and the Economic Community. We are not at, or near, a time of crisis in the relationship, but neither are we as intimately linked as we once were.

The reasons are not hard to fathom, nor should they be surprising. After more than forty years, and against the background of nuclear balance between the two superpowers, there is growing doubt in Europe about the strength of the U.S. commitment to the defense of NATO Europe and to the validity of the American nuclear deterrent. There is, as well, increased concern on both sides of the Atlantic about the whole concept of the use of nuclear weapons.

Generational changes in Europe and the United States have also played a role. That the generations born after the close of World War II should have a different and less emotional view of that experience than those who lived through it can hardly be surprising. Equally, the farther one is removed in time from those events the less likely one is to draw parallels between what happens today and what happened then. This is a reality that is present on both sides of the Atlantic; the frustrations with high defense budgets, the fear engendered by the nuclear arms race, and the belief that domestic concerns must be given greater attention and foreign issues less are as well developed in the United States as in Europe.

The global nature of America's role versus the regional nature of European interests has been another contributing factor. The United States is the West's only *global* power; as such, it has to be concerned with—and respond to—events around the world. Western Europe, on the other hand, has steadily become more concerned with its regional problems and less interested in events far from its borders. This reality has inevitably led to strains, whether caused by European anxiety over American bellicosity, or frustration in the United States over lack of European sympathy and support for actions taken by

Washington in what it considered to be the pursuit of its global responsibilities.

The U.S. attack on Libya, while generally welcomed at home as an appropriate response to Khadaffi-inspired terrorism, was almost universally condemned in Europe. French refusal to permit over-flights enroute to Libya was attacked in the United States with a degree of vehemence usually reserved for enemies. On neither side of the Atlantic was there any discernable effort to understand the motives or concerns of the other partner. Americans failed to recognize that the attack might well lead to further terrorist activity in Europe for which Europeans—not Americans—would pay the price. Europeans remained blind to the mounting American frustration with the international community's inability or unwillingness to deal firmly with the terrorist menace.

The purpose here is not to debate the wisdom of particular American actions or the European response to them. Rather, it is the difference of perspective that is important, whether the issue be Libya, the reflagging of ships in the Persian Gulf, Grenada, Nicaragua, or the pipeline sanctions. In each case a part of the misunderstandings that have arisen has derived from the differing perspective of the players. And these misunderstandings—and European inability to do much to affect American decisions—will continue until Western Europe has organized itself to play a role in the world scene appropriate to its collective wealth, strength, and wisdom.

Europeans are also increasingly disquieted by what they see as American unpredictability and lack of discipline, while Americans are increasingly frustrated by what they consider to be Europe's unwillingness to accept its "responsibilities" and carry its fair share of the burden for our common defense.

American unpredictability and indiscipline, and European failure to accept greater responsibility are in many ways but two sides of the same coin. Vietnam was a body blow to American confidence in itself and its purposes, a blow from which the nation and the institution of the presidency have not fully recovered, and to which the Iran-contra revelations have added their weight. As a consequence, decisions—particularly when they involve the use of force—are inevitably subjects of heated American domestic political debate, with the Congress frequently forcing the president either to compromise his policy to the point of incoherence or to reverse course altogether. In 1983 the United States persuaded a number of our NATO allies to join in sending forces to Beirut, only to have the Congress push the president, thereafter, to withdraw, leaving at least one ally behind. President Reagan's Reykjavik meeting with Chairman Gorbachev, which came within a hair of arriving at a far-reaching strategic arms agreement between the U.S. and the USSR without the least prior consultation with our NATO allies, shocked European capitals, and was seen as but another example of how unpredictable we really were. Such actions are hardly conducive to a high degree of confidence in American steadiness.

A part of the American frustration and doubt about national purpose derives from a perception that the United States has for too long carried more than its share of the burden for the common defense and the maintenance of the international economic order. While Japan is the principal target of American criticism today, Western Europe is also seen as having failed to do its part.

Much of this criticism is unfair: it is the United States that has ended the draft while several European allies have maintained it; it is Western Europe that provides the bulk of the ground, air, and immediate naval defense of NATO Europe. It is the United States that is running budget and trade deficits that threaten the international economic order. But fairness also requires recognition that the United States has shown remarkable—if imperfect—tolerance in the face of less than constructive Japanese and European trade practices. Nor can Western Europe or Japan argue with much conviction that they were averse to taking advantage of America's willingness to be the "engine" of prosperity, or ready to do much to reflate their own economies. And fairness also demands acceptance of the rightness of the proposition that it is, over time, unhealthy and insupportable that Western Europe, with a larger population and GNP than the Soviet Union, should depend so heavily upon the United States for its defense and its prosperity.

Finally, continuing differences in how the Soviet security threat is perceived and dealt with have contributed to transatlantic tensions. These differences are perhaps best illustrated by the history of the intermediate nuclear force (INF) agreement signed by President Reagan and Chairman Gorbachev. The proposal that the U.S. deploy Pershing II and cruise missiles to counter Soviet SS-4 and SS-20 missiles aimed at Western Europe first came from Western Europe. At the time, the United States was less than enthusiastic about the suggestion, arguing that its land- and sea-based missiles were a sufficient deterrent; after months of debate, however, Washington finally acquiesced in the deployment, and then agreed that there should be, in tandem with that deployment, a negotiation with the USSR aimed at securing the elimination of some of the Soviet missiles in return for reduced U.S. deployments. This "two-track" approach led to inevitable problems: as the time neared for the arrival of the first U.S. missiles, violent demonstrations took place throughout Western Europe, accompanied by calls for a delay in deployment while negotiations continued, and charges that the United States was not negotiating in good faith. These charges continued even after the U.S. accepted a further European proposal—the "zero outcome." Indeed, if the USSR had not committed the major blunder of breaking off the negotiations it is unlikely that the deployments could have proceeded without serious political upheaval in a number of Western European countries.

But with the advent of Gorbachev the situation changed radically. Today we have an agreement to withdraw all U.S. INF weapons from Western Europe in return for Soviet elimination of its weapons of the same classes. To say that Western European leaders have been ambivalent about this "success" is to understate the case. The concern of some of them, although seldom openly stated, is twofold: first, that this may be the initial step in the eventual denuclearization of NATO Europe, and second, that as the nuclear deterrent is reduced the Soviet superiority in conventional forces takes on a more substantial character. Others, particularly in the Federal Republic of Germany (FRG), now argue that with the withdrawal of INF Germany is left as the only potential nuclear battlefield in a European war that does not involve exchange of strategic nuclear weapons. As a consequence, there is growing pressure in the FRG for the withdrawal of short-range tactical nuclear weapons from NATO's arsenal.

The history of the INF episode is one of failure on both sides of the Atlantic to arrive at a common strategy *before* undertaking the deployment and the negotiations. It is, as well, a classic example of a European habit of playing domestic politics with defense policy on the assumption that in the end the United States can be blamed for unpopular but necessary decisions. Certainly on the basis of the rhetoric of the first Reagan term, European leaders had good reason to believe that American firmness would save them from themselves. But they failed to foresee the rise of Gorbachev with his so uncharacteristic flexibility, and they failed to take seriously (as did so many Americans) President Reagan's oft-repeated call for the elimination of all nuclear weapons.

Now that Gorbachev has established himself in many Western eyes as a reformer both at home and in terms of Soviet foreign policy, the likelihood of additional disagreements has increased. The United States, despite the greatly transformed character of its dialogue with the USSR in President Reagan's second term, is likely to proceed with more caution in dealing with Moscow, at least on economic matters, than Western Europe. Strategic Arms Reduction Talks (START) will continue, and talks on conventional arms cuts will probably become more serious, but even this will cause problems. When the U.S. is reluctant to negotiate with the Soviets, Western Europeans worry that the Americans are unnecessarily exacerbating tensions with the East; when agreements are reached, the U.S. is criticized for negotiating over the heads of its allies and bringing into question its continued commitment to NATO.

Western Europeans, who have always been more anxious to increase trade ties with Eastern Europe and the Soviet Union than most Americans, will respond enthusiastically to Gorbachev's moves to open the Soviet economy through greater receptivity to joint ventures and expanded trade. Soviet appetite for Western credits to finance both trade and investment has already encouraged European banks to grant large loans; a desire to expand these facilities even further can be expected. The United States, on the other hand, will not want to move so rapidly, and will be particularly resistant to European desires to expand the list of high-technology goods which can be exported to the USSR.

None of these sources of difference or friction between the U.S. and Western Europe are, either singly or collectively, of such magnitude that they threaten to rupture the relationship. But they do have a slow but steady debilitating effect—an effect which, unless checked, will over time make it more difficult for the Atlantic democracies to coordinate their policies, both in the security and economic fields. This, combined with the effects of the pressures the U.S. will be subjected to as it seeks its new role in a polycentric world, can lead to an increasingly less relevant and effective NATO, and a slow drift toward unilateralism on both sides of the Atlantic.

A new factor has entered the picture—a factor which can act as a brake on these trends or can accelerate them, depending on the degree of wisdom demonstrated by Washington and European capitals. That factor is a united European Community. The much touted "single market" to be completed by the close of 1992 will probably be looked upon by historians as one of the seminal events of the latter half of the twentieth century. Even if the single market is not completed in all its ramifications by the target period, the momentum will be such that before the decade is out the European Community will have removed almost all internal barriers and created a market with a population and GNP exceeding that of the United States. That this development will, over time, benefit the member states is beyond question; whether it will contribute as well to a more stable and prosperous international order remains to be seen.

If the European Community's reforms lead to a more productive Western European economy open to the goods, services, and investment of the Common Market's trading partners then the Western democracies as a whole will have been strengthened. If, on the other hand, the single market develops into a restrictive trading bloc intent on insulating itself from foreign competition, then the West will find itself propelled down a path leading to a further erosion of the relatively open international trading system that has served us for the better part of forty years. Advocates of increased protectionism, particularly in the United States, will be strengthened, as will those who espouse the development of competing trading blocs as the only viable alternative to unconstrained protectionism. In either case, the developed West will find itself increasingly divided and less able to deal collectively with the problems inherent in the transit into the twenty-first century.

Neither outcome is foreordained. If there is, on both sides of the Atlantic, a realization of the historic nature of the changes taking place in Western Europe and the need to assure that those changes serve to strengthen the industrialized democracies rather than to divide them, then 1992 will be remembered as the time when the transatlantic relationship entered a new and creative era. To achieve this outcome, however, will require a common recognition that the process of economic "unification" is fundamentally a political rather than an economic matter and, as such, must engage not only the European Community's Brussels bureaucracy, but the political leadership on both sides of the Atlantic as well. For its part, the United States must recognize, and welcome, the fact that a more unified Western Europe will be a more independent Western Europe, less ready to accept and support decisions taken in Washington. Europeans, on the other hand, will have to accept that their unity carries with it responsibilities for assuring international economic, political, and military stability that they earlier could largely leave to others.

While it is possible that the establishment of a single market will mark the end of the process of Western European unification, the opposite is more likely to be the case. Some greater political unity would seem almost the inevitable consequence, over time, of the economic union the single market implies. Also, although less certain, is the possibility that the most significant of the EC countries—France, the FRG, the United Kingdom, and perhaps Italy—will, over a longer period of time, begin to integrate their military establishments, thereby preparing the ground for a more balanced sharing of roles and responsibilities with the United States in the defense of NATO Europe.

If all this sounds more like a sermon than an analysis of likely events so be it. The point remains as stated earlier: the United States will of necessity play a lesser role—albeit a critical one—in future decades than is now the case. If that change is managed with wisdom in Washington and other Western capitals, then stability will be maintained while the realities of the shifting balance of power will be reflected in the burdens we put down and our friends and allies assume. If that change is not managed well then the West will find itself increasingly in a struggle with itself and ever less able to control events and shape outcomes.

Not least among the challenges the Western democracies will have to contend with both now and for decades to come is the changing nature of the Soviet Union and its Eastern European empire.

Transition in the East is, as in the West, already underway. Mikhail Gorbachev, whatever else he may be, is a formidable adversary. He has moved with great courage to force political and economic reform at home, and has fashioned a less confrontational stance abroad. His drive for internal reform reflects his recognition of the sorry state of the Soviet economy. *Perestroika* and *glasnost* are, in a word, for his reasons, not ours; his objective is a stronger Soviet Union. Whether his foreign policy shifts—which thus far are more rhetorical than substantive—reflect a permanent redirection of Soviet policy or simply a clever device to charm the West remains to be seen. At this stage, no one can even be sure that the reforms will ever really take root; Gorbachev may yet go the way of Khrushchev and be followed by another Brezhnev, or worse. Nor is it self-evident that a successful effort to rejuvenate the stagnating

Soviet system is to the advantage of the West. A stronger USSR is not necessarily a more benign USSR.

It is evident that the Gorbachev era presents the U.S. and its allies with a far more nuanced challenge than was the case before his rise to power. It is too early, at this stage, to suggest just how the West should adjust to the changes that may be taking place in the Soviet Union. That must await developments in Moscow.

It is not too early, however, to suggest that as the West shifts to meet the Gorbachev reality, it should also keep a watchful eye on some disturbing developments in Eastern Europe. There are signs that the countries of the region are in the early stages of a time of substantial instability engendered in part by Gorbachev's reforms. All are in various stages of economic disrepair; all are governed by regimes that lack legitimacy or substantial popular support. The East German and Czech Communist parties have in large measure rejected the Soviet reform program; the Hungarian party is moving in the other direction at a pace that exceeds that of its Soviet brethren. The Polish party continues in a state of turmoil and uncertainty that threatens to degenerate into an inability to govern, while Romania remains the personal Stalinist preserve of Ceaucescu. Nationality questions plague several of these regimes and have led to substantial and open dispute between the "fraternal" regimes of Hungary and Romania.

If history has any relevance, we know that earlier efforts at reform in Eastern Europe have usually foundered because once they began they could not be contained short of Soviet military intervention (as in Hungary and Czechoslovakia) or violent action by the central government (as in East Germany and Poland). In each case the "conservatives" could look to Moscow for support: today it is Moscow that is pushing for the very reforms that may unleash the long-repressed desires for fundamental change.

It may be that the Eastern European regimes—as well as the Soviet Union—will prove capable of tolerating far reaching reform. In such a case, however, it is likely that the relationship between Moscow and its Warsaw Pact allies would undergo significant change as a consequence. The economic pull of the West would be enormous and could, over the course of several decades, lead to a significant reduction in Moscow's influence in the region.

In either scenario the potential for change—dangerous or benign—in the East-West relationship is obvious. Equally obvious is the fact that Western cohesion in the face of these changes would greatly enhance the chances for a productive and peaceful outcome. Conversely, Western confusion or disagreement on how to deal with them could either make a dangerously unstable situation worse, or limit our ability to take advantage of a possibly unique opportunity to undo some of the consequences of the postwar division of Europe.

Japan

The rise of Japan to economic superpower status in the brief span of some thirty years must rank as one of the most significant events of the postwar era. The contemporary question, for Japan and for the developed democracies, is whether the single-mindedness, dedication, and creativity that transformed the nation can now be harnessed for the broader interests of the West. In the period of American predominance the United States realized relatively quickly that its position brought not only advantages, but also responsibilities. Whether for reasons of enlightened self-interest or something more, the United States bore much of the burden for the common defense, contributed generously to the rebuilding of Europe and Japan, and sustained an open international financial and trading system without which neither Europe nor Japan could have recovered so quickly from the aftermath of war. Whether Japan can be brought to a similar recognition of the need to accept greater responsibility for the maintenance of international stability remains to be seen.

Despite the many transatlantic differences that plague the relationship, the ties of blood, culture, language, and institutions have made it possible for the United States and Western Europe to contain their differences within reasonable bounds.

Those ties should also assist in the development of a more cooperative relationship in the decades to come as Europe creates a more distinct personality.

In the case of Japan, however, the ties are much more ephemeral and of much shorter duration. Japan, despite its phenomenal growth, is still a society largely isolated from outside influences. Its people are highly motivated, educated, and competitive, yet to some degree convinced of their racial superiority. Their decision-making process is consensual and beyond the ken of most Westerners. The role of women is highly confined; consumerism is as yet far less well developed than in the United States or Western Europe.

Given such disparate cultural circumstances, it is hardly surprising that the level of acerbity in the U.S.–Japanese (and Japanese–Western European) relationship has risen as Japan has come to play an increasingly significant role in world trade and financial markets. Nor is there any reason to believe that the strains on the relationship will abate much in the absence of major and fundamental changes that are beyond the ken of this chapter. Clearly the U.S. budget deficit, the ability of U.S. industry to compete effectively, and Japanese economic nationalism, protectionism, and provincialism are at the core of the problem. Clearly the solution to any one of these issues, much less all of them, will require painful compromise on all sides over decades. The immediate issue is how to prevent or contain further transpacific deterioration while easing the process of adaptation to new circumstances in both countries. One possible answer is to involve Tokyo more intimately in Western councils. The instruments for effective consultation with Japan are not as well developed as those between the United States and Western Europe. Seven nation summit meetings are important, but they do not permit the kind of close and continuing discourse that is available to the U.S. and Western European governments through NATO.

Obviously the NATO structure cannot be duplicated with Japan; neither can Japan be brought into the alliance consultative process. But it should be possible to establish—even if only informally—a mechanism that permits regular consultation on the range of political, economic, and military questions that increasingly concerns Japan, the U.S., and the Western Europe of NATO or the EC. The reality of the closing years of this century is that the world of the democracies is increasingly a world of three centers of power; the institutional framework for consultation and coordination among those power centers has not yet been revised to reflect that reality.

Third World Debt

If there is a single international issue that best exemplifies the proposition that the problems of the last decade of the twentieth century and beyond exceed the capacity of any one nation to resolve, it is the question of developing world debt. Throughout much of Latin America, in Poland and Yugoslavia, in the Philippines, and in Africa the weight of external debt has stiffled growth. Most governments cannot pay even the interest without periodic rescheduling agreements, much less reduce the principal. What has for too long been looked upon by the lending governments and private banking institutions as a purely financial matter is rapidly becoming a political problem threatening the survival of governments and potentially the stability of the international order. In almost every case the debtor government has been guilty of serious mismanagement, which has contributed substantially to the weakened state of the economy, but this fact will be of little solace in the event of debt default or political violence.

The magnitude of the problem far exceeds the ability of the private banks or any single government to handle alone. What is needed is a coordinated multilateral program, including both government and private bank creditors, to reduce the drain on scarce resources and return the developing world to a rate of growth that will foster internal stability. A plethora of workable proposals aimed at achieving this result has been put forward by concerned observers, but thus far none of them has received substantial international support. Instead, creditors have resorted to a series of band-aid measures which have but postponed the day of reckoning.

Mexico is a classic case in point, and of particular relevance to the United States. That nation is burdened by an external debt that approaches $100 billion, an economic structure in great need of reform, and an increasingly restive populace. Bailout programs have several times saved the country from default, but none has begun to arrest the steady deterioration in economic and political stability that has gone on for the better part of a decade.

The governing political party, the PRI, long served the country admirably as the mechanism for balancing diverse interests while maintaining an adequate rate of growth and a stable political environment. But rapid population growth, an increasingly urban populace, regional disparities, and a precipitous drop in the price of oil have all contributed to growing dissatisfaction with the way in which the country is governed and the PRI as the instrument of that governance. The result is a growing restiveness that could, within the next decade or so, generate rising civil unrest bordering on revolution.

By the end of the century, if current trends remain unchecked, Mexico could be one of the United States' most serious foreign policy problems. The rate of illegal immigration from Mexico to the United States could expand beyond anything known before, while serious political instability to America's south could lead the U.S. to an obsessive concern with that problem, while ignoring other international issues of equal importance but more geographically remote.

Serious as the Mexican problem is and will continue to be, it is not beyond solution. A multilateral debt relief program supported by Western governments and the private banking sector could, with time and appropriate domestic reforms (the price for the assistance program), return Mexico to economic growth and a more stable political environment. But the emphasis here must be on the word "multilateral." The support of Japan and Western Europe, as well as the United States, will be necessary, not only because of the magnitude of the resources needed, but also because the peculiar history of Mexican-American relations means that the role of the United States must be managed discreetly. A program made in Washington would have little chance of success when it comes face-to-face with Mexican nationalism.

Conclusion

These are but a few examples of the kinds of problems that will face the Western democracies as they move into the twenty-first century. They are complicated and, if badly handled, potentially dangerous. Yet they by no means cover the spectrum of challenges inherent in an increasingly complicated and polycentric world. One could add, for example, the problems of the environment, which have been dealt with for too long as domestic issues, despite the fact that they do not respect borders. They are inherently international in scope and, in the end, will have to be dealt with cooperatively by those nations wealthy enough to mobilize the resources necessary to their solution.

The Western democracies, to steal from Franklin Roosevelt, have a rendezvous with destiny. If they act together, the twenty-first century can be a time of building and creation. If they fail to cooperate, it will be a time of turmoil and tragedy. As another Franklin (Benjamin) said in another revolutionary time, "Either we hang together or we shall surely hang separately."

7

American Public Opinion:
Evolving Definitions
of National Security

JOHN MARTTILA

I n the closing moments of the 1984 presidential election, the Reagan campaign unveiled the most celebrated television advertisment of that year—the so-called bear in the

---

JOHN MARTTILA is a partner in Marttila & Kiley, a national market research and strategic consulting firm. Mr. Marttila has been actively involved in U.S. politics for more than fifteen years. During that time he has worked with several presidential candidates, numerous U.S. senators, governors, members of the U.S. House of Representatives, and big city mayors. Mr. Marttila is a frequent speaker on national political issues and expects to publish a volume on the results of the Americans Talk Security (ATS) project.

The Americans Talk Security project is a series of nationwide surveys examining American attitudes toward national security issues. Funded by Massachusetts businessman Alan Kay, ATS was designed to enhance the dialogue between presidential candidates and the public on all aspects of national security during the 1988 campaign. To this end, a bipartisan consortium of prominent opinion research

woods commercial. In the ad, a giant grizzly bear was seen roaming through the wilderness, while muffled drumbeats, meant to evoke the sound of a heart beating, were heard in the background.

If the setting for the commercial was unconventional, the narration was remarkable for its subtlety in this era of "punch them in the mouth, make sure they get the point" political advertising:

> There's a bear in the woods
> For some people, the bear is easy to see.
> Others don't see it at all.
> Some people say the bear is tame.
> Others say it's vicious and dangerous.
> Since no one can really be sure who's right,
> Isn't it smart to be as strong as the bear
> . . . If there is a bear?

The ad closed with a smiling photograph of President Reagan appearing above the words "Prepared for Peace."

Pity the poor visitor from another country trying to make sense of this campaign commercial. Yet to millions of Ameri-

---

firms was assembled to conduct twelve national surveys from November 1987 to November 1988 in what many believe to be the most comprehensive study of public attitudes on these issues ever undertaken.

Four nationally recognized research firms were involved in each survey: Market Opinion Research, which works exclusively with Republican clients; Marttila & Kiley, which works with Democrats; and two organizations that are not active in partisan politics—The Daniel Yankelovich Group and the Public Agenda Foundation. Each company participated in the drafting of the questionnaires and the review of the results; the execution of each survey alternated among the firms. This rigorous approach was meant to guarantee the most accurate and unbiased results possible.

The surveys were shared at no cost with each Republican and Democratic presidential campaign, the entire Congress, all fifty governors, news organizations across the country, policy organizations that have a special interest in national security issues, and prominent Americans who have been active in these issues.

cans, the advertisement made complete sense; it was a metaphor for President Reagan's approach to the Soviet Union, and most people understood its intent perfectly. Moreover, the ad was widely accepted as a devastating indictment of the president's opponent and his party, without even mentioning Walter Mondale or the word Democrat. The notions of Republican strength and Democratic lack of resolve with respect to U.S.–Soviet relations had insinuated themselves into the American political consciousness so thoroughly that the words did not even need to be spoken.

Strength, Caution, Negotiation

Given the importance of the superpower rivalry, it should come as no surprise that Americans hold very strong views about what their government's basic approach to the Soviet regime should be. In fact, poll results show that a truly unshakable national consensus exists on the matter. Simply put, the American people believe the U.S. government should be involved in continuing negotiations with the Kremlin to reduce the threat of nuclear war. But because the public also harbors grave suspicions about the Soviet system and its leadership, they believe our leaders should negotiate very cautiously and from a position of strength.

This seemingly simple conviction is one of the enduring political truths of the post–World War II era; but many political leaders have failed to realize it has three components. By relying on fragmentary evidence, i.e., poll results that have testified to Americans' desire for arms control through negotiation, these politicians have ignored the public's simultaneous commitment to strength and caution as preconditions of any negotiations. Gorbachev's genuine popularity with Americans notwithstanding, polls consistently indicate that our people are deeply suspicious of the Soviet regime and have little interest in pursuing a drastic new approach with the Kremlin.

This fundamental American attitude is highly significant because it is almost impossible to overstate the impact of U.S.–Soviet relations on our national political life. The issue has dominated the foreign policy debate of virtually every presidential campaign since 1948, and it has played a critical role in helping Americans evaluate national candidates and their party platforms. While concern about other international developments has ebbed and flowed, the Soviets have remained a central preoccupation of the American people for more than forty years, as they will continue to be for the foreseeable future.

In a very real sense, the issue of U.S.–Soviet relations is the gateway through which all aspiring national politicians must pass before they can credibly discuss other international issues. Presidential candidates who are thought to be naive about the Soviets are unlikely to be fully trusted by the American people, no matter how impressive their other policy proposals or personal credentials might be.

In spite of the American public's skepticism about the Soviets, however, recent poll results indicate that the people believe our relationship with the Kremlin leaders has become increasingly predictable and, consequently, less likely to result in an unanticipated blow-up that would threaten world peace. This perception of relative stability has been enhanced by the positive impression the new Soviet leader has made upon the American people, and by the news coverage arising out of the Reagan-Gorbachev summit meetings.

Thus the perception of a more stable U.S.–Soviet relationship, coupled with a series of new international and domestic developments, pointed to the possibility of a national security debate during the 1988 presidential campaign that would deal with some powerful new topics. Moreover, the continued progress between the United States and the USSR could have reassured the public that they had the "luxury" of debating other pressing international issues, something that they were definitely anxious to do. For reasons rooted in the tactics employed by the respective campaigns, however, these new concerns received less attention than one would have expected. Nevertheless, the polls indicated they are bound to be a major presence in the national security debates of the early 1990s.

New Threats to U.S. National Security

These shifting priorities of the American people were documented in a series of twelve national surveys that were conducted during the 1988 presidential campaign by Americans Talk Security (ATS), an unprecedented program of bipartisan opinion research on a single topic. ATS was the creation of Massachusetts businessman Alan Kay. Its sole purpose was to study public attitudes toward national security issues and foreign policy questions.

The ATS surveys indicated Americans wanted to focus less on the U.S.–Soviet rivalry during the 1988 campaign and more on a new set of international issues. Then and now, Americans are struggling to cope with the new challenges of the rapidly changing world we live in; and they are not having an easy time. Traditional international relationships are being turned on their heads: former military adversaries look less menacing; current economic allies look like possible threats to our future; and the proper American role in the world seems a little less certain. Moreover, the oceans and international borders no longer provide us the convenience of separating domestic from foreign policy issues—distinctions that have less relevance in our increasingly interconnected world.

Thus in the 1988 ATS polling, when the public was regularly asked to identify the most serious threats to U.S. national security in the next five years, they consistently indicated that international drug trafficking, terrorism, and the spread of nuclear weapons to Third World countries were greater threats to our country than the threat of Soviet expansionism.

NATIONAL SECURITY THREATS IN THE NEXT FIVE YEARS AUGUST, 1988					
	Extrmly Serious	Very Serious	Smewht Serious	Not vry Serious	Not Sure
International drug trafficking	44%	42	11	2	*
Spread of nuclear weapons to Third World countries	36%	45	14	4	2
Terrorist activities around the world	34%	45	17	3	1
Damaging our environment from things like air & water pollution or the greenhouse effect – the heating of the earth's atmosphere	32%	45	16	7	1
Domestic problems – unemployment, homelessness and crime.	26%	47	22	5	1
Undermining of our constitutional government	22%	36	24	13	4
Economic competition from countries like Japan & W. Germany	19%	36	32	12	3
Unnecessary U.S. involvement in conflicts around the world.	19%	33	31	14	4
Increase in Soviet military strength relative to the U.S.	18%	32	31	18	2

Throughout its twelve surveys, ATS extensively documented the public's belief that threats to U.S. national security are changing. This was one of the project's most important contributions to an increased understanding about the public mood regarding our international future. Indeed, in one important ATS summary result, nearly 60 percent of the people supported the general proposition that threats to our national security are changing, and that these new threats require different kinds of national security policies than the ones the United States has relied upon in the past.

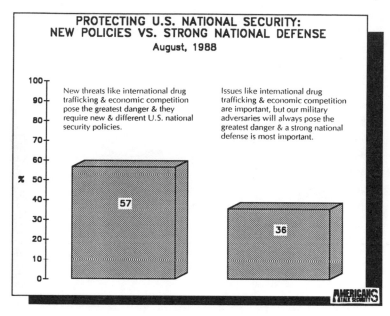

**PROTECTING U.S. NATIONAL SECURITY:
NEW POLICIES VS. STRONG NATIONAL DEFENSE**
August, 1988

New threats like international drug trafficking & economic competition pose the greatest danger & they require new & different U.S. national security policies.

Issues like international drug trafficking & economic competition are important, but our military adversaries will always pose the greatest danger & a strong national defense is most important.

57

36

    Not surprisingly, some of the public's greatest anxiety about
our international future centers on the United States' ability to
compete successfully in the new, more challenging world
economy. One of the most important findings in the ATS series dramatically underscored American concern on this issue:
only 22 percent of the people believe the United States is the
top economic power in the world today; and 34 percent actually think the United States has less economic power than
countries like Japan or West Germany. This finding was so
startling that it was verified before it was fully reported. This
remarkable poll result speaks volumes about growing American apprehension regarding U.S. economic competitiveness.

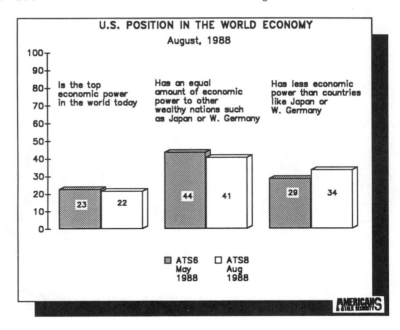

Americans are very worried about our country's economic future, and these mounting concerns are bound to have an important impact on our national politics in the coming years. Barring an actual military conflict in which U.S. forces see action, this issue is certain to be one of the major foreign policy issues of the 1990s. Also, these troubled attitudes are clearly responsible for some of the public's change of mind about threats to our national security.

It is not surprising, therefore, that more and more Americans are defining national power in economic terms, and that many are actually linking economic strength to their definitions of national security. In another key ATS finding, majorities of the public indicated that economic competitors like Japan pose a greater threat to our national security than military adversaries like the Soviet Union.

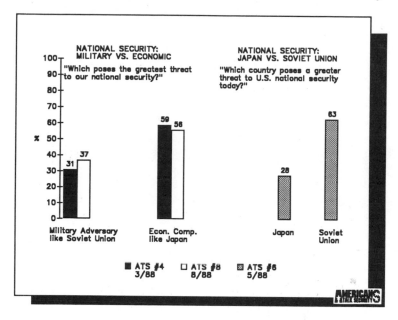

As the chart shows, however, this result does not mean Americans believe Japan poses a greater threat to U.S. national security than the Soviet Union does. When the comparative threats of the two countries were directly compared, nearly two-thirds of the Americans polled thought the Soviets were a greater threat to U.S. national security, while less than 30 percent chose the Japanese. The results from these two questions overlap, but they do not necessarily contradict one another. The evidence suggests that the American people believe our economic competitors will ultimately prove to be a greater threat to U.S. national security than our traditional military adversaries. But make no mistake about it, the Soviet Union is still seen as a major threat to our country. And any assessment of public attitudes about the global challenges we will face in the 1990s must begin with a review of American attitudes toward the USSR and its popular leader, Mikhail Gorbachev.

American Attitudes Toward
the Soviet Union

In considering the possibilities for improvements in the superpower relationship, one should never underestimate the
inherent suspicion the American people harbor toward the Soviet Union. This steadfast wariness, which was confirmed yet
again in the ATS polling, is truly impressive, especially since
all of the surveys were conducted during the very height of the
Reagan-Gorbachev era of improved relations.

While the Soviet leader is remarkably popular in the United
States, Americans remain extremely skeptical about the Soviet
system. Thus much of the public's hope for improved superpower relations is invested in the person of Gorbachev. If he
were to lose power, the public's cautious optimism about U.S.–
Soviet relations would almost certainly evaporate overnight,
and Americans would revert to their deeply guarded attitudes
of the early 1980s. A few examples of American attitudes toward the Soviets should amply demonstrate the profound level
of ongoing public distrust.

In the seventh ATS survey, nineteen possible Soviet actions—ranging from reducing the power of the Soviet secret
police to increasing the freedom of press and speech in the
USSR—were tested to see if any would increase Americans'
trust in the Soviets. The written analysis concluded that

only three out of the nineteen potential Soviet initiatives emerge as
likely to increase the trust of a majority of the people: cutting back the
power of the secret police; stop trying to win over our allies; and
greatly reducing the amount of spying and covert activity against the
U.S. Moreover, less than one out of five voters will acknowledge that
any action on the part of the Soviets would increase trust a great deal.

One could argue that so theoretical a consideration of potential Soviet actions was bound to produce results that are
ambiguous or highly speculative and, therefore, not all that
useful in assessing the evolution of long-term American attitudes. Nevertheless, when the public was asked to evaluate one
of the most widely publicized actual Soviet actions in 1988—

the beginning of the withdrawal of their troops from Afghanistan—the American people were similarly unimpressed. Less than 30 percent of the people felt that the Afghan pullout meant the Soviets may eventually end their policy of military intervention in other countries; two-thirds thought the Soviet decision to withdraw their troops from Afghanistan was unique and was no reason to believe the Soviets would cease military intervention elsewhere. Even more telling, only 20 percent of the people said the Soviet withdrawal from Afghanistan made them trust the Soviets more, 70 percent said they continued to trust them to about the same degree, while 10 percent said the evacuation actually made them trust the Soviets less.

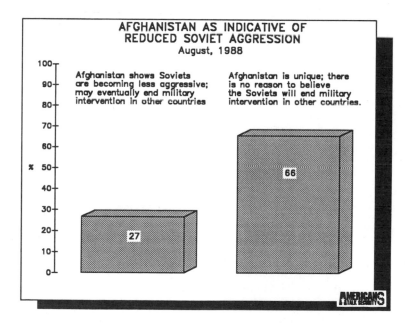

When the withdrawal of Soviet forces from Afghanistan began, many analysts speculated the pullout might mark the beginning of a softening of American attitudes toward the Soviets. But these findings confirmed the results of much of

the other ATS research: the Soviets will have to win the trust of
the American people on a step-by-step basis, rather than
through any single action, no matter how noteworthy it may
be.

The surprisingly indifferent public response to the Soviet
withdrawal from Afghanistan can be fully understood only
when it is considered in the context of fundamental American
attitudes toward the Soviet regime. Listed below are some simple measures of these beliefs as they were measured in the
ATS polling. Most of these questions have been asked in surveys dating back five or six years and, for the most part, the
ATS results indicated improved levels of public trust.

	Agree	Disagree
The Soviets lie, cheat, and steal—they'll do anything to further the cause of communism	52%	41%
The Soviets only respond to military strength	55%	40%
If we are weak, the Soviet Union, at the right moment, will attack us or our allies in Europe and Japan	56%	37%
Communism threatens our religious and moral values	66%	30%
The Soviets aren't fanatics about spreading communism, they won't take any reckless chances	49%	44%
Because the Soviets will not keep their end of the bargain, we should not sign any agreements limiting nuclear arms	53%	41%

As one further indication of public wariness about the Soviets, 70 percent of the American people still embrace the policy

of containment that was formulated after World War II to contain future Soviet expansion in Europe.

Even more revealing about American attitudes, 40 percent of the people support the strategic theory known as rollback, which was conceived to force the Soviets out of Eastern Europe and eventually overthrow the Soviet government itself! To be entirely fair, 50 percent reject this notion, a figure that would have surely increased if the financial, military, and human costs of achieving such a victory were part of this theoretical question. Nevertheless, these top-of-the-mind responses are truly useful in illuminating the underlying attitudes through which new information about Soviet behavior is filtered.

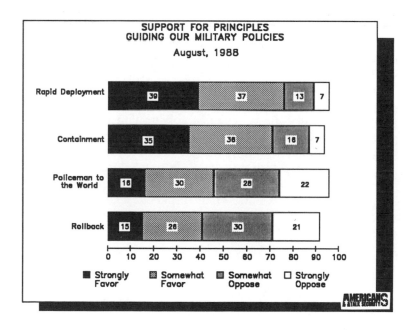

Women Without College Educations: The Surprising Conservatives on U.S.–Soviet Relations

The ATS polling shows a strong correlation between education and income levels and attitudes toward the Soviet Union. As Americans move up the income and education ladder, they are likely to be more hopeful (optimistic is the wrong word) about the future of the superpower relationship; people with lower income and education levels, on the other hand, are much more skeptical. Higher levels of education and income also correlate with more interest in, and more knowledge about, foreign affairs: college educated men, postgraduates of both sexes, and people who make more than $50,000 per year are consistently the most well-informed demographic subgroups about international issues. These three audiences are also the most hopeful about U.S.–Soviet relations.

One of the most consistently useful demographic approaches for analyzing foreign policy issues is to divide the population into four subgroups: college educated men; college educated women; men without a college education; and women without a college education. In virtually every survey, the views of these four subgroups produced meaningful distinctions and assumed great predictive value in anticipating future ATS survey results. Their respective shares of the electorate are indicated in the chart below.

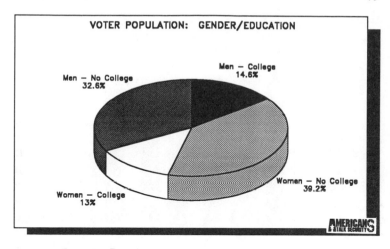

Surprisingly, among these four gender/education audiences, women without college educations were the least receptive in the ATS surveys to encouraging interpretations about improving U.S.–Soviet relations, and they consistently gave Gorbachev lower personal ratings as well. Also, on any number of survey questions about the Soviet Union, the views of non–college educated women and college educated men contrasted the most sharply within the four gender/education quadrants, with college educated men being the most hopeful and non–college educated women being the most skeptical. From the standpoint of the partisan structure of American politics, what is especially noteworthy about these contrasting views is that college educated men are the most Republican of these four audiences, and women without college educations are the most Democratic.

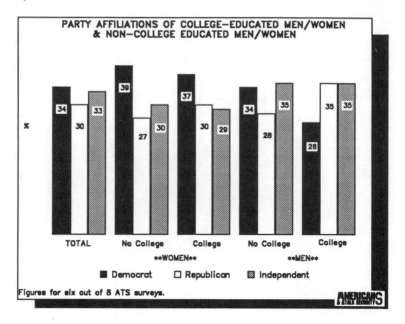

The stunningly anti-Soviet views of women without college educations are revealed in the following ATS data. These findings upset longstanding notions about the political values of American men and women on the issues of war and peace, and the origins of the "gender gap," which has long been recognized as a feature of our political landscape.

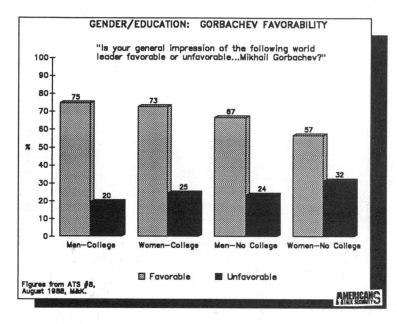

GENDER/EDUCATION: GORBACHEV FAVORABILITY

"Is your general impression of the following world
leader favorable or unfavorable...Mikhail Gorbachev?"

Figures from ATS #8,
August 1988, M&K.

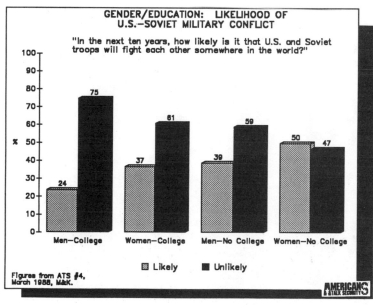

GENDER/EDUCATION: LIKELIHOOD OF
U.S.–SOVIET MILITARY CONFLICT

"In the next ten years, how likely is it that U.S. and Soviet
troops will fight each other somewhere in the world?"

Figures from ATS #4,
March 1988, M&K.

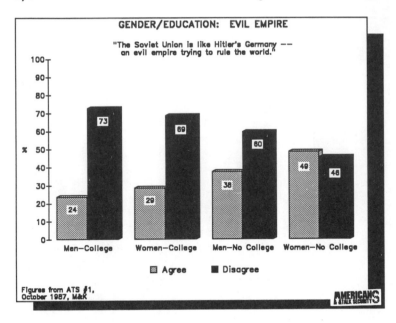

GENDER/EDUCATION: EVIL EMPIRE

"The Soviet Union is like Hitler's Germany —— an evil empire trying to rule the world."

Men—College: Agree 24, Disagree 73
Women—College: Agree 29, Disagree 69
Men—No College: Agree 38, Disagree 60
Women—No College: Agree 49, Disagree 46

Agree   Disagree

Figures from ATS #1, October 1987, M&K

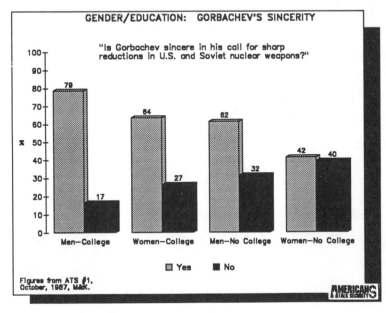

GENDER/EDUCATION: GORBACHEV'S SINCERITY

"Is Gorbachev sincere in his call for sharp reductions in U.S. and Soviet nuclear weapons?"

Men—College: Yes 79, No 17
Women—College: Yes 64, No 27
Men—No College: Yes 62, No 32
Women—No College: Yes 42, No 40

Yes   No

Figures from ATS #1, October, 1987, M&K.

Peace Through Strength

One practical measure of American concern about the Soviets is the amount of money we spend on them. Today, staggering amounts of our national resources are directed at the USSR through our nation's military apparatus. The analysis contained in William Kaufman's book, *A Reasonable Defense,* indicates that defending Europe from Soviet attack alone consumes nearly 40 percent of the Defense Department budget, or approximately $130 billion. Another $55 billion is required to cover the cost of our nuclear capability, most of which is directed at the Soviet Union or its military installations.

Mission	Budget Authority
The Fiscal 1986 Defense Budget by Major Mission*	
Strategic nuclear retaliation.	51.5
Theater nuclear retaliation.	3.2
Conventional defense of:	
Central Europe	80.2
North Norway	17.2
Greece and Turkey	9.8
Atlantic and Caribbean.	25.8
Persian Gulf States.	20.9
Republic of Korea	12.9
Pacific and Indian Oceans.	21.7
Continental United States, Alaska and Panama. . . .	16.2
Intelligence and communications.	36.5
Subtotal	$295.9
Retired pay accrual	17.8
Total budget authority	**$313.7**

* *Figures are in billions of dollars; taken from William Kaufman, A Reasonable Defense, page 14.*

In total, nearly two-thirds of our defense budget is aimed directly or indirectly at our greatest military foe, and the public is strongly supportive of these allocations. The ATS surveys revealed the depth of the country's commitment to military strength, even during a time when increasing numbers of Americans are troubled by the negative impact that defense spending may be having on our economy and on our country's ability to address pressing social problems.

Perhaps the most striking evidence of the breadth of support for President Reagan's military build-up was found in a proposition that was tested in several ATS surveys. When asked if the Reagan military build-up was necessary or unnecessary, an overwhelming majority (two-thirds) of the people consistently responded that it was necessary. Even when this question was asked following a sequence of inquiries about America's growing economic problems, 58 percent of the people indicated the build-up was necessary.

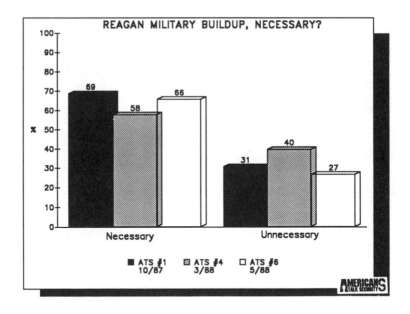

Also, while the ATS surveys and many other national polls have found support for defense cuts, these results must be balanced against other opinion research that has measured

American attitudes regarding the relative military strength of
the United States and the Soviet Union. Surprisingly, in light
of President Reagan's massive military build-up, there appears
to be a slight deterioration in public confidence about the relative strength of the United States during the years since 1985.

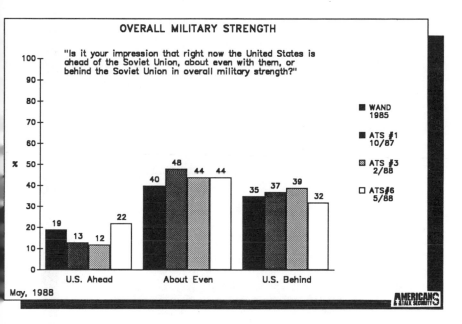

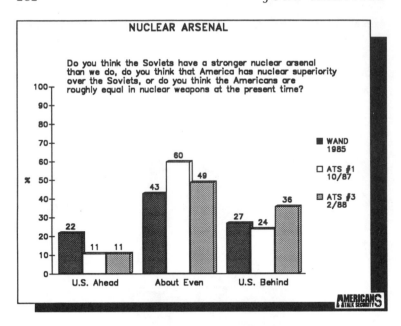

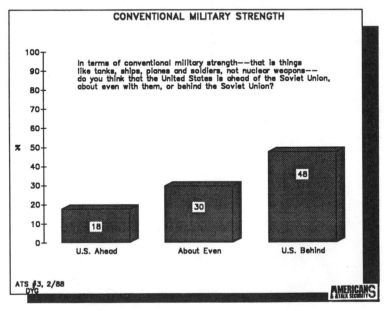

These findings provide the clearest possible warning against accepting at face value poll results that indicate the public wants the defense budget reduced. While such proposals have obvious top-of-the-mind appeal, they inevitably succumb to Americans' deeper anxiety about perceived Soviet military strength. In my view, these results indicate that the public would accept reduced U.S. military expenditures only if there were compensating strategic developments that would make such cuts less risky, e.g., increased military spending by our allies, or a reduced Soviet military presence in Eastern Europe. In other words, the people will not accept defense budget cuts without a new conceptual framework for our national security requirements.

The Strategic Defense Initiative (SDI)

Perhaps the most interesting recent case study of Americans' ambivalent attitudes toward military expenditures—and one that has been frequently misunderstood by its critics—is Star Wars. The system was proposed during a period of political turmoil for the president. Reagan's bellicose attitude toward Moscow during the early years of his administration had played an important role in launching the nuclear freeze movement. This movement, a genuine citizen-based protest against Reagan's policies, swept across the country like a prairie fire during the early 1980s. Although the real political impact of the freeze movement has been frequently overestimated, this was a difficult time for the Reagan White House.

This difficulty stemmed from the fact that the American people are of two minds about our national defense; they seek both peace and strength. As much as they seek strong leaders capable of handling the Soviets, Americans also expect these leaders to keep our nation at peace. Someone who is seen as militarily reckless will lose the trust of the American people just as rapidly as someone who is seen to be naive about the Kremlin. Leaving aside questions about its scientific, military, and diplomatic potential, SDI proved to be one of the most masterful political counteroffensives of our time; it played a major role in stopping the freeze movement's momentum because it simultaneously tapped the popular desire for peace through strength and Americans' nearly religious faith in the potential of high technology. Moreover, in spite of the increased criticism Star Wars received during the presidential campaign, a majority of the public continued to support the program through 1988, although by slightly diminished margins.

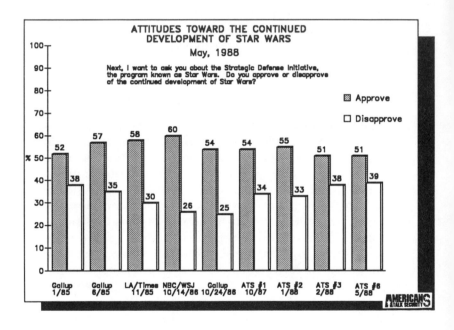

Parenthetically, one of the most interesting aspects of the freeze and SDI battles was that they left the defense, scientific, and diplomatic communities—the traditional arbiters of this esoteric subject matter—largely on the sidelines. As these experts looked on from a distance, the president and the citizen groups who supported these widely divergent proposals leapfrogged over the experts and took their own, allegedly "flawed," ideas directly to the people. The dichotomy between the values of the average citizens and the opinions of the expert community is a continuing presence in any debate about the arms race and, for his part, Reagan took full advantage of this division in his defense of SDI. While the Democrats used experts to discredit Star Wars, the president used a public relations campaign to take his case directly to the people. Star Wars is one of the most controversial, and most widely criticized, ideas ever proposed by the Defense Department. Yet it has remained politically viable because it enjoys broad public support; in other words, the doubts of the scientific community have been offset by the dominant currents of public opinion.

The ATS surveys revealed that the public had many reservations about the costs of SDI at a time of record deficits and during a period when social and economic problems were seen as needing federal attention. Moreover, most Americans believe the Soviets will eventually develop ways to overcome the technology, thereby only speeding up the arms race. But critics of SDI, unlike the system's supporters, have rarely spoken with a unified voice, and opponents have consistently underestimated the breadth of support for Star Wars and its deeper psychological appeal to the public. As a result, they have never fully appreciated how difficult it would be to change public opinion on the issue. The American people showed themselves to be receptive to criticisms of SDI, but they also indicated that these criticisms must be sharply focused and presented as part of a broader definition of national security needs.

But even the most focused criticism of Star Wars would run into difficulties when SDI is considered in the context of the Soviet threat, as the table by that name shows.

S.D.I. IN CONTEXT OF SOVIET THREAT

WAND (M&K, 1985)	Agree	Disagree
The Soviet leaders are extremely concerned about "Star Wars," which means we must be on the right track with this idea	64%	26

ATS #1 (M&K, Oct. 1987)		
"Star Wars" has already proven to be an effective bargaining issue in getting the Soviet Union to seriously negotiate reductions in nuclear weapons . . .	60%	28
"Star Wars" has shown that Ronald Reagan is right: the best way to achieve progress with the Soviets is to deal with them from a position of strength	60%	33

AMERICANS TALK SECURITY

Finally, in the ATS surveys the people consistently rejected any notion of sharing Star Wars technology with the Soviets. Strong majorities also opposed abandoning SDI research in exchange for arms control progress. The American people know "the Bear" does not like Star Wars, and, given their deep anxieties about Soviet military strength, that suits them just fine.

Arms Control: INF & START

Nowhere were Americans' skeptical instincts about the Soviets more evident than in the poll results reporting the public's appraisal of the intermediate nuclear force (INF) treaty and the Strategic Arms Reduction Talks (START). At a surface level, both treaties were supported by overwhelming majorities of the American people, but there was less enthusiasm for them than most politicians and analysts believed. As an exam-

AMERICAN PUBLIC OPINION   287

ple, in one of the ATS surveys, nearly 90 percent of the respondents agreed that INF is a good way to find out if the Soviets can be trusted *before* we agree to more arms reduction through START. Even more revealing, a majority of the people favored an amendment to the INF treaty "requiring President Reagan to certify that the Soviet Union is adhering to all past arms control agreements before the treaty can take effect—even if requiring it would kill the treaty." And, if the American people were sitting at the START negotiating tables, they would drive a tough bargain and demand additional concessions before agreeing to further reductions in our nuclear arsenal. The Conditions on START table shows the demands the majority of our citizen negotiators would make.

Conditions on START

"Here are some examples of changes in Soviet policy that we should require. For each one, please tell me if the U.S. should or should not require the Soviets to make that change before we agree to another nuclear arms reduction."

	Should Require	Should Not Require
ATS #2 (MOR, 1/88)		
The Soviets should remove their restrictions on Jews who wish to leave the Soviet Union before we agree to another nuclear arms reduction	53%	41
The Soviets should establish freedom of the press in their country before we agree to another nuclear arms reduction	36%	59
The Soviets should withdraw their troops from Afghanistan before we agree to another nuclear arms reduction	63%	31
The Soviets should stop their military assistance to revolutionary forces in Africa and Central America before we agree to another nuclear arms reduction	60%	33

If the American people were collectively doing the negotiating, would they really kill INF and START by making too many

tough demands on the Soviets? Probably not. What is very
clear, however, is that their deep skepticism of the Soviet regime can even raise doubts about the wisdom of reducing the
superpowers' stockpiles of nuclear weapons, something that
all opinion research has shown to be one of the public's highest priorities. That these reservations about reducing nuclear
weapons are expressed at a time when the popular Gorbachev
is at the helm is even more revealing of the public's mood and
its fundamental attitude toward the Kremlin regime.

The Popular Gorbachev

In spite of the American public's inherent caution about the
Soviets, the ATS polls indicated that most Americans believe
our relations with the Soviets are getting better, in large measure because of the positive impression Mikhail Gorbachev has
made upon the American people. By any measure, Gorbachev
is genuinely popular with the American people. The ATS polling tested the popularity in the United States of more than
twenty world leaders, and the Soviet leader was the third most
well-liked, trailing only Margaret Thatcher and the Pope. Gorbachev's personal ratings were even higher when he was rated
individually.

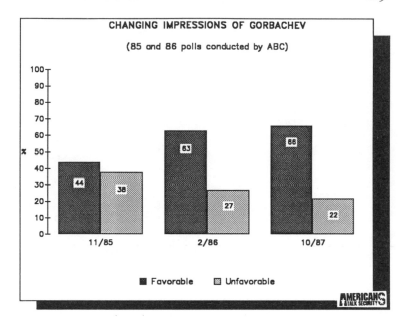

CHANGING IMPRESSIONS OF GORBACHEV

(85 and 86 polls conducted by ABC)

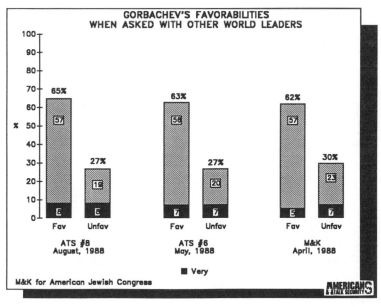

GORBACHEV'S FAVORABILITIES
WHEN ASKED WITH OTHER WORLD LEADERS

M&K for American Jewish Congress

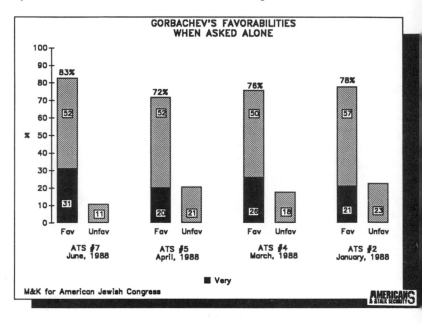

Gorbachev's popularity with the American people is probably best explained by their belief that he is unlike past Soviet
leaders—seven out of ten Americans hold this view. Two-
thirds of the respondents believe Gorbachev can be trusted
more than past Soviet leaders; 60 percent believe he is more
interested in peace with the West than his predecessors; and
55 percent believe the changes taking place in the Soviet
Union are primarily the result of Gorbachev's leadership,
rather than reflections of deeper changes taking place within
the Soviet system itself.

These impressive findings were reinforced even further by
the American public's expectations regarding the potential impact on Soviet society if Gorbachev is successful in implementing his reforms: clear majorities believe the Soviets will
become more westernized in their style and fashions; they will
build a more competitive economy; they will move toward a
more open and free society; and they will become more com-

mitted to reducing nuclear arms. Nevertheless, decisive majorities reject the notion that the Kremlin leaders will pull back from their attempts to expand their influence in the Third World.

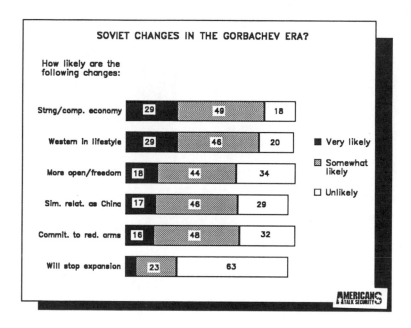

SOVIET CHANGES IN THE GORBACHEV ERA?

How likely are the following changes:

	Very likely	Somewhat likely	Unlikely
Strng/comp. economy	29	49	18
Western in lifestyle	29	46	20
More open/freedom	18	44	34
Sim. relat. as China	17	46	29
Commit. to red. arms	16	48	32
Will stop expansion		23	63

AMERICANS & ATALK SECURITY

Gorbachev's obvious popularity notwithstanding, 70 percent of Americans reject the notion that the United States should seize the opportunity to engage in accelerated negotiations with him because he represents the best opportunity in decades to achieve real breakthroughs with the Soviets. Even when Gorbachev is given every benefit of the doubt, most Americans still want to proceed cautiously with him.

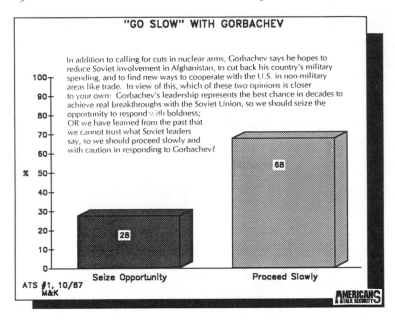

"GO SLOW" WITH GORBACHEV

In addition to calling for cuts in nuclear arms, Gorbachev says he hopes to reduce Soviet involvement in Afghanistan, to cut back his country's military spending, and to find new ways to cooperate with the U.S. in non-military areas like trade. In view of this, which of these two opinions is closer to your own: Gorbachev's leadership represents the best chance in decades to achieve real breakthroughs with the Soviet Union, so we should seize the opportunity to respond with boldness; OR we have learned from the past that we cannot trust what Soviet leaders say, so we should proceed slowly and with caution in responding to Gorbachev?

Seize Opportunity: 28
Proceed Slowly: 68

ATS #1, 10/87
M&K

AMERICANS
& ATALK SECURITY

Nevertheless, Gorbachev has had an important impact on the American public's assessment of U.S.–Soviet relations: two-thirds of the people believe relations between the United States and the Soviet Union are getting better; only a negotiable minority believe relations are getting worse. Moreover, compared to ten years ago, 44 percent of the people believe we can now trust the Soviets more than in the past.

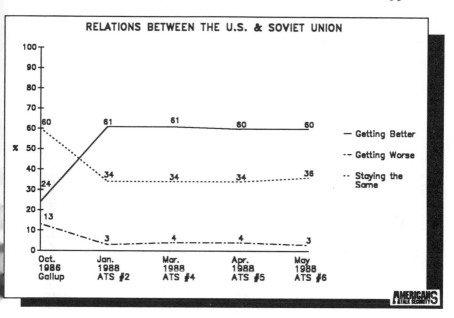

RELATIONS BETWEEN THE U.S. & SOVIET UNION

The Soviets: Increasingly Predictable Adversaries

Another contributing factor to the public's view that U.S.–Soviet relations are getting better is that the Soviet Union is seen as an increasingly predictable adversary. In an era when explosive regional conflicts and terrorism seize the headlines, this possibility is somewhat of a comfort—at least Americans *think* they know what to expect from the Soviets.

Very few Americans polled (10 percent) believe a nuclear war will be started by the Soviets launching a surprise attack on the United States or by their invading Western Europe. Only slightly more (21 percent) feel that such a war is most likely to be started by the superpowers' being drawn into a regional conflict. In contrast, two-thirds believe a nuclear war, if begun, will be started by a terrorist, a madman, or a nonsuperpower involved in a regional conflict.

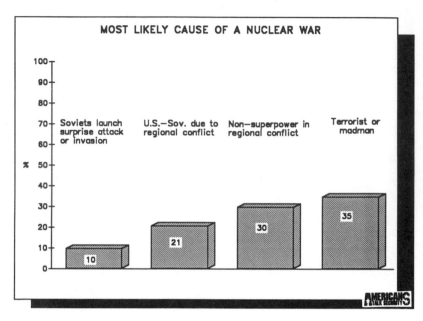

Three-fourths of the Americans polled think the United States' being drawn into a Third World regional conflict poses a greater threat to our national security than a direct conflict between the superpowers.

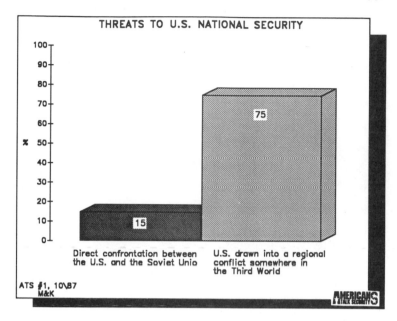

THREATS TO U.S. NATIONAL SECURITY

ATS #1, 10\87
M&K

AMERICANS
& ATALK SECURITY

And when asked which of the countries with a nuclear capability is most likely to "explode a nuclear bomb," twice as many American voters chose Iraq as chose the Soviet Union.

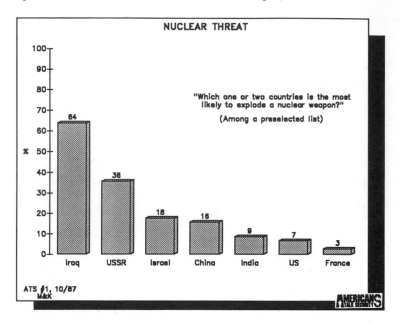

NUCLEAR THREAT

"Which one or two countries is the most likely to explode a nuclear weapon?"

(Among a preselected list)

ATS #1, 10/87
M&K

AMERICANS
TALK SECURITY

These changing perceptions about the likely cause of nuclear war help explain why the American public appears to be growing less fearful about the possibilities of the United States' becoming involved in a nuclear war. Over the twelve-month course of the ATS surveys, there was a decline in the number of respondents who believed the United States was going to become involved in a nuclear war within the next twenty-five years. But if the United States were to become involved in a nuclear war, a majority of the American people believe both the United States and the Soviet Union would be destroyed; thus, there has been no lessening of concern about the ultimate impact of such a conflagration.

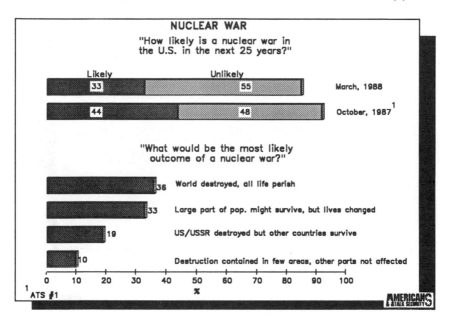

NUCLEAR WAR

"How likely is a nuclear war in the U.S. in the next 25 years?"

Increased U.S.–Soviet Cooperation

When Americans were asked to evaluate the likelihood of nine possible future developments in U.S.–Soviet relations, they consistently predicted the superpowers would *collaborate* on projects such as increased economic trade or joint space exploration rather than engage in *conflict,* e.g., the Soviets invading Western Europe. In fact, all but one of the six projections of cooperation ranked higher than the three possible areas of conflict. A significant minority (41 percent) thought it is even likely that the superpowers would enter into a long-term military alliance.

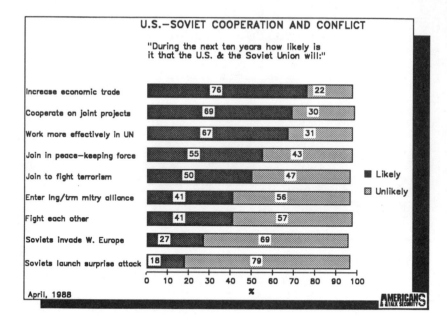

U.S.–SOVIET COOPERATION AND CONFLICT

"During the next ten years how likely is
it that the U.S. & the Soviet Union will:"

	Likely	Unlikely
Increase economic trade	76	22
Cooperate on joint projects	69	30
Work more effectively in UN	67	31
Join in peace-keeping force	55	43
Join to fight terrorism	50	47
Enter lng/trm mltry alliance	41	56
Fight each other	41	57
Soviets invade W. Europe	27	69
Soviets launch surprise attack	18	79

April, 1988

AMERICANS TALK SECURITY

Beyond the American public's sense of what is likely to happen, the data also suggest that there is a variety of cooperative ventures with the Soviets that Americans would support. Cases in point include stopping illicit drug trade (85 percent); halting environmental pollution (85 percent); expanding cultural exchanges (84 percent); fighting terrorism around the world (78 percent); resolving the Middle East crisis (72 percent); working toward the elimination of most nuclear weapons by the year 2000 (71 percent); and cooperating with the Soviets on a joint trip to Mars (59 percent). Nevertheless, most Americans draw the line at certain other suggested cooperative ventures, which they believe require too much trust of the Soviets.

LIMITS TO U.S.-SOVIET COOPERATION

	Proceed	Don't Trust	Not Sure
Agree with the Soviets to a 50% reduction in long-range nuclear weapons without any reduction in Soviet conventional weapons in Europe	36%	50	14
Agree with the Soviets to a 50% reduction in long-range nuclear weapons even before we see how the new INF Treaty with the Soviets is working out	36%	52	12
Sell nonmilitary high technology, like advanced computer equipment and software, to the Soviets	36%	56	8
Agree to stop work on the Strategic Defense Initiative, "Star Wars," as part of a nuclear arms agreement with the Soviet Union	34%	55	11
Share the Strategic Defense Initiative, also known as "Star Wars," with the Soviets as it is being developed	26%	62	10

AMERICANS TALK SECURITY

Thus while Americans remain suspicious of the Soviets, the impact of Gorbachev's leadership and the belief that the Soviets are becoming increasingly predictable adversaries has caused the people to conclude that a superpower military conflict is unlikely and a nuclear war is extremely remote. As a result, a majority of the public supports carefully specified areas of increased cooperation between the two nations to reduce tensions over the long run. Nevertheless, Americans' basic level of trust of the Soviets will only increase on a step-by-step basis and slowly, over time. This, the polls suggest, is the foundation of public opinion on the superpower relationship as we move into the 1990s.

Burden Sharing Among the Western Allies

As Americans have become less fearful about the possibilities of a superpower military conflict, and more concerned

about the U.S. economy, they have become increasingly convinced that America's allies should be paying more for their
own defense. A clear majority of the people believe we should
be spending less on the defense of Western Europe and Japan.
If the United States and the USSR continue to make progress
at the negotiating tables, this sentiment seems certain to gain
further public support. These feelings run so deep that it is
quite possible President George Bush will preside over one of
the most historic debates about U.S. defense policy since the
end of World War II, despite the public's commitment to a
strong national defense. Americans appear ready to reexamine
the traditional priorities of U.S. defense policy and the amount
of money we spend to achieve our objectives.

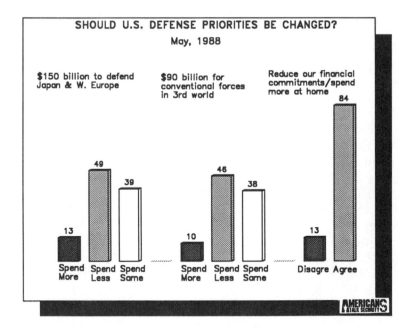

In other ATS findings, the people were more inclined to cut
the Defense Department budget once they understood the
strategic objective of the spending, i.e., $150 billion to defend

Western Europe and Japan, than they were when they learned how the money was used inside the department, i.e., $78 billion for armed forces pay and benefits. The one exception was the $55 billion spent for U.S. strategic nuclear forces: the public was less inclined to cut money spent for nuclear weapons when they understood the strategic objective of the spending. This is one more indication that Americans are willing to maintain current levels of spending in order to defend U.S. national security, but they appear willing to cut spending for the defense of our allies.

Thus in a comprehensive national debate that included a thorough discussion of the relative importance of U.S. economic and military power—and providing they believed the Soviets would gain no undue advantage—the American people might consider a reduction in our overall military expenditures. In any event, a majority certainly seems ready to make reductions in the amount of money America is spending to defend its allies around the world.

First Use of Nuclear Weapons

Over the years, many national surveys have indicated that Americans do not believe it is the policy of the United States to use nuclear weapons against the Soviets if they invade Europe using only conventional forces and weapons. Four out of five Americans mistakenly believe it is our policy to use nuclear weapons if, and only if, the Soviet Union attacks the United States with nuclear weapons first.

Beyond documenting this continuing public misunderstanding of American policy concerning first use, the ATS surveys also found that the public rejects the underlying principles behind this long-established doctrine. When asked under what circumstances the use of nuclear weapons might be justified, Americans rejected using nuclear weapons except in the event an American city were destroyed by a limited nuclear attack. Using nuclear weapons to repel a successful, but conventional, Soviet invasion of Europe was rejected by an eleven-to-one margin.

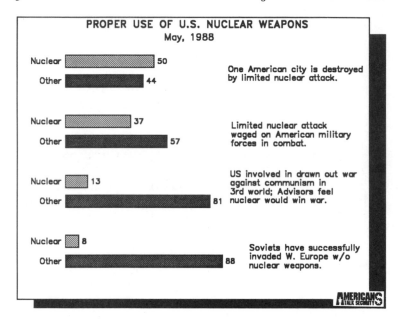

The Public Agenda Foundation (PAF) conducted an exhaustive three-year study of American attitudes on U.S.–Soviet relations. The proper use of nuclear weapons was a frequent topic of the project's focus group research. PAF found that even when the first use doctrine is carefully explained, Americans refuse to believe the U.S. government would ever implement the policy. The ATS and PAF findings about public understanding and support of the first use doctrine is another example of the dissonance that often exists between popular attitudes and official U.S. policy toward our allies. This lack of popular support for U.S. policy also spills over into discussions about U.S. foreign aid.

Lukewarm Support for U.S. Foreign Aid

While Americans support the humanitarian and pragmatic arguments for U.S. foreign aid, nearly 90 percent believe that such aid frequently does not reach the needy people for whom it was intended. Also, three-fourths of the people question whether the countries we help appreciate our efforts. Both as a general proposition, and on a country-by-country basis, many more Americans would rather cut foreign aid than increase it, although most people would continue to fund such aid at current levels. In part, these attitudes reflect concern about U.S. overextension abroad and the perceived need to pay attention to domestic problems at home.

Clear majorities of Americans accept the humanitarian and pragmatic arguments for U.S. foreign aid: 71 percent agree it reminds other nations that the United States is a positive moral force in world affairs; 68 percent agree that if we implement our aid wisely, the nations we help will become more friendly to the United States; 60 percent agree it helps to reduce the influence of the Soviets; and 59 percent agree it has been effective in improving poor people's lives in the Third World.

Nevertheless, the ATS survey questions on foreign aid that evoked the most intense public response were those that were critical of the program. Nearly 90 percent of the people agreed that all too often the aid ends up in the pockets of corrupt officials rather than in the hands of the needy people for whom it was intended; and 80 percent agreed that too many countries we help never seem to appreciate our efforts. Moreover, two-thirds of the people disagreed that we have a moral responsibility to help the disadvantaged of the world, even if it means putting off spending on domestic problems. Finally, 56 percent agreed that the United States can no longer help so many countries, no matter how worthy this help may be.

The lukewarm support for foreign aid is also revealed by the public's unenthusiastic attitudes about funding the program: while more Americans would continue to finance the aid program at current levels, a large minority would decrease it, while only 12 percent would increase the funding.

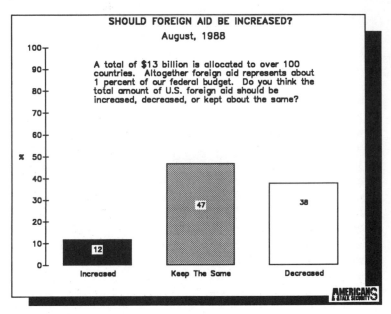

As a final measure of the public's attitudes toward spending money on foreign aid, 50 percent of the people believe "the U.S. foreign aid program is one of the best places to cut federal government spending." Forty-five percent disagree with this proposition, however.

Few Americans have any understanding that Japan will soon provide more foreign aid to countries around the world than the United States does. But two-thirds believe the foreign aid provided by Japan, which is almost exclusively economic and humanitarian, is more likely to win friends than the foreign aid of the United States, which is largely military or directly related to security agreements.

Once Americans are informed that two-thirds of U.S. foreign aid is security-based assistance, decisive majorities support *increasing* the amount of humanitarian foreign aid and *decreasing* the amount of military aid.

Eighty-four percent of the American people believe the United States provides more foreign aid to countries around

the world than does Japan; only 5 percent think Japan dis-
burses more than the United States does. While this response
is still technically correct, it suggests that the people have little
idea that Japan is currently providing almost as much foreign
aid as the United States is and that soon the Japanese will
actually be distributing more. Once Americans are informed
that the Japanese aid almost exclusively takes the form of economic development loans or humanitarian assistance and that
two-thirds of U.S. aid is security-related assistance, 68 percent
conclude that the Japanese aid is more likely to win friends
around the world, while 21 percent think the U.S. military emphasis will be more successful. Moreover, clear majorities of
the people believe economic and humanitarian aid is more
likely to advance our national security interests, while one-
fourth think military assistance is more effective. Finally, by
reasonably decisive margins, Americans believe we should increase our economic and humanitarian aid and decrease our
military aid.

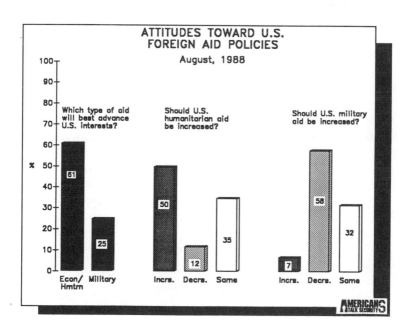

Is Isolationism Growing in America?

Growing concerns about U.S. international economic competitiveness, coupled with increased support for defense cost
burden sharing by our allies *and* lukewarm support for U.S.
foreign aid, all point to the possibility of a modestly resurgent
American isolationism. In the ATS surveys, Americans consistently acknowledged our special leadership role in the world,
and also recognized the need for the country to increase its
participation in the world economy if the U.S. economy is to
keep growing. Nevertheless, there were some intriguing poll
findings that seemed to suggest that latent isolationist tendencies might be creeping to the surface.

In one important finding from the third ATS survey, 47 percent of the people agreed with the following proposition: "We
should bring our troops home and limit our military involvement to defending our own borders—and we should gradually
end our treaty commitments and let our allies take care of
themselves." To be fair, only 17 percent of the respondents
strongly favored this notion, while 51 percent rejected it altogether. Also, there were no consequences attached to this
question, which made agreement with it relatively painless.
Nonetheless, it is probably not insignificant that a near majority of the country responded affirmatively to this rather
strongly isolationist proposition.

Obviously, a case for resurgent isolationism cannot be made
on the basis of a handful of poll questions, but there was an under-
current in the ATS data that consistently reflected a desire
among some Americans to pull back from world responsibility
or, at least, reflected a profound sense of unease about our
international future. And most of this anxiety can be attributed
to the mounting concern about the U.S. economic future.

The Dominant Foreign Policy
Issue of the 1990s

When only 22 percent of the people believe the United
States is the number one economic power in the world, it

should come as no surprise that 50 percent of the public believes the U.S. economy is "slipping dangerously when compared to other industrialized nations." This ATS finding showed a 9 percent increase from a Roper poll taken in January of 1987, when 41 percent held the same view.

Moreover, most Americans believe that Japan is a stronger competitor in the world economy than the United States is—only one-third characterize the United States as a very strong competitor, while two-thirds describe Japan in the same terms. When people look to the future, however, they are slightly more optimistic about U.S. possibilities.

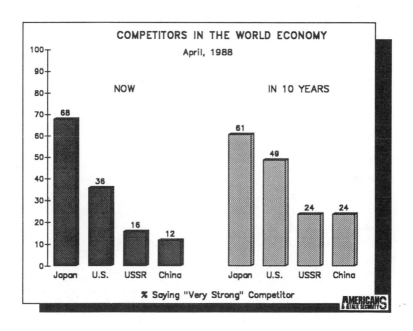

If the ATS economic data were not telling enough, consider this remarkable poll result: 45 percent of the American people agree that "the economic competition from Japan and West Germany poses more of a threat to our nation's future than the threat of Communist expansion ever did." Forty-eight percent disagree with this assertion.

Even though the issue of our country's ability to compete in the world economy was never fully joined during the 1988 presidential campaign, all of the ATS polling data indicated that this concern will be one of the major foreign policy issues of the 1990s; indeed, it has the potential to become as important to the American people in the future as the issue of U.S.–Soviet relations has been in the past.

And if foreign investment in the United States continues at its current pace, added political fuel will be poured onto this profound national concern. The combination of domestic and international economic worries, impatience with our allies, and signs of creeping isolationism could make this one of the most difficult and complicated foreign policy debates our country has ever experienced.

		Close Ally	Friend Not Ally	Not Friend Not Enemy	Enemy	Not Sure
		TIER ONE				
Great Britain	AJC	76%	18%	3%	1%	2%
Canada	ATS6	72%	21%	4%	1%	3%
		TIER TWO				
Australia	ATS6	53%	33%	6%	1%	7%
West Germany	AJC	52%	30%	8%	5%	5%
Japan	ATS6	38%	40%	12%	3%	5%
	ATS5	43%	40%	7%	3%	—
	AJC	47%	38%	9%	2%	4%
Israel	AJC	44%	32%	10%	5%	8%
Mexico	ATS5	34%	48%	8%	1%	8%
France	ATS6	38%	38%	15%	3%	6%
New Zealand	ATS6	35%	33%	8%	1%	23%
		TIER THREE				
Egypt	AJC	19%	48%	19%	2%	12%
China	ATS6	9%	50%	27%	6%	8%
India	ATS6	15%	42%	19%	3%	21%
Brazil	ATS6	16%	38%	15%	2%	28%
Saudi Arabia	AJC	17%	36%	24%	10%	14%
Jordan	AJC	12%	34%	24%	5%	26%
Panama	ATS5	10%	34%	27%	15%	14%

American Reaction to
Countries Around the World

None of these mounting international concerns appears to have turned Americans against our closest allies—at least not yet. When these nations and their leaders are evaluated amidst a wide range of countries and world leaders, our traditional loyalties seem to be intact.

In total, the ATS series measured public attitudes toward eighteen countries using a classic evaluation technique developed by the Chicago Council on Foreign Relations. When these results are supplemented by a 1988 American Jewish Congress poll, a total of twenty-seven countries were evaluated through this process. The responses about a particular

		Close Ally	Friend Not Ally	Not Friend Not Enemy	Enemy	Not Sure
		TIER FOUR				
South Africa	ATS6	9%	31%	39%	7%	13%
Nigeria	ATS6	5%	22%	22%	9%	42%
El Salvador	ATS5	7%	25%	27%	16%	25%
Iraq	AJC	7%	24%	33%	24%	12%
Soviet Union	ATS6	3%	28%	33%	30%	6%
	ATS5	3%	26%	30%	11%	5%
	AJC	3%	30%	31%	33%	4%
Syria	AJC	3%	19%	34%	21%	24%
Nicaragua	ATS5	3%	19%	29%	32%	16%
	AJC	4%	15%	36%	33%	4%
Vietnam	ATS6	3%	14%	36%	36%	12%
Lebanon	AJC	3%	15%	33%	34%	15%
		TIER FIVE				
Cuba	ATS5	1%	9%	25%	58%	7%
Iran	ATS5	0%	5%	11%	76%	8%
	AJC	2%	4%	15%	76%	3%

American Jewish Congress (AJC), April 1988, Marttila & Kiley.
ATS5, April 1988, Market Opinion Research.
ATS6, May 1988, Marttila & Kiley.

country fluctuated from survey to survey, but the relative standing among countries remained constant. Therefore, the countries have been grouped below according to five general rating categories, rather than by any one specific finding. As an example, Japan's ratings appear to decline over three consecutive surveys; yet its relative standing remains unchanged.

American Reaction to World Leaders

The American people may have more well-developed attitudes about world leaders than many analysts might have assumed. Margaret Thatcher, the Pope, and Mikhail Gorbachev received the highest personal ratings in the ATS polling. The Ayatullah Khomeini, Mohammar Khaddafi, Fidel Castro, Yassir Arafat, and Daniel Ortega were the most disliked, some of them intensely. With the exception of Gorbachev and the Soviet Union, most of the personal ratings correlate strongly to the preceding evaluations of the countries. The public also has surprisingly consistent views of these world figures. Twenty-three world leaders were evaluated in three national surveys conducted between April and August 1988. Whenever these individuals were measured in more than one poll, they received virtually identical ratings in the subsequent research.

These personal evaluations do more than simply measure the popularity or unpopularity of a particular individual. Often, the intensity of the voter response to these figures serves as a useful additional insight into the salience of the foreign policy issues that are associated with their countries or regions of the world. Finally, the ability to evaluate a majority of these world leaders has been shown to be an extremely reliable predictor of the respondents' general knowledge of foreign policy issues.

The Reagan Legacy

No analysis of the global challenges the United States will face in the 1990s would be complete without some evaluation of the Reagan foreign policy/national security legacy. Even his

WORLD LEADER FAVORABILITIES

		Very Favor	Favor	Unfav	Very Unfav	DK/ Nvr Hrd
Margaret Thatcher, Prime Minister of Great Britain	ATS8	21	48	20	8	2
	ATS6	20	64	6	1	9
	AJC	24	63	4	1	7
Pope John Paul II	AJC	25	56	10	2	8
Mikhail Gorbachev, General Secretary of the Soviet Union	ATS8	8	57	19	8	8
	ATS6	7	56	20	7	10
	AJC	5	57	23	7	9
Brian Mulroney, Prime Minister of Canada	ATS8	6	48	6	1	39
Rajiv Ghandi, Prime Minister of India	ATS8	4	40	13	3	40
King Hussein of Jordan	AJC	2	41	15	2	39
Noboru Takeshita, Prime Minister of Japan	ATS8	3	35	14	3	44
Helmut Kohl, Chancellor of West Germany	ATS8	2	35	9	2	52
Shimon Peres, Foreign Minister of Israel	AJC	3	32	19	4	41
Francois Mitterrand, President of France	ATS6	1	31	14	3	51

Hosni Mubarak,

WORLD LEADER FAVORABILITIES *(Continued)*

		Very Favor	Favor	Unfav	Very Unfav	DK/ Nvr Hrd
President of Egypt	ATS8	2	29	10	3	56
	AJC	2	31	11	2	53
Deng Xiaoping, leader of China	ATS6	2	29	10	2	57
Hafez al Assad, President of Syria	AJC	0	10	25	9	56
Yitzhak Shamir, Prime Minister of Israel	ATS6	3	28	26	7	37
	AJC	2	27	28	7	37
Yitzhak Rabin, Defense Minister of Israel	AJC	2	23	22	4	49
Carlos Salinas de Gortari, President of Mexico	ATS8	1	12	13	4	70
P.W. Botha, President of South Africa	ATS6	1	12	27	15	45
Augusto Pinochet, President of Chile	ATS6	0	6	15	5	74
Daniel Ortega, President of Nicaragua	ATS6	1	9	44	24	21
Yassir Arafat, Head of the PLO	AJC	0	7	42	37	14
Fidel Castro, President of Cuba	ATS8	1	7	43	42	7
Mohammar Khaddafi, Libya's Head of State	AJC	1	4	33	55	7
Ayatullah Khomeini, Leader of Iran	ATS8	1	3	22	71	4
	AJC	1	3	28	64	4

critics would agree that President Reagan cast a large shadow in the world arena and that many of his decisions will continue to have a major impact well into the 1990s.

First, Reagan left office as a very popular figure. In the final ATS poll, the president's personal favorable ratings had climbed to 69 percent, while his unfavorable ratings fell to 28 percent. For someone who had occupied the White House for eight years, these were truly outstanding ratings. His substantive ratings were no less impressive.

Since World War II, when Americans have evaluated a president's performance in the area of national security and foreign policy, they have traditionally placed major emphasis on his ability to deal effectively with the Soviets, to reduce the threat of nuclear war, to develop a strong national defense, to make appropriate use of military power, and to keep America out of war. On these classic tests of presidential performance in the national security area, President Reagan received extraordinary ratings from the American people.

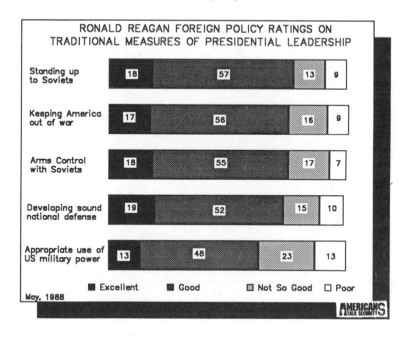

RONALD REAGAN FOREIGN POLICY RATINGS ON TRADITIONAL MEASURES OF PRESIDENTIAL LEADERSHIP

	Excellent	Good	Not So Good	Poor
Standing up to Soviets	18	57	13	9
Keeping America out of war	17	56	16	9
Arms Control with Soviets	18	55	17	7
Developing sound national defense	19	52	15	10
Appropriate use of US military power	13	48	23	13

■ Excellent   ■ Good   ▨ Not So Good   ☐ Poor

May, 1988

AMERICANS TALK SECURITY

Reagan also received very strong marks from the public on another series of traditional measures of presidential leadership, foreign policy ratings.

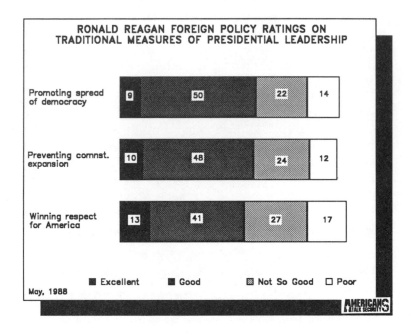

The president's overall ratings, however, were tarnished somewhat by a generally poor evaluation on a number of more contemporary foreign policy issues.

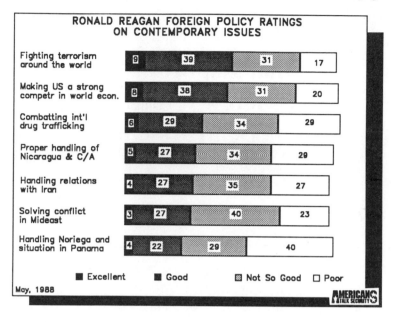

RONALD REAGAN FOREIGN POLICY RATINGS
ON CONTEMPORARY ISSUES

Fighting terrorism around the world — 9 | 39 | 31 | 17

Making US a strong competr in world econ. — 8 | 38 | 31 | 20

Combatting int'l drug trafficking — 6 | 29 | 34 | 29

Proper handling of Nicaragua & C/A — 5 | 27 | 34 | 29

Handling relations with Iran — 4 | 27 | 35 | 27

Solving conflict in Mideast — 3 | 27 | 40 | 23

Handling Noriega and situation in Panama — 4 | 22 | 29 | 40

■ Excellent   ■ Good   ▧ Not So Good   □ Poor

May, 1988

AMERICANS & ATALK SECURITY

These more negative evaluations notwithstanding, President Reagan left office with a truly impressive level of public support for his foreign policy leadership. The substantive foreign policy contributions of his administration will be debated for many years to come, but the political support he marshaled for his policies among the American people is unlikely to be duplicated in the foreseeable future.

Final Report of the Seventy-fifth American Assembly

At the close of their discussions, the participants in the Seventy-fifth American Assembly on U.S. Global Interests in the 1990s: A New Approach, at Arden House, Harriman, New York, November 17–20, 1988, reviewed as a group the following statement. This statement represents general agreement; however, no one was asked to sign it. Furthermore, it should be understood that not everyone agreed with all of it.

Preamble

Four decades of effort have vindicated the foresight of the brave spirits who looked beyond the devastation of World War II to a community of prosperous Western democracies secured by an effective deterrent against aggression. History offers no more compelling example of a vision formed and then realized. But the very successes of postwar American foreign policy bring with them new risks and opportunities, many of them unimaginable in any other time. Once again, the wellsprings of American inspiration are tested. Once again, fundamental American interests require a creative response.

The cold war has dominated the international arena for forty years. Perhaps it will continue to do so. While there are important signs of change in Soviet behavior, there are many respects in which Soviet actions do not match the new rhetoric. Sheer containment of Soviet aggression—critical though it remains—does not by itself constitute an adequate American policy response to the questions and opportunities that may arise if these still preliminary signs of change are verified by experience. The goal of postwar U.S. policy has always extended beyond containment to peaceful competition with the Soviet system if and when the Soviets were prepared to turn their attention inward and cease their systematic attempts to undermine Western security. Since 1950 American policy has contemplated that successful containment of Soviet expansionism, combined with the inherent inefficiencies and inequities of the Soviet system, could eventually lead to a reordering of Soviet priorities and a spirit of cooperation between the United States and the Soviet Union.

Despite the refreshing new tone of recent rhetoric from Moscow and some encouraging contributions to the reduction of regional conflicts, there is still limited hard evidence of a broad change in Soviet military force structure. Nevertheless, should evidence of far-reaching change materialize, the Western allies must be prepared to use the easing of cold war tensions to pursue policies that build on the success of the containment effort—policies that promise to leave our children with something better than a world perpetually crouched in fear of a nuclear exchange.

While signals from Moscow are still mixed, challenge on the economic front is all too real and imminent. Postwar U.S. policy sought to stimulate the growth of independent Western economies, each powerful in its own right and all beneficiaries of an open trading system and stabilizing financial and monetary institutions. This economic pluralism has now been achieved. Average standards of living in the Western democracies are at levels that could hardly have been dreamt of forty years ago.

But in a community of thriving trading nations, pluralism

necessarily means interdependence. Dominance by a single nation is not merely inadvisable, it is impossible. The diffusion of economic power transforms the very concept of leadership. The common stake in a balance of national fortunes requiring some coordination of national policies exerts great stress upon traditional notions of autonomous domestic economic policy. When a major trading nation evades its internal responsibilities—as we believe America has in recent years—both the means of adjustment and the decision to employ them shift to foreign hands. America's sustained economic recovery during the 1980s notwithstanding, a nation that borrows heavily to finance its current consumption mortgages its future and magnifies the risks of painful foreclosure by forces over which its government has no direct control.

In an interdependent system, the tools of leadership must shift from subsidy and sanction to example and suasion. Nationalism, though still powerful, must be refined to take into account the extremely high price of autonomous disregard for the interlocking interests of other nations. Hierarchical decision making must give way to negotiation among partners, and maximization of narrow national gains must defer to optimization among the shared interests of the participant economies. Although all of these changes were the implicit aims of a postwar U.S. policy encouraging economic pluralism, the fact that pluralism now exists requires profound transformation of the traditional attitudes and expectations of American leaders and populace. We concentrate on these changes here, but emphasize the need for similarly profound changes in other countries' attitudes.

Recent years have seen many constructive developments: lower inflation, lower unemployment, sustained growth, Soviet withdrawal from Afghanistan, and the INF treaty. Nevertheless, we believe that failure to recognize and adapt adequately to the new world of economic interdependence has created a crisis in American governance. The United States has drawn on the debt financing capacity of other economies to evade the discipline necessary to maintain the soundness of its own. By delaying needed internal corrections that have been widely recognized for years, America has created an ominous cloud over its own prosperity. Unless dissipated by timely and credible U.S. action, continued excessive borrowing could condemn this nation to a downturn of major proportions. Any new approach to American global interests, as well as effective preservation of those interests, is, in our judgment, vitally dependent upon early, decisive action to right the twin imbalances in the nation's national budget and external accounts.

However, the challenge to American vision transcends the imperatives of the moment. Unanswered questions about long-term U.S. objectives posed by developments in the Soviet Union and in the international economy are symbols of the broader need to reexamine those objectives in light of current conditions and prospects. No single group can presume to perform this massive task in a comprehensive or authoritative way. We make no such claim. We simply offer our considered thoughts on possible long term goals and on the immediate issues that strike us as most pressing. Our findings and recommendations are offered in the hope that they will help to stimulate the broad public debate about the ends and means of American foreign policy that we believe to be vital to the national interest.

The worldwide changes addressed herein will precipitate many difficult policy choices for the United States. These discussions and the accompanying past debate about them could make the next ten years among the most challenging and traumatic for the American people in our recent history.

These times require extraordinary leadership. Our political and business leaders, policy makers, academic institutions, and news organizations should tap the most patriotic interests of our people by presenting them with the most candid possible discussion about the challenges and policy questions we face.

Inherent in this recommendation is a conviction that, as always, the American people are prepared to face hard realities and are ready to make necessary sacrifices for this country's well-being. Indeed, we believe the American people yearn to be constructively involved in solving the problem of our nation's future.

Economic Issues

Long-term Objectives. The globalization of markets for goods and capital and the greater openness of the U.S. economy create both opportunities and challenges. They magnify the gains from technological progress and capital formation, but, by intensifying economic interdependence, they make it more difficult for the United States to manage its own economy, they increase the influence of other countries' policies on the functioning of the U.S. economy, and they make domestic economic stability depend more heavily on the stability of the world economy.

To take full advantage of the opportunities provided by an open and growing world economy, the United States must invest more in physical and human capital, and it must save more in order to invest more. This will require some moderation of domestic consumption. The United States must raise the rate of growth of productivity in order to increase its competitiveness and assure a rising standard of living over the long run shared by all citizens. Low growth in productivity will make it increasingly difficult for the United States to achieve its international and domestic aspirations.

The United States must collaborate closely with its principal partners to achieve macroeconomic stability, sustain and promote the growth of the world economy, and foster greater exchange-rate stability over the long run. This collaboration will require the gradual intensification of international policy coordination, especially in monetary and exchange rate matters, including stricter collective surveillance over fiscal policies. To increase the effectiveness of these processes, they must be given more prominence and publicity, and the United States must demonstrate an increasing willingness to abide by the advice that emerges from the process of surveillance. Such cooperation should not be regarded as an inhibition on the making of fiscal policy but rather as a way of broadening support for sound macroeconomic decision making.

The United States must not diminish its commitment to an open trading system and should work vigorously to assure that other nations share this commitment. It should resist and urge others to resist the ever-present tendency to view the world economy as a set of loosely connected regions, each featuring one dominant country or group of countries. However, while maintaining its basic commitment to the international trading system, the United States should retain a careful balance between attention to global interests and to its own national interests. America should continue to support efforts at regional economic cooperation, such as the European Community, but should remain alert to the risk that these arrangements will build new barriers to trade with the outside world.

Finally, the United States must assist the developing countries to step up their growth rates. It can act on its own, when appropriate, but should strongly support the World Bank and regional development banks, and should promote multilateral initiatives by the industrialized countries, including those achieved within the OECD framework, to remove or reduce external constraints on the development process.

The Immediate Challenge. The most urgent economic problem facing the new administration is reducing the deficit in the federal budget. This is crucial for stabilizing financial markets throughout the world and setting the United States on a course for regaining equilibrium in its external trade and payments and thereby reducing its heavy and growing dependence on foreign borrowing.

The United States cannot hope to grow out of its budget deficit simply by expecting tax revenues to grow faster than government expenditures. The budget deficit persisted at a high level even during the past six years in which the U.S. economy was expanding from the depths of the severe 1981–82 recession. Now, starting from a low level of unemployment and a high rate of capacity utilization, real growth can be expected to slow down, and revenue growth will therefore slow as well. To attempt to solve the budget problem through inflationary finance would obviously aggravate all of the nation's problems, particularly the problem of stabilizing its currency.

The only way to preserve stable growth in the years ahead is to reduce the budget deficit. We expect that some combination of expenditure reductions and tax increases will be required. No part of the federal budget should be exempt from scrutiny. This will necessitate a realistic examination of America's evolving national security and civilian needs. We did not take it as our charge in this study of the nation's global problems to recommend specific revenue-raising measures or spending cuts, but we note that a significant proportion of any tax increase should be dedicated to deficit reduction.

We believe the president and the Congress should act expeditiously to deal with the deficit, after careful review of both revenues and expenditures. An agreement on a credible, multi-year deficit reduction package should be negotiated in a collaborative spirit and concluded as quickly as possible.

We welcome foreign investment in the United States when it is in new productive facilities or other activities that enhance U.S. prosperity. But we warn against expecting foreign investors or foreign governments to relieve the president and Congress of the need to reduce the budget and trade deficits. It would be equally imprudent to believe that a further depreciation of the dollar can by itself reduce the trade deficit. The impressive recovery of exports and of domestic capital formation in 1988 could be choked off by capacity constraints and labor shortages unless private and public consumption are reduced to make room for more exports and investment. Delay will make the problem harder. Interest payments get larger when debts get larger, and deficits add to debts. This arithmetic applies to both the budget deficit and the current-account deficit.

While reviewing its budget options, the United States should study and take into account the causes of such major changes in our domestic economy as leveraged buyouts, declining saving rate, increasing foreign ownership of U.S. assets, and the defense implications of a shrinking U.S. industrial base.

Debt and Development. Prompt action must also be taken to reduce the debt burdens of the heavily indebted countries in Latin America and Africa. Those burdens interfere with the countries' own efforts to stabilize their own economies and start to grow again. They also complicate the elimination of imbalances in the world economy. If the developing countries cannot increase their imports because they must use export earnings to make debt-service payments, it is harder for the United States to increase its own exports.

There has been an important shift of emphasis in the management of the debt problem, from an unsuccessful effort to increase commercial bank lending, which would have raised total indebtedness, to an endorsement of voluntary debt reduction on market-related terms. But this shift is not likely to produce a sufficiently large or rapid reduction in the burdens borne by the highly indebted countries. The United States and other industrialized countries must therefore reconsider their declared opposition to debt forgiveness or relief from servicing costs. The costs of managing and reducing the debt problem must be shared fairly among the debtor countries, the commercial banks, and the governments of the industrialized countries, all of which bear some responsibility for the creation of the problem.

Debt reduction for African countries is more directly and immediately the responsibility of the major industrialized countries, because the debts are to governments and international institutions, not to commercial banks. Other governments have acted more boldly than the U.S. government, which should make a larger contribution to the solution of this special problem.

Trade Policy. To assure the continued expansion of international trade and to participate fully in the benefits it can confer, U.S. foreign trade and commercial interests should be given higher priority in a broader range of policy decisions than has been true in the past. The United States must resist domestic protectionist pressures, work to facilitate positive adjustment and to strengthen multilateral arrangements for resolving trade disputes, and strive for the successful completion of the Uruguay Round of trade negotiations, which is now reaching its mid-point. America must also move aggressively, by national action under the Omnibus Trade Act and through multilateral action under GATT, to induce other governments to remove trade barriers that unfairly impede the expansion of American exports of goods and services.

As economies become more open and more closely connected, differences between domestic policies and regulatory regimes become more important both economically and politically. The United States must work with other like-minded governments to harmonize domestic policies affecting international competition. The recent agreement among the major industrialized countries concerning the prudential regulation of their commercial banks may serve as a model for this purpose. It need not involve the creation of new international institutions or the writing of new international law. It involves the development and application of common standards and, in some cases, modifications in domestic legislation. In this process, the United States must be receptive to initiatives by other countries; it should not try dogmatically to make them mimic U.S. institutions and practices.

Energy Dependence. The United States is at risk of becoming excessively dependent on imported oil, a development that could threaten its security during the next decade. Higher taxes on fossil-fuel use, most particularly higher gasoline taxes, are the most effective remedy because energy conservation will reduce import dependence, improve environmental equality, and encourage innovation by energy producers as well as energy consumers. Higher taxes on energy use will also raise needed revenue.

Political and Security Issues

A new administration and a new Congress enjoy specific opportunities to work together on a positive foreign policy agenda.

Long-term Objectives. Preventing a nuclear war stands as the first and perpetual obligation of superpower diplomacy. More broadly, enhancing the quality of Soviet-American relations in the interest of greater stability remains a fundamental interest that American policy should pursue into the next century.

Success in managing Soviet-American relations should permit the United States, over the long haul, to adapt its policies in other areas as well. Deliberate movement toward more equilateral alliances with Europe and Japan, engaging the full range of security, economic, and political factors, should prove feasible. Freed of preoccupation with ideological competition in the Third World, the United States can and should adopt a discriminating posture toward regional conflicts and issues. And a geopolitical reorientation of this magnitude, while not eliminating all traditional tensions among sovereign states, will facilitate more coordinated attention on the part of the developed nations toward the emerging problems of the global commons, world population, and poverty.

Transforming East-West Relations. Is the chance to end the cold war real or illusory? The only way to find out is through an activist U.S. policy toward the Soviet Union on such issues as arms control, regional conflict, and human rights. U.S. policy must remain skeptical with respect to Soviet goals unless and until there is evidence of an enduring change in Soviet intentions. Soviet withdrawal from Afghanistan, support for a settlement in Angola, and encouragement of Vietnamese disengagement from Cambodia give reason to hope that essential change may be happening.

Much depends on whether Soviet actions in other spheres

match their words. U.S. engagement strategy should be based on a plan that hedges against damage to important U.S. interests in the event that Moscow fails to fulfill its undertakings. We recommend that the United States, in consultation with its allies, put forth a program of specific advances in various areas that would challenge Soviet behavior to correspond to recent shifts in announced Soviet foreign policy objectives.

It is imperative that the momentum initiated in the Reagan administration on START and conventional arms policy in Europe not be lost. Both should be high priorities for action, but completion of a START agreement that enhances U.S. security may be in prospect and would be a very desirable achievement.

In defining a stable strategic balance for the future, two possible objectives are too implausible to serve as ambitions for policy: neither abolition of nuclear weapons nor a perfect defense against nuclear weapons is a realistic guideline. It remains to be seen whether more modest applications of defensive technologies may someday play a constructive role in an agreed regime for reducing reliance on massive offensive forces.

Eventually, success in lowering the mutual threats posed by the superpowers and their alliances should alleviate the dominant preoccupation with the East-West confrontation that has defined the cold war. Such a historic transformation should enable the United States to address other political and security problems freshly and free from the ideological distortions that have infected policy in many regions.

For the indefinite future, containment of the threat of Soviet expansionism will remain a crucial goal of U.S. policy. However, if Soviet conduct confirms a move toward normalization of relations, additional objectives should inform U.S. policy. We recommend that one of those objectives should be measured progress toward as high a degree of Soviet involvement in Western economic and financial arrangements as prudent pursuit of U.S. interests may permit.

Changes in Eastern Europe may offer opportunities but could also lead to instability. U.S. policy must be alert to both.

A policy of differentiation, recognizing the particular circumstances of each Eastern bloc country, continues to make sense. For example, the achievements of Hungarian liberalization and reform warrant a more forthcoming Western response than the less ambitious and less successful endeavors in Poland.

Alliances. Cohesion of the alliance among the Western democracies endures as a primary American interest for the foreseeable future. The alliance is not only a vital institution in itself, but also a bulwark of economic, as well as political, cooperation in dealing with issues in other parts of the world.

U.S. policy must guard against the danger that General Secretary Gorbachev's success in gaining the confidence of Western publics will breed a complacency in Europe undermining necessary defense cooperation. At the same time, the United States should welcome the signs of increased European defense cooperation, illustrated by the strengthening of the Western European Union, as a viable path to a more balanced division of labor within NATO.

The United States should seek greater burden sharing by its allies, understanding that with it will go a shift in the balance of decision-making power. This redistribution of responsibility should not be achieved through confrontation but through consultation. Recent quiet but effective cooperation in the Persian Gulf provides a model for future coordination.

In East Asia, greater efforts by Japan to assume larger economic and aid responsibilities on a global basis are clearly desirable. By contrast, it would be unwise to press Japan for significant increases in defense expenditures, although an American priority should be that Japan fully implement its stated defense commitments. To go beyond this would threaten to destabilize important relationships in the region. Rather, the guiding concept for burden-sharing policy should be one of comprehensive security, acknowledging that not every contribution is measured by defense budgets.

The U.S. security role in NATO and in East Asia must be maintained, although its scale and focus may change as threats to peace evolve. Conversations with respect to possible adjustments in the level and nature of U.S. involvement should proceed consistent with events.

Regional. Finally, challenges and opportunities to expand peace through the resolution of conflict in the Middle East, Central America, and southern Africa exist and should be exploited. It is critically important in these areas in particular that the United States seize available openings to help bring peaceful settlements. Escalation of violence in one or more of these areas could still lead to superpower involvement.

Such escalation is all the more threatening given the spread of ballistic missiles and the use of chemical weapons, especially in the Middle East. These are worrisome features of the political-military environment. Enlisting wider participation (by the Soviet Union, China, and other producers) in the Missile Technology Control Regime should be an early priority of the next administration.

Quite apart from the lingering problems of Soviet-American relations and other immediate issues, the long-term goals of the United States should include tapping the vast potential of international cooperation in many areas where unilateral approaches are outmoded or unworkable. As a specific objective, the United States should promote an international order to instill new standards and habits of accountability for the consequences of acts that affect citizens of other countries, new methods of dispute resolution, and new techniques to ensure the rights afforded individuals. These ambitions for American policy would reflect the historic national support for democratic values and principles in developing countries and elsewhere.

In this connection, we note that the United States has benefitted in the past by upholding adherence to the rule of law as an essential element of its foreign policy and of a just international order. It would serve its interests and enhance its leadership role in the world to demonstrate a strong commitment to do so in the future.

Global Imperatives

Long-term Objectives. Powerful evidence has been advanced that a number of problems, some still very imperfectly understood, threaten the planet's capacity to support human life and prosperity. One such problem is the possibility that oxidation of fossil fuels is aggravating a "greenhouse effect," systematically warming the earth's climate, melting its polar ice caps, and threatening consequences which range from submerging heavily populated coastlines to turning croplands into deserts. Another problem, now substantially documented, is the effect of release of chlorofluorocarbons that deplete the stratospheric ozone layer, increasing the exposure of animal and plant life to the sun's ultra-violet rays and resulting in increased incidence of skin cancer and interfering with biological processes. The common thread among these very different problems is that they are global consequences of human activity on a scale that can only be effectively addressed through global cooperation.

These recently discovered threats do not exhaust the list of global dangers. Others include the consequences of nuclear accidents and the mismanagement of natural resources, especially the loss of genetic diversity, the oceans, and the atmosphere, the so-called "global commons."

Existing multilateral mechanisms for developing or implementing coordinated policy to deal effectively with problems of this scope need to be strengthened. Similarly, inadequate attention is paid to developing global perspectives and cross-cultural communication skills that must underpin effective multilateral collaboration on global issues in a world of diversity. An objective of U.S. policy in the 1990s must be to lead an aggressive long-term international effort to devise imaginative, technically expert, global vehicles for researching, monitoring, ameliorating, and, if possible, eliminating such global threats.

Near-term Actions. *Environmental Problems*—The initial exercise of this new exertion of U.S. leadership might be to develop bilateral or multilateral interest coalitions of countries upon which a global response could be built. The warming trend (and its contributory elements) and acid rain are critical matters requiring urgent attention. Tropical deforestation and the expected loss of 20 percent of the world's plant and animal species by the year 2000 also demonstrate the extent to which the absence of a global environmental policy allows for "unplanned experiments on unknown subjects" with potential catastrophic consequences to us all.

The United States should further its existing efforts in this area by developing a comprehensive strategy encompassing, but exceeding, existing initiatives on greenhouse warming, ozone depletion, fossil fuel, and chemical waste pollution. Such a strategy should, initially, intensify the work of the coalition and develop initial objectives including comprehensive information gathering and a global consensus on information sharing.

Population—Unchecked population growth could produce economic disaster, uncontrollable migration, and social instability. Nigeria had a population of 41 million people in 1950 and 105 million in 1986. In the same time frame, Mexico's population tripled, going from 27 million to 82 million, Ethiopia's went from 16 million to 44 million, and Bangladesh's went from 44 million to 104 million.

Numerous studies demonstrate that economic growth and development contribute to reducing fertility rates. Two of the variables most highly associated with declining fertility rates are increased education levels and increased percentages of women in the work force. These facts are a compelling reason for the United States to help promote integral development in poor countries. But we can do more. Many governments of the less developed countries now have noncompulsory responsible parenthood programs in place but lack the financial resources to implement these programs. The United States should renew its support of family planning activities and other such efforts of Third World governments to reduce their birth rates. These efforts should include improved health-care delivery and education, not merely the distribution of contraceptive devices.

Special Note On Drugs

We are virtually unanimous in our belief that drugs constitute a growing threat to the quality of American life. We are also virtually unanimous that the United States must do everything it can to reduce the domestic demand for narcotics. We urge the allocation of increased governmental expenditures to enhance the quality and availability of education and rehabilitation programs.

There was sharp disagreement, however, about how to handle, or even to conceptualize, the international dimension of the drug trade. Some participants argued that a special foreign policy priority should be attached to control of drug trafficking, while others argued that, important as the problem is, it is more appropriately dealt with in the normal course of U.S. foreign activities. Even the question of sanctions against countries involved in drug trade created controversy. Some participants argued for the prohibition of any U.S. aid to a country that did not give complete cooperation to U.S. drug interdiction activities in that country. However, some of our colleagues cautioned that strict adherence to recent U.S. legislation might force the United States to deny aid to many countries, such as Mexico, that are important to U.S. security, and that most certainly would need some U.S. aid to construct stronger anti-drug enforcement policies. Virtually everyone felt that the existing domestic and international policies need more intense attention, thought, and resources.

Marshalling Domestic Support
for Effective Foreign Policy

Polling data and other evidence suggest to us that American public opinion does not pose an insurmountable barrier to reformulation of foreign policy along the lines we recommend. There appears to be ample room for effective leadership from the president and Congress. But such leadership will require important changes in curent conditions. Longer-term U.S. policy objectives should include renewal of the tradition of closer cooperation on foreign policy matters between the executive and legislative branches and timely harmonization within the executive branch.

We also believe that public support would benefit greatly from a more candid public debate of foreign policy options. Too often, critical information is withheld from official announcements for the convenience of the speaker and at the expense of information to which the public is entitled. When the truth is later disclosed, the result is deepened public suspicion of and disillusionment with government-supplied information. As a matter of policy, foreign affairs authorities should cultivate a tradition of full and frank disclosure of all critical information relevant to each event or decision except for any portion the disclosure of which would involve appreciable risk to the national security or to another vital American interest. Nor can we progress if every suggestion that American power to act unilaterally has grown more limited is equated with an "unpatriotic" belief in American decline.

Finally, we believe that the substantial broadening of the cross-section of the American populace actively interested and engaged in foreign affairs that has occurred over the past twenty years has been an extremely healthy phenomenon. But we do not think it has yet gone far enough. American policy should aim at even greater outreach within the citizenry, both in recruitment of professional foreign affairs practitioners and in informing more diverse publics.

Participants
The Seventy-Fifth American Assembly

† MICHAEL H. ARMACOST
Under Secretary of State for
  Political Affairs
U.S. Department of State
Washington, DC

LINCOLN PALMER
  BLOOMFIELD
Professor
Department of Political
  Science
Massachusetts Institute of
  Technology
Cambridge, MA

GODFREY E. BRIEFS
Economist, Minority Staff
Committee on Banking,
  Finance and Urban Affairs
U.S. House of
  Representatives
Washington, DC

SEYOM BROWN
Professor
Department of Politics
Brandeis University
Waltham, MA

WILLIAM P. BUNDY
Writer
Princeton, NJ

** MICHAEL J. CALHOUN
Partner
Laxalt, Washington, Perito &
  Dubuc
Washington, DC

DAVID P. CALLEO
Dean Acheson Professor of
  European Studies
School of Advanced
  International Studies
The Johns Hopkins
  University
Washington, DC

ARNOLD CANTOR
Assistant Director
Department of Economic
  Research
AFL-CIO
Washington, DC

PAT CHOATE
Vice President, Policy
  Analysis
TRW, Inc.
Arlington, VA

CHARLES A. COOPER
Consultant
The RAND Corporation
Santa Monica, CA

MICHAEL P. COREY
Vice President
Champion International
  Corporation
Stamford, CT

WILLIAM J.
  CUNNINGHAM
Legislative Representative
  for Federal Taxation and
  International Trade
AFL-CIO
Washington, DC

† AMITAI ETZIONI
Thomas Henry Carroll Ford
Foundation Professor
(1987–1989)
Graduate School of Business
Administration
Harvard University
Boston, MA

GEZA FEKETEKUTY
Counselor to the U.S. Trade
Representative
Office of the U.S. Trade
Representative
Washington, DC

* ALTON FRYE
Vice President & Washington
Director
Council on Foreign Relations
Washington, DC

LEON FUERTH
Aide for International and
Security Affairs
Office of Senator Albert
Gore, Jr.
Washington, DC

† RICHARD N. GARDNER
Henry L. Moses Professor of
Law
School of Law
Columbia University
New York, NY

WILLIAM GORHAM
President
The Urban Institute
Washington, DC

EDWARD K. HAMILTON
President
Hamilton, Rabinovitz &
Alschuler, Inc.
Los Angeles, CA

RITA E. HAUSER
Senior Partner
Stroock & Stroock & Lavan
New York, NY

ELEANOR HICKS
Advisor for International
Liaison
University of Cincinnati
Cincinnati, OH

JOHN HILLEY
Assistant Director
Committee on the Budget
U.S. Senate
Washington, DC

JAMES HOGE
President and Publisher
New York Daily News
New York, NY

† SAMUEL P. HUNTINGTON
Director
The Center for International
Affairs
Harvard University
Cambridge, MA

ROBERT B. KEATING
Executive Director, United
States
International Bank for
Reconstruction and
Development
Washington, DC

** PETER B. KENEN
Professor of Economics and
Director of the International
Finance Section
Department of Economics
Princeton University
Princeton, NJ

JEFFREY M. LANG
Chief International Trade
  Counsel
Committee on Finance
U.S. Senate
Washington, DC

ROGER E. LEVIEN
Vice President, Corporate
  Strategy Office
Xerox Corporation
Stamford, CT

WILLIAM H. LUERS
President
Metropolitan Museum of Art
New York, NY

RICHARD W. LYMAN
Director
Institute of International
  Studies
Stanford University
Stanford, CA

JOHN MARTTILA
Marttila & Kiley
Boston, MA

JESSICA TUCHMAN
  MATHEWS
Vice President
World Resources Institute
Washington, DC

CHARLES WILLIAM
  MAYNES
Editor
Foreign Policy
Washington, DC

MARCIA MILLER
Professional Staff Member
  for Trade
Committee on Finance
U.S. Senate
Washington, DC

MILTON D. MORRIS
Director of Research
Joint Center for Political
  Studies Inc.
Washington, DC

MICHAEL W. MOYNIHAN
Head of Center
Organization for Economic
  Cooperation and
  Development
Washington, DC

RICHARD MURPHY
Assistant Secretary of State
  for Near Eastern & South
  Asian Affairs
U.S. Department of State
Washington, DC

JOSEPH S. NYE, JR.
Director
Center for Science and
  International Affairs
John F. Kennedy School of
  Government
Harvard University
Cambridge, MA

VAN DOORN OOMS
Acting Executive Director
  and Chief Economist
Committee on the Budget
U.S. House of
  Representatives
Washington, DC

CHARLES PETERS
Editor
Washington Monthly
Washington, DC

EDWARD POLLAK
President & CEO
Olin Hunt Specialty Products
West Paterson, NJ

ROBERT REILLY
Executive Director,
 Corporate Strategy Staff
Ford Motor Company
Dearborn, MI

† DONALD B. RICE
President & CEO
The RAND Corporation
Santa Monica, CA

NATHANIEL SAMUELS
Managing Director
Shearson Lehman Hutton
 Inc.
New York, NY

† ISABEL V. SAWHILL
Senior Fellow
The Urban Institute
Washington, DC

DAVID J. SCHEFFER
Staff Consultant
Committee on Foreign
 Affairs
U.S. House of
 Representatives
Washington, DC

† SUSAN C. SCHWAB
Legislative Director
Office of Senator John C.
 Danforth
Washington, DC

JOHN W. SEWELL
President
Overseas Development
 Council
Washington, DC

FRANK A. SIEVERTS
Senior Staff

Committee on Foreign
 Relations
U.S. Senate
Washington, DC

** LEONARD S. SILK
Economics Columnist
The New York Times
New York, NY

THEODORE C. SORENSEN
Paul, Weiss, Rifkind,
 Wharton & Garrison
New York, NY

STEPHEN STAMAS
President
New York Philharmonic
New York, NY

*ALFRED STEPAN
Dean
School of International and
 Public Affairs
Columbia University
New York, NY

*ADLAI E. STEVENSON
Of Counsel
Mayer, Brown & Platt
Chicago, IL

IRA WOLF
Legislative Assistant
Office of Senator John D.
 Rockefeller IV
Washington, DC

*CASIMIR YOST
Executive Director
World Affairs Council of
 Northern California
San Francisco, CA

* Discussion Leader
** Rapporteur
† Panel Member

Index

Acheson, Dean, 43, 167
acid rain, 80, 182, 216, 330
acquired immune deficiency
  syndrome (AIDS), 80
advertising, political, 261–63
Afghanistan, 70
  Soviet relations with, 46, 66, 70,
    128, 160
  Soviet withdrawal from, 29, 59,
    66, 160, 226, 271–72, 318, 325
  U.S. relations with, 46, 160
Africa, 46, 137, 190, 258, 323
  Cubans in, 60, 67, 226
  democracy in, 129
  southern, 47, 48, 68–69, 151, 161
  see also North Africa; specific
    countries
African National Congress, 67
agriculture, 55, 93
Air Force, U.S., 144
Algeria, 69
  Soviet relations with, 178
Alliance for Progress, 47
allies, U.S., 148–51, 157, 159–60,
    169–70, 214
  burden sharing and, 102–3,
    149–50, 232–33, 327
  in cold war, 41–42
  out-of-area cooperation and,
    150–51

U.S. Global Interests report and,
    325, 327–28
U.S. security strategy for the
    1990s and, 229–36
  see also specific allies
Allison, Graham, 20–24, 198, 241
  background of, 198n
Ambrose, Stephen, 43
American Assembly, 3–4, 34
  see also Seventy-fifth American
    Assembly
"American Century," 200
American Jewish Congress, 309
Americans Talk Security (ATS)
    project, 261n–62n, 265–315
  arms control and, 286–88
  burden sharing and, 299–301
  foreign aid and, 302–6
  gender/education factors and,
    274–78
  Gorbachev and, 288–92
  isolationism and, 306
  new threats to U.S. national
    security and, 265–69
  nuclear weapons and, 301–2
  peace through strength and,
    279–83
  predictability in Soviet-American
    relations and, 293–96
  Reagan legacy and, 310, 313–15

Americans Talk Security (*continued*)
  Strategic Defense Initiative and,
    283–86
  U.S. attitudes toward Soviet
    Union and, 270–73
  U.S. economy and, 306–8
  U.S.-Soviet cooperation and,
    297–99
  world leaders and, 310, 311–12
Angola, 69, 226
  Soviet relations with, 60, 67, 68,
    325
  U.S. relations with, 161
anticommunism, 18, 128, 176–77
  see also cold war
ANZUS, 41
Aqaba, Gulf of, 65
Arab-Israeli conflict, 64, 65, 131,
    139, 145, 159
Arab nationalism, 45–46
Arafat, Yassir, 310
Argentina, 72
  U.S. relations with, 178
arms control, 20, 23, 24, 159, 232
  in Bush administration, 156
  Gorbachev and, 225
  INF and, 29, 58–59, 171, 226, 231,
    250–51, 286–88, 318
  in 1950s vs. 1990s, 34, 39–40,
    63–64, 127–28
  START and, 29, 140, 251, 326
  U.S. public opinion and, 28, 29,
    286–88
arms race:
  in 1950s vs. 1990s, 39–40, 63–64
  regional, 40, 63
arms suppliers, 39–40, 44–45, 63
Asia, *see* East Asia; Indochina; South
    Asia; *specific countries*
Association of Southeast Asian
    Nations (ASEAN), 65, 76–77,
    135, 244
"Atoms for Peace," 40
ATS, *see* Americans Talk Security
Australia, U.S. relations with,
    41

Baker, James A., III, 91
ballistic missiles, 137, 142, 210, 228,
    328
  intercontinental (ICBMs), 141,
    156, 171, 240
  intermediate-range (IRBMs), 171
Bangladesh, 330
Bank for International Settlements,
    117
Baruch plan, 208
Bay of Pigs, 44
Belgium, 48, 100
Bergsten, C. Fred, 11–15, 31,
    82–125
  background of, 82*n*
  economic recommendations of,
    11–13, 87–112
  Laffer's commentary on, 14–15,
    122–25
  Roberts's commentary on, 13–14,
    113–21
Berlin blockade, 36, 45
Berlin crisis (1958–1962), 45
Bipartisan Economic Commission,
    218
bipolarity, 22, 25, 214–15
  in 1950s, 35–39
  reduction of, 57–63
  see also cold war
Bolivia, 99
bonds, bond market, 86, 99, 103
Botswana, 77
Brady Commission, 220
Brazil, 52, 80, 133
  debt of, 68
  democracy in, 135
  economy of, 76
  as regional power, 135, 137, 153,
    214
  U.S. relations with, 68
Bretton Woods agreement, 37, 51,
    207, 230, 240, 243
Brezhnev doctrine, 152
Brodie, Bernard, 204–5
Brown, Harold, 15–18, 21, 126–65
  background of, 126*n*–27*n*

Brown, Seyom, 18–21, 166–97
  background of, 166*n*
Brzezinski, Zbigniew, 167, 173
budget deficit, U.S., 74, 249
  Allison on, 23, 218–19
  Bergsten on, 11, 82–83, 88–91
  elimination of, 88–91, 218–19
  Roberts on, 13, 14, 113–14,
    117–19
  U.S. Global Interests report and,
    321–23
Bundy, William P., 9–11, 33–81,
    127
  background of, 33*n*
burden sharing:
  economy and, 102–3, 150
  Japan and, 102–3, 150, 232–33,
    327
  security issues and, 149–50,
    163–64, 232–33, 299–301
  U.S. public opinion and, 299–301
  West Germany and, 102–3, 150
Burma, 77
Bush, George, 218, 300
Bush administration:
  arms control and, 156
  economy and, 11, 82–89, 106–12,
    218

Cambodia (Kampuchea), 61, 65, 77,
    226, 325
Canada, 101, 105, 179
  debt of, 95, 117
  U.S. border with, 181
  U.S. trade with, 52, 93
capital, 320, 322
  foreign, U.S. reliance on, 90–91
  Laffer on, 14–15, 123
  selective capital increase (SCI)
    and, 102–3
  surplus of, 14–15, 100, 123
  Third World debt and, 99
  trade flows and, 114–16
capitalism, 18
  contradictions of, 219–20
Caribbean, *see specific countries*

Caribbean Basin Initiative, 180
Carter, Jimmy, 87
Carter administration, 71, 84
Castro, Fidel, 47, 310
CENTO (Central Treaty
    Organization) Alliance, 45, 135
Central America, 79, 129, 151
  Cuban role in, 60
  Gorbachev on, 226–27
  Soviet Union and, 23, 67, 128, 227
  U.S. role in, 47, 68, 136, 160–61
  see also specific countries
Central Intelligence Agency (CIA),
    41, 43, 45, 46
Central Treaty Organization
    (CENTO) Alliance, 45, 135
Chernobyl nuclear accident, 79, 182
Chicago Council on Foreign
    Relations, 309
Chile, 99
  U.S. relations with, 68
China, People's Republic of (PRC),
    60–61, 79, 129–30, 144, 163,
    244
  economy of, 10, 54, 73, 214
  Japan and, 151
  nuclear weapons and, 71, 170
  as regional power, 135, 137, 153
  Soviet relations with, *see*
    Sino-Soviet relations
  U.S. rapprochement with, 176–77
  U.S. relations with, 34, 60, 128,
    328
China, Republic of, *see* Taiwan
China, U.S. "loss" of, 56
"China lobby," 56
chlorofluorocarbons (CFCs), 80,
    182–83, 329
Chun Doo-Hwan, 72
Churchill, Winston, 213
CIA (Central Intelligence Agency),
    41, 43, 45, 46
coal, 79
coalition strategy, 157
coexistence, 175
cold war, 7, 18, 317

cold war (*continued*)
  Azerbaijan confrontation and, 46
  containment and, 20, 21, 22,
    203–4, 206–10, 214, 221, 273,
    317, 326
  economics and, 51
  evolution of geostrategic
    environment and, 171–74
  expectations vs. realities of, 170
  geopolitical legacy and, 166–70,
    196–97
  "heartland/rimland" concept and,
    168–69
  national security strategy for the
    1990s and, 23, 211–40
  in 1950s, 35–47, 51, 127
  polyarchy and, 20
  restoration of, 190–91
  Third World and, 23, 177
  United Nations and, 50
  U.S. alliance system in, 41–42
  weakening of, 174–77
Colombia, 77
Cominform, 41
Comintern, 41
Commission on Integrated
  Long-Term Strategy, 173
Commission on National Goals, 34
Common Market, *see* European
  Economic Community
communications, 172–73
  human rights and, 51
communism, 18, 68
  loss of prestige of, 59, 77, 128
  "outer circle" of countries and, 60
  rolling back, 45, 128, 273
  see also cold war; *specific countries*
competitive interdependence,
  12–13, 106–12
  premises of, 110–11
comprehensive security, 24, 232–
  34
Congo, 48, 50
Congress, U.S., 11, 54, 56, 81, 249,
  322, 325

economy and, 82–86, 89, 90,
  107–12
pro-Israel lobby in, 65
consumption:
  ethic of, 219–20
  savings vs., 219–20, 320
Contadora process, 226–27
containment, 20, 22, 203–4, 206–10,
  214, 273, 317, 326
  NSC-68 and, 21, 221
conventional weapons and forces,
  37, 38, 43
  cost of, 63–64
  of Soviet Union, 58, 133–34,
    250–51
  of United States, 131, 143–46,
    157–60
cooperation, 79, 204, 327
  economic, 22, 320–21, 324
  out-of-area, 150–51
  security and, 132, 150–51
  U.S.-Soviet, 29, 239, 297–99
corporate strategy, 201–2
Council on Competitiveness,
  94
creative adaptation, 20, 187–88,
  191–97
  accountability and, 195–96
  depolarization and, 192–93
  new statecraft and, 194–95
  nuclear proliferation and, 193–94
cruise missiles, 250
Cuba, 60, 67
  in Africa, 60, 67, 226
  Soviet relations with, 60, 67, 128,
    178
  U.S. relations with, 47, 160
Cuban missile crisis, 171
currency, 12, 72–74, 181
  target zones and, 12, 104–5, 108
  see also exchange rates; *specific
    currencies*
current accounts:
  adjustment of U.S. deficit in, 106,
    107

international allocation of changes
in, 100, 101
Cyprus, 44
Czechoslovakia, 36, 213, 233, 255
Prague Spring in, 175–76

debt, debt financing, 318–19
of Canada, 95, 117
GNP and, 14, 87, 117–19
of Japan, 14, 117, 124
of Mexico, 27, 68, 77, 99, 259–60
oil prices and, 78, 100
Third World, see Third World
debt; specific countries
of United States, see budget
deficit, U.S.; trade deficit, U.S.
of West Germany, 14, 117, 124
Declaration of Human Rights, U.N.,
230
decolonization, 34, 47–48, 205, 208
Defense Department, U.S., 43, 172,
279, 285, 300–301
defense spending:
GNP and, 75, 131, 150, 154, 162,
163, 233, 234
of Japan, 234, 327
of Soviet Union, 23, 224–25
of United States, 29, 75, 131, 150,
154, 158, 161–63, 233, 279–83,
300–301
de Gaulle, Charles, 48, 170
deliberate depolarization, U.S.
strategy of, 20
democracy, 50–51, 68, 71–72, 129,
135, 209, 211
Democrats, Democratic party, U.S.,
56, 188, 263, 275, 285
Depression, Great, 207
detente, 175, 176, 177, 191, 209
deterrence, 239
limited wars and, 172
nuclear, 22–23, 37, 71, 127,
130–31, 133–34, 140, 143, 156,
171, 208, 215–16, 230–31,
237–38, 250–51

development:
debt and, 323
North-South issues and, 177–80
U.S. national security and, 152–53
unevenness of, 211
see also less developed countries
Discriminate Deterrence (Commission
on Integrated Long-Term
Strategy), 173
diseases, 54–55, 80
dollar, New Taiwan, 104
dollar, U.S., 12, 51, 53, 72–73, 83,
85, 322
decline of, 86–87, 88, 103, 105–6
monetary system and, 103–6
Draper, William H., 54
drugs, 77, 331
Dubos, Rene, 183
Dulles, John Foster, 43, 167

Eagleburger, Lawrence S., 24–27,
242–60
background of, 242n
East Asia, 64, 72, 129, 133, 327–28
Japanese role in, 52, 62, 327
U.S. policy in, 42–43, 45
see also specific countries
Eastern Europe, 10, 26, 36, 79, 128,
129, 134, 136, 163, 204,
230–31, 231, 233–34, 326–27
"Finlandization" of, 234
nationalism in, 60
21st century foreign policy
challenges and, 247–56
U.S. vs. Soviet influence in,
145–46
Warsaw Pact and, 39, 143, 170,
175–76, 226, 238–39, 255–56
Western Europe's relations with,
151, 234, 251–52
see also specific countries
East-West struggle, see bipolarity;
cold war
economics, economy:
burden sharing and, 102–3, 150

economics (*continued*)
of China, 10, 54, 73, 214
cooperation and, 22, 320–21, 324
governmental vs.
  nongovernmental control of,
  181–82
of India, 53–54, 73, 76
of Japan, 10, 12, 14, 27, 28, 30,
  52, 53, 62, 73, 74–75, 81, 85,
  88, 100–103, 108–9, 129, 133,
  138, 189, 191, 214, 216, 235,
  307
Keynesian, 114–17
in 1950s vs. 1990s, 51–55, 72–81
North-South issues and, 177–80
of South Korea, 77, 88, 100, 102,
  108, 244
Soviet-American relations and, 17,
  146–48
of West Germany, 12, 14, 28, 30,
  52, 85, 88, 93, 100, 108, 214,
  307
economic security, U.S., 15, 17–18
economy, Soviet, 36, 41, 147, 209,
  252
decentralization of, 227
stagnation of, 15, 58, 130, 134,
  140, 245, 254
economy, U.S., 82–125
activist trade policy and, 91–95
budget deficits and, *see* budget
  deficit, U.S.
Bush administration and, 11,
  82–89, 106–12, 218
competitive interdependence and,
  12–13, 106–12
competitive position of, 52–53,
  73–76
complacency about, 216–17
"comprehensive security" and, 24
decline of competitiveness of, 12,
  15, 73–76
exports and, 11, 12, 15, 85, 87, 88,
  89, 92, 102, 104, 133, 322
foreign dimension of, 95–103

imports and, 15, 91, 92, 133
innovation and, 8
interest rates and, 12, 87, 89, 90,
  94, 96, 106, 114, 181
investment and, *see* investment
long-term objectives of, 320–21
management mistakes and, 22
national security and, 10–11, 15,
  17–18, 23, 132, 133, 149
in 1950s vs. 1990s, 10, 36–37,
  51–53, 72–76, 80–81
pluralism and, 317–18
productivity and, *see* productivity
public opinion and, 28, 30,
  267–69, 300–301, 306–8
restoration of base of, 218–20
savings and, *see* savings
security commitments and, 74–76,
  102
trade deficit and, *see* trade deficit,
  U.S.
urgency of policy action and,
  85–88
U.S. Global Interests report and,
  318–24
Western economic system and,
  51–52, 73
world economy and, 11–12,
  82–125, 320
economy, world, 8, 11–15
national mistakes and, 22
postwar, 207, 209
uneven development and, 210–11
U.S. economy and, 11–12,
  82–125, 320
Western economic system and,
  51–52, 73, 74, 76
education, public opinion and, 29,
  274–78
EEC, *see* European Economic
  Community
Egypt:
Nasserite, 45–46, 170
Soviet relations with, 45
U.S. relations with, 65

Eisenhower, Dwight D., 34, 37, 38, 43, 46, 54, 56, 65, 167
election of 1960, 34–35
election of 1984, 261–63
election of 1988, 167, 265
El Salvador, U.S. relations with, 136
EMS (European Monetary System), 104, 105
energy, 183
  future of, 79–80
  synthetic fuels, 155
  U.S. dependence and, 324
  see also oil
environmental problems, 194
  acid rain, 80, 182, 216, 330
  chlorofluorocarbons and, 80, 182–83, 329
  greenhouse effect, 16, 31, 80, 139, 183, 329
  long-term objectives and, 329
  national security and, 139
  in 1950s vs. 1990s, 54, 80
  technological revolution and, 182–83
  U.S. Global Interests report and, 329–31
  U.S. public opinion and, 28
Epstein, Joshua, 143
Ethiopia, 330
  Somalia's conflicts with, 131
  Soviet relations with, 68, 178
  U.S. relations with, 42, 44, 172
Eurocommunism, 68
Europe:
  U.S. security strategy for the 1990s and, 229–36
  see also Eastern Europe; Western Europe; *specific countries*
European Economic Community (EEC) (Common Market), 12, 51, 52, 53, 61, 92–93, 179, 181, 214, 243, 244, 247, 252–54, 321
European Monetary System (EMS), 104, 105
exchange rates, 72, 73, 82, 83, 88

  floating, 12, 105
  stability of, 320
exit bonds, 99, 103
"Export Expansion and Removal of Disincentives Act," 92
Export-Import Bank of the United States, 92, 99

family planning, 330–31
Federal Bureau of Investigation (FBI), 40
Federal Reserve Bank (Fed), 87
Feldstein, Martin, 111
first strike capacity, 24, 30, 208, 225, 237, 301
Food and Agricultural Organization (FAO), 50
foreign aid, Japanese, 304, 305
foreign aid, U.S., 29, 131
  drugs and, 331
  economic, 34, 42, 46, 55, 304
  in 1950s, 34, 40, 42, 46, 47, 55
  public opinion and, 302–5
foreign policy, U.S.:
  assumptions of, 5–8, 35
  bipartisan, 167
  consensus on, 34–35, 187, 190–91
  creative adaptation and, 20, 187–88, 191–97
  current problems resulting from, 21–22
  domestic support and, 331–32
  economic assumptions of, 6
  future aspirations of, 8, 21
  geopolitical assumptions of, 6
  geopolitical legacy and, 166–70, 196–97
  human rights and, 17, 23, 42, 50–51, 71–72, 135, 147, 209, 211, 227, 230
  isolationism, 29, 306, 308
  NSC-68 and, 21, 22, 23, 202–3, 206, 211, 212, 221–22, 227
  passive adaptation and, 187–90
  postwar objectives of, 202–3

foreign policy (*continued*)
    public opinion and, 8, 28–29,
        302–15, 331–32
    21st century challenges and,
        24–27, 242–60
    Western alliance changes and,
        25–26
    see also cold war; *specific countries*
Formosa Straits crisis, 170
France, 46, 61, 62, 68, 95, 105, 150,
        213, 248, 254
    as arms supplier, 39
    decolonization and, 48
    Israel and, 42
    NATO and, 170
    nuclear weapons and, 40, 71,
        238
    Soviet relations with, 59, 204
    U.S. relations with, 37
Franco, Francisco, 42
Franklin, Benjamin, 260
FRG, *see* Germany, Federal Republic
    of
full employment, 12, 90, 105
    trade deficit and, 123
fundamentalism, 128
    Muslim, 10, 64, 66, 69, 129

gas tax, 218–19
gender, public opinion and, 29,
        274–78
General Agreement on Tariffs and
    Trade (GATT), 84, 108, 207,
        227, 243, 324
Genscher, Hans Dietrich, 222
geopolitics, 6, 18–20
    evolution of geostrategic
        environment and, 171–74
    expectations vs. realities in, 170
    legacy of, 166–70, 196–97
    military strategy and, 158, 160–61
    in 1950s vs. 1990s, 35–51, 57–72
    North-South axis of tension and,
        177–80
    polyarchy and, *see* polyarchy
    S. Brown on, 166–97

technological change and, 171–74,
        180–83
    U.S. foreign policy choices and,
        187–97
    U.S. Global Interests report and,
        325–27
    weakening of cold war ideology
        and, 174–77
    world order crisis and, 180–83
German Democratic Republic (East
    Germany), 61, 255
Germany:
    in nineteenth century, 78
    postwar, 204, 205
    reunification of, 45, 138
Germany, Federal Republic of (West
    Germany) (FRG), 45, 61, 116,
        146, 209, 230, 232, 254
    burden sharing and, 102–3, 150
    capital surplus of, 100
    debt of, 14, 117, 124
    economy of, 12, 14, 28, 30, 52, 85,
        88, 93, 100, 108, 214, 307
    nuclear weapons and, 232, 251
    Soviet Union and, 131, 134, 138,
        146
    U.S. relations with, 134
Germany, Nazi, 35–36, 213
glasnost, 136, 148, 223, 227, 245, 254
GNP, *see* gross national product
Goodpaster, Andrew, 173
Gorbachev, Mikhail, 102, 134, 147,
        148, 167, 175, 191, 327
    Allison on, 23, 24, 212–13, 216,
        222–28, 230–37
    Bundy on, 10, 58, 59, 71
    "common security house" concept
        of, 225
    Eagleburger on, 25, 26, 245, 249,
        250–52, 254–55
    perestroika of, 58, 135–36, 227, 245
    pragmatism of, 223
    public opinion and, 28–29, 231,
        263, 264, 269, 270, 288–92,
        299, 310
    testing of, 222–28

Gramm-Rudman-Hollings schedule,
    89
Great Britain, 18, 46, 48, 78, 105,
    124, 213, 254
  as arms supplier, 39
  Iran and, 46
  nuclear weapons and, 40, 71, 238
  Soviet relations with, 59
  Suez crisis and, 37, 170
  U.S. relations with, 37, 168
Great Leap Forward, 39
Greece, 44
  Soviet Union and, 34, 36, 204
  U.S. relations with, 64
greenhouse effect, 16, 31, 80, 139,
    183, 329
"green revolution," 55
Greenspan, Alan, 91
gross national product (GNP), 17,
    37, 72, 114, 137, 209, 214, 217
  capital surplus and, 100–102
  client regimes and, 178
  debt and, 14, 87, 117–19
  defense spending and, 75, 131,
    150, 154, 162, 163, 233, 234
  development and, 179
  investment and, 120
  Soviet, 224, 249
  Western European, 249, 252
Group of Five, 105
Group of Seven, 105, 220
Group of 77, 179
Guatemala:
  Soviet relations with, 227
  U.S. relations with, 47
Gulf Cooperation Council, 135

Haig, Alexander, 167
Hamilton, Edward K., 4–32
  background of, 5n
Hammarskjold, Dag, 50
Harman, Sidney, 38
health concerns, in 1950s vs. 1990s,
    54–55, 80
Helsinki Accords, 72, 230
Hitler, Adolf, 204, 207, 213

Hoffman, Stanley, 209
Holland, see Netherlands
Hong Kong, 52
Horn of Africa, 46
human rights, 17, 135, 209, 211, 230
  in 1950s vs. 1990s, 42, 50–51,
    71–72
  in Soviet Union, 23, 147, 227
Hungary, 255, 327
  revolution in, 45, 170, 233

ICBMs (intercontinental ballistic
    missiles), 141, 156, 171, 240
IDB (Inter-American Development
    Bank), 84, 98
Ikle, Fred, 173
ILO (International Labor
    Organization), 49–50
IMF, see International Monetary
    Fund
imperial overstretch, 17–18, 130,
    162–63, 216
income:
  U.S. distribution of, 86
  worldwide distribution of, 22
income transfers, defense spending
    and, 161–62
India, 34, 40, 50, 77, 129–30, 133,
    139, 205
  democracy in, 129, 135
  economic development of, 53–54,
    73, 76
  nuclear weapons and, 71
  Pakistan's conflicts with, 131
  as regional power, 135, 153, 214
  U.S. relations with, 46
Indochina, 34, 37, 45
  see also Vietnam War; specific
    countries
Indonesia, 34, 80
  U.S. relations with, 45, 48, 178
INF, see intermediate nuclear forces
    (INF) treaty
inflation, 181
  U.S. economy and, 12, 13, 83, 85,
    86, 87, 90, 114, 119, 318

Inner Alliance, 37, 41, 75
innovation, U.S. economy and, 8
Inter-American Development Bank
(IDB), 84, 98
intercontinental ballistic missiles
(ICBMs), 141, 156, 171, 240
interdependence:
competitive, 12–13, 106–12
economic pluralism and, 318
interest rates, 181
decline in, 89, 94, 96, 114
increase in, 12, 87, 90, 106
intermediate nuclear forces (INF)
treaty, 29, 58–59, 171, 226, 231,
250–51, 318
public opinion and, 286–88
intermediate-range ballistic missiles
(IRBMs), 171
International Bank for
Reconstruction and
Development (World Bank), 49,
78, 84, 98–99, 103, 207, 243,
321
International Labor Organization
(ILO), 49–50
International Monetary Fund (IMF),
49, 78, 84, 98–99, 103, 105,
207, 243
investment:
Bergsten on, 11, 14, 88, 89, 90,
92, 94
in debtor countries, 99
defense spending and, 161–62
foreign, in United States, 53, 92,
116, 119, 124, 125, 308, 322
foreign, of United States, 116, 146
Laffer on, 15
as lending, 116
Roberts on, 13, 14, 116, 119, 120
tax and, 14, 76
trade deficits and, 15, 124
Iran, 61, 135, 160
revolution in, 10, 64, 65–66, 69,
172
Soviet Union and, 34, 36, 46, 145

U.S. relations with, 42, 43, 46, 66,
153, 172, 208, 248
Iran-Iraq War, 66, 70, 131, 145, 159
Iraq, 45, 295
Iran's war with, 66, 70, 131, 145,
159
Soviet relations with, 65, 145, 178
IRBMs (intermediate-range ballistic
missiles), 171
Islamic fundamentalism, *see* Muslim
fundamentalism
isolationism, 29, 306, 308
Israel, 129
French relations with, 42
nuclear weapons and, 71
United Nations and, 70
U.S. relations with, 42, 43, 46, 65,
144, 178
see also Arab-Israeli conflict
Italy, 95, 105, 117, 209, 254
Soviet relations with, 204

Japan, 22, 25, 34, 62–63, 78, 79,
162, 179, 209
burden sharing and, 102–3, 150,
232–33, 327
capital surplus of, 100, 101
China and, 151
comprehensive security and, 24,
232–34
currency of, 73, 103, 105, 125
debt of, 14, 117, 124
defense spending of, 234, 327
demand in, 101
democracy in, 129
East Asian role of, 52, 62, 327
economy of, 10, 12, 14, 27, 28, 30,
52, 53, 62, 73, 74–75, 81, 85, 88,
100–103, 108–9, 129, 133, 138,
189, 191, 214, 216, 235, 307
foreign aid of, 304, 305
postwar, 204–7
reconstruction of, 51, 52, 129,
206–7
Soviet Union and, 109, 131, 144

21st century foreign policy
    challenges and, 244–46, 249,
    256–58
U.S. public opinion and, 28, 30,
    268–69, 304, 305, 307, 310
U.S. relations with, 8, 27, 41, 52,
    129, 137, 138, 168, 207, 212,
    220, 229–35, 240, 244–46, 249
U.S. security strategy for the
    1990s and, 229–36
Jarvis, Howard, 123
Johnson administration, 167
Jordan, U.S. relations with, 178

Kampuchea (Cambodia), 61, 65, 77,
    226, 325
Kant, Immanuel, 235–36
Kaufman, William, 279
Kay, Alan, 261*n*, 265
Kennan, George, 34, 41, 167, 203–4,
    206, 210
Kennedy, John F., 35, 55, 119, 171
Kennedy, Paul, 61, 64, 75, 188,
    198–99
Kennedy administration, 167
Kenya, 79
Keynesian economics, 114–17
Khaddafi, Mohammar, 310
Khomeini, Ayatullah Ruhollah, 137,
    310
Khrushchev, Nikita, 34, 41, 58, 171,
    254
Kissinger, Henry, 167, 173, 176,
    191–92, 209, 215, 233–34
Korean War, 34, 36, 43, 45, 49, 52,
    155, 159, 163
    armistice in, 38
    Chinese role in, 39

labor unions, cold war and, 40, 41
Laffer, Arthur B., 14–15, 122–25
    background of, 122*n*
Lance missiles, 232
Latin America, 50, 98, 137, 190,
    258, 323

democracy in, 129, 135
U.S. policy in, 34, 46–47,
    67–68
see also Central America; *specific
    countries*
Law of the Sea Conference, 50
LDCs, *see* less developed countries
leadership, 319, 332
    economic pluralism and, 318
    faith in, 56, 57
    U.S. public opinion and, 310,
    311–12
League of Nations, 204
Lebanon crisis (1958), 45
less developed countries (LDCs), 98,
    151, 216, 330–31
    in 1950s vs. 1990s, 53–54, 76–78
Liberia, U.S. relations with, 42
Libya, 68, 69
    Soviet relations with, 178
    U.S. relations with, 42, 248
Lincoln, Abraham, 69
Lome Conventions, 179
Louvre Accord (1987), 83
Luce, Henry, 200

McCarthy, Joseph, 34, 56
McCarthyism, 34, 55
McNamara, Robert, 215
MAD (mutual assured destruction),
    208, 228, 238, 239
Magsaysay, Ramon, 42
Malaysia, 135
Marcos, Ferdinand, 72
maritime strategy, 157–58
mark, German, 104
Market Opinion Research, 262*n*
Marshall Plan, 34, 37, 51, 55, 202,
    206–7
Marttila, John, 27–31, 261–315
    background of, 261*n*–62*n*
Marttila & Kiley, 27–28, 262*n*
Marxism (Marxism-Leninism), 18,
    145, 175, 179, 190, 192–93
    pluralism and, 175–76

"massive retaliation" strategy,
  37
Mexico, 78, 330
  debt of, 27, 68, 77, 99, 259–60
  democracy in, 135
  U.S. relations with, 27, 52, 68, 77,
    129, 136, 259–60, 331
Middle East, 45–47, 62, 129, 151,
  190
  arms sales in, 39
  oil and, 43, 64
  U.S. vs. Soviet role in, 65–66,
    144–45
  see also specific countries
Middle East War (1973), 64
military strategies and dispositions,
  U.S., 154–61
  conventional forces, 131, 143–46,
    157–60
  nuclear, 140–43, 156–57, 208,
    210, 236–40
  regional balances and, 160–61
Millikan, Max, 53
missiles, 63, 64
  ballistic, *see* ballistic missiles
  cruise, 250
  Jupiter, 171
  Lance, 232
  Pershing II, 250
  Soviet testing of, 36
  SS-4, 250
  SS-18, 225
  SS-20, 250
  zero-option and, 231–32
Missile Technology Control Regime,
  328
Miyazawa, Kiichi, 235
Mohammed Reza Shah Pahlavi,
  46
Mondale, Walter, 263
monetary system, U.S. dollar and,
  103–6
Monroe Doctrine, 47
Montreal Convention, 182–83
Morgenthau, Henry, 205

Morocco, 46
Mosadeq, Mohammed, 46
Moscow summit (1988), 225
Mozambique, 69
multipolarity, 129
  Allison on, 22, 215
  Eagleburger on, 25, 245
Muslim fundamentalism, 10, 64, 66,
  69, 129
mutual assured destruction (MAD),
  208, 228, 238, 239
Mutual Balanced Force Reduction
  Talks, 226

nationalism, 205, 210
  Arab, 45–46
  in eastern Europe, 60
  Marxism and, 176
  North-South issues and, 177–
    78
  in South Africa, 68–69
national security, U.S.:
  allies and, 148–51, 157, 159–60,
    169–70
  burden sharing and, 149–50,
    163–64
  choices for the 1990s and, 16–17,
    126–65
  comprehensive, 24, 232–34
  conventional forces and, 131,
    143–46, 157–60
  dominance strategy for, 142
  economy and, 10–11, 15, 17–18,
    23, 132, 133, 149
  foreign aid and, 40, 42, 131
  future changes in, 133–39
  gradualist policy of, 16, 155
  introduction to, 126–33
  issues and options in, 139–61
  long-term objectives of, 325
  military strategies and dispositions
    and, 154–61
  minimalist policy of, 16, 141–42,
    154, 156, 157
  new threats to, 265–69

in 1950s vs. 1990s, 10–11, 74–76,
127–30
nuclear forces strategies and,
140–43, 156–57
out-of-area cooperation and,
150–51
postwar strategy for, 199–211,
317; *see also* postwar national
security strategy, U.S.
public opinion and, 8, 27–31,
261–315
redistribution of responsibilities
and influence in, 132
Third World and, 17, 151–53,
207–8
U.S. Global Interests report and,
325–27
withdrawal policy and, 130–32
see also national security strategy
for the 1990s, U.S.; political
security, U.S.
National Security Council (NSC)
document #68, 21, 22, 23,
202–3, 206, 211, 212, 227
objective of, 221–22
national security strategy for the
1990s, U.S., 20–24, 198–241
changes in postwar concepts and,
22–23
cold war and, 211–40
environment of, 213–17
microstrategies and, 217–40
objectives of, 213
postwar period and, 199–211; *see
also* postwar national security
strategy, U.S.
Soviet-American relations and, 22,
23–24, 211–16, 220–29
nation-state:
core accountability principle and,
195–96
technological development and,
19, 216
NATO, *see* North Atlantic Treaty
Organization

natural gas, 79
natural resources, in 1950s vs.
1990s, 54, 79–80
Navy, Soviet, 158
Navy, U.S., 43, 158
Nazi Germany, 35–36, 213
Necessity for Choice (Kissinger),
209
"negative financial transfer,"
proposal for elimination of,
95–98
Nehru, Jawaharlal, 44
Netherlands, 100, 117, 150
New International Economic Order,
179
newly industrializing countries
(NICs), 75, 90, 100, 108–9,
129–30, 135, 137, 151, 163
U.S. national security and, 148–49
see also specific countries
newly industrializing economies
(NIEs), *see* newly industrializing
countries
New Zealand, U.S. relations with, 41,
71
Nicaragua:
Soviet relations with, 128, 227
U.S. relations with, 68, 136,
160–61, 227
NICs, *see* newly industrializing
countries
NIEs (newly industrializing
economies), *see* newly
industrializing countries
Nietzsche, Friedrich, 202
Nigeria, 330
1950s vs. 1990s, 33–81
areas of concern and conflicts in,
45–47
arms race and arms control issues
and, 39–40, 63–64, 127–28
change indicators and, 53–54
decolonization and, 47–48
demographic change and, 54,
78–79

1950s vs. 1990s (*continued*)
  East-West struggle and, 40–45,
    57–63, 65, 127
  economics and, 51–55, 72–81, 128
  environment, resources, and
    health issues and, 54–55, 79–80
  global issues and, 54–55, 79–80
  human rights and democracy and,
    42, 50–51, 71–72
  ideological challenge in, 128
  intermediate and regional powers
    and, 57–58, 64–69
  international organizations and
    law and, 40, 48–50, 69–70
  less developed countries and,
    53–54, 76–78
  military/technological challenge
    in, 127–28
  national security and, 10–11,
    74–76, 127–30
  nuclear proliferation and nuclear
    attitudes in, 70–71
  political challenge in, 128–29
  power and, 35–39, 57–63
  strategic and political setting and,
    35–51, 57–72
  terrorism and, 69
  U.S. capacity to support security
    commitments and, 74–76
  U.S. competitive position and,
    52–53, 74–76
  U.S. situation and, 55–57, 80–81
  Western economic system and,
    51–52
1999 (Nixon), 60
Nitze, Paul, 167
Nixon, Richard, 55, 59, 60, 167
  China policy and, 176–77
Nixon administration, 84, 111, 167
Nixon Doctrine, 173
nonaligned countries, 42, 44, 46, 70,
    135, 170, 179
Non-Proliferation Treaty, 70–71,
    194
North Africa, 34, 42, 45–46, 65
  see also specific countries

North Atlantic Treaty Organization
  (NATO), 34, 36–39, 41, 62,
    135, 138, 151, 170, 191, 192,
    207, 240, 327–28
  burden sharing and, 150
  "flexible response" strategy of,
    215
  French withdrawal from, 170
  Lisbon goals and, 208
  nuclear weapons and, 71, 215–16,
    238–39
  21st century foreign policy
    challenges and, 243, 247, 249,
    251, 252, 257
North Korea, 144
  Soviet relations with, 178
  U.S. security strategy for 1990s
    and, 212, 214, 215–16, 220,
    225–26, 231–33
nuclear accidents, 79, 182, 329
nuclear power, 79
nuclear proliferation, 20, 28, 66,
    70–71, 228
  creative adaptation and, 193–94
nuclear weapons, 17, 18, 20, 70–71,
    204–6
  Allison on, 22–23, 24, 204–6, 208,
    236–40
  China and, 71, 170
  deterrence and, 22–23, 37, 71,
    127, 130–31, 133–34, 140, 143,
    156, 171, 208, 215–16, 230–31,
    237–38, 250–51
  fire break and, 238
  first strike capacity and, 24, 30,
    208, 225, 237, 301
  Great Britain and, 40, 71, 238
  INF treaty and, 29, 58–59, 171,
    226, 231, 250–51, 286–88, 318
  mobilization timetable and,
    237
  national security strategy for the
    1990s and, 22–23, 24, 140–43,
    156–57
  NATO and, 71, 215–16, 238–39
  Soviet testing of, 34, 36

in *U.S. Global Interests* report, 326
U.S. public opinion and, 28, 29, 38, 63, 293–96, 301–2
U.S. strategy for, 140–43, 156–57, 208, 210, 236–40
U.S. superiority in, 37–38, 140–41
West Germany and, 232, 251

OAS (Organization of American States), 41–42, 135
OECD (Organization for Economic Cooperation and Development), 51, 117, 243, 321
Offshore Islands crisis (1958), 39, 43, 45
oil, 43, 54, 79, 128, 132, 155
debt crisis and, 78, 100
U.S. dependence and, 324
Omnibus Trade and Competitiveness Act (Omnibus Trade Act) (1988), 83, 94, 110, 324
Only One Earth (Ward and Dubos), 183
Organization for Economic Cooperation and Development (OECD), 51, 117, 243, 321
Organization of African States, 135
Organization of American States (OAS) Treaty, 41–42, 135
Organization of Petroleum Exporting Countries (OPEC), 100, 129, 137
Ortega Saavedra, Daniel, 310

PAF (Public Agenda Foundation), 262n, 302
Pakistan, 40, 66, 160
India's conflicts with, 131
nuclear weapons and, 71
U.S. relations with, 44, 46, 178
Palestine, 69
Paley Report, 54
Panama, U.S. relations with, 136

passive adaptation, 187–90
peace, Kant on, 235–36
pereduishka, 212
perestroika, 58, 136, 227, 245, 254
Perpetual Peace (Kant), 235–36
Pershing II missiles, 250
Persian Gulf, 132, 144–45, 151, 153, 155, 174, 327
Philippines, 77, 79, 98, 135, 139, 258
Marcos regime in, 72
U.S. relations with, 41, 42, 48, 64, 65, 138, 178, 208
Plaza Agreement (1985), 83, 105
Poland, 36, 45, 60, 255, 258, 327
Solidarity in, 175–76
political prisoners, Soviet, 227
political security, U.S., 15–16, 24
politics, U.S.:
long-term objectives of, 325
see also geopolitics
pollution, 182, 216
polyarchy, 19–20, 183–87, 189, 194
benign form of, 19–20, 184–86
dangerous tendencies of, 186–87, 190
in 1950s vs. 1990s, 54, 77, 78–79
population growth, 137, 330–31
warlord phenomenon and, 19–20
Portugal, 48, 68
postwar national security strategy, U.S., 199–211, 317
environment of, 203–5
microstrategies and, 205–8
objectives of, 202–3
performance and, 208–11
poverty:
passive adaptation and, 189–90
uneven development and, 210–11
power, political:
concentration of, 35–39
diffusion of, 10, 57–63
Prague Spring, 175–76
PRC, *see* People's Republic of China

Primacy or World Order (Hoffmann),
    209
productivity:
    consumption vs., 220
    security policy and, 132
    U.S. growth rate in, 23, 88, 90,
        119, 123, 219, 320
protectionism, 91, 111, 149, 220,
    246, 253
Public Agenda Foundation (PAF),
    262n, 302
public opinion, Soviet, 36, 59
public opinion, U.S., 261–315
    arms control and, 28, 29, 286–88
    burden sharing and, 299–301
    defense spending and, 279–83,
        300–301
    economy and, 28, 30, 267–69,
        300–301, 306–8
    foreign aid and, 302–5
    foreign policy and, 8, 28–29,
        302–15, 331–32
    gender/education factors in, 29,
        274–78
    Gorbachev and, 28–29, 263, 264,
        269, 270, 288–92, 299, 310
    national security and, 8, 27–31,
        261–315
    in 1950s, 42, 43, 49, 56
    nuclear weapons and, 28, 29, 38,
        63, 293–96, 301–2
    peace through strength and,
        279–83
    reactions to countries around the
        world and, 309–10
    Reagan legacy and, 310, 313–
        15
    Soviet-American relations and,
        262–65, 268–303
    Strategic Defense Initiative and,
        283–86
    Vietnam War and, 176
    world leaders and, 310, 311–12

Quirino, Elpidio, 42

Reagan, Ronald, 71, 87, 123, 215,
    218, 225, 249
    anticommunism and, 177
    in election of 1984, 261–63
    foreign policy/national security
        legacy of, 310, 313–15
    Gorbachev compared with, 59,
        231
    INF and, 250–51, 287
    military build-up of, 280, 281
    Strategic Defense Initiative of, 29,
        127–28, 283, 285
Reagan administration, 84, 111, 120,
    124, 140, 147, 167, 326
    cold war consensus in, 187,
        190–91
    geopolitical legacy of, 167
    zero-option of, 231–32
Reasonable Defense, A (Kaufman), 279
recession, 86, 90, 106, 181
    of 1981–1982, 13, 114, 321
reconnaissance systems, 171–72,
    173
Regan, Donald, 74
regionalism, 135, 328
Republicans, Republican party, U.S.,
    45, 56, 188, 275
    in election of 1984, 261–63
Reykjavik agreement, 71, 142, 249
Rise and Fall of the Great Powers
    (Kennedy), 198–99
Roberts, Paul Craig, 13–14, 113–21
    background of, 113n
rollback theory, 45, 128, 273
Romania, 255
Roosevelt, Franklin D., 260
Roosevelt, Theodore, 198
Roper poll, 307
Rostow, Walt, 53, 167

SACEUR (Supreme Allied
    Commander, Europe), 143
Sandinistas, 227
satellites, reconnaissance, 171–72,
    173

Saudi Arabia, U.S. relations with, 42,
    139, 178
savings, 132
    consumption vs., 219–20, 320
    defense spending and, 161–62
    U.S. rate of, 14, 23, 73–74, 89, 90,
        120, 219, 320
Schelling, Thomas, 237
Schmidt, Helmut, 215
Schumpeter, Joseph, 219
SCI (selective capital increase),
    102–3
SDI, *see* Strategic Defense Initiative
SEATO (Southeast Asian Treaty
    Organization), 41, 65, 135
second strike capacity, 156
security, U.S., *see* economic security,
    U.S.; national security, U.S.;
    national security strategy for the
    1990s, U.S.; political security,
    U.S.
selective capital increase (SCI),
    102–3
Seventy-fifth American Assembly:
    final report of, 4, 316–32; *see also*
        U.S. Global Interests in the 1990s
    participants in, 333–36
Singapore, 52, 72, 135
Sino-Soviet relations, 10, 65, 170,
    175, 178
    in 1950s, 39
    split in, 39, 60–61, 190
SLBMs (submarine-launched
    ballistic missiles), 141
socialism, 179
    "many roads to," 175–76
Solidarity, 175–76
Somalia, Ethiopia's conflicts with,
    131
South Africa, 51, 68–69, 129, 161
    nuclear weapons and, 71
    Soviet Union and, 67
South Asia, 129, 137, 190
    U.S. policy in, 46
    see also specific countries

Southeast Asian Treaty
    Organization (SEATO), 41, 65,
    135
South Korea, 52, 72, 139
    economy of, 77, 88, 100, 102, 108,
        244
    U.S. relations with, 41, 65, 102,
        135, 138, 144, 178, 208
    see also Korean War
South Vietnam:
    U.S. relations with, 178
    see also Vietnam War
Soviet-American relations, 29, 102,
    133–36, 138–48, 164
    change in, 8
    coexistence and, 175
    conventional force strategies and,
        143–46
    cooperation and, 29, 239, 297–99
    creative adaptation and, 192–93,
        196
    detente and, 175, 176, 177, 191,
        209
    economic issues in, 17, 146–48
    election of 1984 and, 262–63
    in 1950s, 34–47
    1990s national security strategy
        and, 22, 23–24, 211–16, 220–29
    nuclear force strategies and,
        140–42
    passive adaptation and, 189
    peaceful competition and, 228–29
    predictability in, 293–96
    public opinion and, 262–65,
        268–303
    Reykjavik meeting and, 71, 142,
        249
    rollback theory and, 45, 128,
        273
    strategic balance and, 16–17
    21st century foreign policy
        challenges and, 245, 249–52,
        254–56
    U.S. Global Interests report and,
        325–27, 328

Soviet-American relations (*continued*)
  U.S. public opinion and, 28–29
  worldwide alliances and, 18
  see also bipolarity; cold war
Soviet Union, 18, 57–61, 64–68, 79,
    162, 163
  Afghanistan's relations with, 46,
    66, 70, 128, 160
  Afghanistan withdrawal of, 29, 59,
    66, 160, 226, 271–72, 318, 325
  Algeria and, 178
  Angola and, 60, 67, 68, 325
  British relations with, 59
  in Central America, 23, 67, 128,
    227
  China and, *see* Sino-Soviet
    relations
  conventional weapons and forces
    of, 58, 133–34, 250–51
  Cuba's relations with, 60, 67, 128,
    178
  defense spending of, 23, 224–25
  economic stagnation in, 15, 58,
    130, 134, 140, 245, 254
  economy of, 36, 41, 147, 209, 227,
    252
  Egypt and, 45
  Ethiopia and, 68, 178
  expansion of, 20, 28, 34, 66,
    203–4, 317, 326
  glasnost and, 136, 148, 223, 227,
    245, 254
  GNP of, 224, 249
  Greece and, 34, 36, 204
  guerrillas aided by, 227
  human rights in, 23, 147, 227
  intelligence estimates on, 58
  Iran and, 34, 36, 46, 145
  Iraq and, 65, 145, 178
  Italy and, 204
  Japan and, 109, 131, 144
  Libya and, 178
  multipolarity and, 25
  North Korea and, 178
  political evolution in, 15, 130

  power base of, 35–36, 57–61
  public opinion in, 36, 59
  South Africa and, 67
  Stalinist era in, 10, 210, 212
  Syria and, 65, 178
  in Third World, 10, 23, 66–67,
    131; *see also specific countries*
  Turkey and, 34, 36
  United Nations and, 50, 70
  U.S. relations with, *see* bipolarity;
    cold war; Soviet-American
    relations,
  Vietnam and, 60, 65, 178, 226,
    325
  West Germany and, 131, 134, 138,
    146
Spain, 68
  U.S. relations with, 42, 64
Sputnik, 41
SS-4 missiles, 250
SS-18 missiles, 225
SS-20 missiles, 250
Stalin, Joseph, 34, 58
START, *see* Strategic Arms
    Reduction Talks
Starting with the People (Yankelovich
    and Harman), 38
Star Wars, *see* Strategic Defense
    Initiative
State Department, U.S., 48
Steiger, Bill, 123
stock market, 86
Strategic Arms Reduction Talks
    (START), 29, 140, 251, 326
  public opinion and, 286–88
Strategic Defense Initiative (SDI)
    (Star Wars), 29, 127–28, 139,
    147, 162
  public opinion and, 283–86
strategy:
  defined, 201
  future of, *see* national security
    strategy for the 1990s, U.S.
  postwar, *see* postwar national
    security strategy, U.S.

submarine-launched ballistic
    missiles (SLBMs), 141
Suez crisis (1956), 34, 37, 45, 46, 49,
    170
Sukarno, 44
Supreme Allied Commander,
    Europe (SACEUR), 143
Switzerland, 100
Syria, Soviet relations with, 65, 178

Taiwan, 88, 100, 108, 135, 244
    U.S. relations with, 41, 52, 65,
        178, 208
target zones, currency, 12, 104–5,
    108
tax credits, 94
taxes, 11, 13, 120, 123, 124, 321
    cuts in, 14
    on energy, 218–19, 324
    increases in, 15, 89, 322
    investment and, 14, 76
Taylor, Maxwell, 43, 167
technology, technological change,
    18, 194
    geopolitics and, 171–74, 180–83
    military strategy and, 158
    national security and, 136–39
    nation-state affected by, 19, 216
    U.S. lead in, 53, 59
    world order crisis and, 180–83
technology transfer, 146, 148
television, 51
terrorism, 28, 29, 69, 71, 228
    polyarchy and, 186–87, 190
    state, 19, 69, 128, 248
    U.S. national security and, 153
Thatcher, Margaret, 28, 288, 310
thermonuclear weapons, 36, 40,
    156
Third World, 13, 61, 128
    appeal of communism in, 41, 128
    cold war and, 23, 177
    democracy in, 129, 135
    development in, U.S. national
        security and, 152–53

North-South axis of tension and,
    177–80
regional powers in, 135, 137, 153
Soviet behavior in, 10, 23, 66–67,
    131; *see also specific countries*
United Nations and, 49, 69–70,
    179
U.S. national security and, 17,
    151–53, 207–8
U.S. policy in, 17, 23, 34, 42–44
U.S. public opinion and, 265
see also specific countries
Third World debt, 12, 68, 124, 150,
    178, 235
    Bergsten on, 84, 88, 95–99, 108
    capital flow increases and, 99
    continued lending and, 98–99,
        120–21
    debt relief and, 99, 323
    Eagleburger on, 27, 258–60
    elimination of "negative financial
        transfer" and, 95–98
    U.S. Global Interests report and, 323
    see also specific countries
Tito, Marshal (Josip Broz), 44
Tocqueville, Alexis de, 211
trade:
    of Japan, 62
    liberalization of barriers to, 101,
        108, 109, 220
    Omnibus Trade Act and, 83, 94,
        110
    protectionism and, 91, 111, 149,
        220, 246, 253
    security policy and, 132, 133
    Soviet, 59, 146, 227
    surpluses in, 12
    U.S. activist policy for, 91–95
    U.S.-Canadian, 52, 93
    U.S. Global Interests report and,
        321, 323–24
    U.S. role in, 52, 84, 85, 149
    Western European-Soviet bloc,
        62
trade deficit, U.S., 74, 249, 322

trade deficit (*continued*)
  Bergsten on, 11, 83, 85, 86,
    88–91, 106
  elimination of, 88–91, 218–19
  Laffer on, 14, 122–25
  Roberts on, 13, 113, 114
transitional power structures,
    passive adaptation and, 189–90
Truman, Harry S., 37, 56
Tuchman, Barbara, 243
Tunisia, 46
Turkey, 44, 77, 129
  Soviet Union and, 34, 36
  U.S. relations with, 46, 64, 171,
    178, 208

UNCTAD (United Nations
    Conference on Trade and
    Development), 179
UNESCO (United Nations
    Educational, Scientific, and
    Cultural Organization), 50, 70
United Kingdom, *see* Great Britain
United Nations (U.N.), 34
  Assembly of, 49, 70
  Charter of, 49, 70, 230
  Declaration of Human Rights of,
    230
  human rights and, 51, 230
  in 1950s vs. 1990s, 48–50, 69–70
  Security Council of, 49, 70
  Third World and, 49, 69–70, 179
United Nations Conference on
    Trade and Development
    (UNCTAD), 179
United Nations Educational,
    Scientific, and Cultural
    Organization (UNESCO), 50,
    70
United States:
  conventional weapons and forces
    of, 131, 143–46, 157–60
  currency of, *see* dollar, U.S.
  defense spending of, 29, 75, 131,
    150, 154, 158, 161–63, 233,
    279–83, 300–301

economy of, *see* economic security,
    U.S.; economy, U.S.
  energy dependence of, 324
  foreign policy of, *see* cold war;
    foreign policy, U.S.; *specific*
    countries
  image of, 55
  national security of, *see* economic
    security, U.S.; national security,
    U.S.; national security strategy
    for the 1990s, U.S.; political
    security, U.S.
  nuclear strategy of, 140–43,
    156–57, 208, 210, 236–40
  nuclear superiority of, 37–38,
    140–41
  overseas base structure of, 42
  power base of, 36–37
  public opinion in, *see* public
    opinion, U.S.
  United Nations and, 48–50, 70
  unpredictability and indiscipline
    of, 248–49
Uruguay Round, 84, 92, 93, 94, 108,
    324
U.S. Global Interests in the 1990s
    (American Assembly report), 4,
    316–32
  alliances and, 325, 327–28
  budget deficit and, 321–23
  drugs and, 331
  economic issues in, 320–24
  global imperatives and, 329–31
  marshalling domestic support
    and, 331–33
  political and security issues in,
    325–28
  preamble of, 316–20
U.S.-Japan Mutual Defense Treaty,
    240

Vietnam, 77, 161
  Soviet relations with, 60, 65, 178,
    226, 325
Vietnam War, 44, 57, 66, 81, 155,
    163, 164, 176, 248

Volcker, Paul, 91, 123
voluntary restraint agreements
  (VRAs), 93–94

Ward, Barbara, 183
warlord phenomenon, 19–20
Warsaw Pact, 39, 143, 170, 192, 226,
  238–39, 255–56
  pluralism in, 175–76
Western Europe, 22, 25, 34, 61–62,
  64, 129, 137–38, 146, 189
  Eastern Europe's relations with,
    151, 234, 251–52
  GNP of, 249, 252
  INF weapons and, 250–51
  market unification of, 26, 61,
    92–93, 149, 252–54
  Soviet Union and, 131, 133–34,
    136
  Third World economic relations
    with, 179
  21st century foreign policy and,
    25–26, 244–56
  U.S. power in, 37, 38
Western European Union, 138
"Why America's Piggy Banks Aren't
  Bulging" (Roberts), 120

Wohlstetter, Albert, 173
won, Korean, 104
World Bank, see International Bank
  for Reconstruction and
  Development
World Health Organization (WHO),
  54–55
World War I, 159, 163, 209
World War II, 36–37, 41, 159, 163,
  213, 230, 237
  geopolitics inherited from,
    166–70
  world change since, 3, 7

"X" article, 34

Yankelovich, Daniel, 38, 63
  Daniel Yankelovich Group,
    262n
yen, Japanese, 73, 103, 105,
  125
Yew, Lee Kuan, 72
Yugoslavia, 40, 258
  U.S. relations with, 40

zero-option, 231–32, 250
Zhou en-Lai, 44